Instructor's Manual with Test Bank to Accompany

ENTREPRENEURSHIP:
A PLANNING APPROACH

Fred L. Fry

Bradley University

WEST PUBLISHING COMPANY

St. Paul/Minneapolis   New York   Los Angeles   San Francisco

WEST'S COMMITMENT TO THE ENVIRONMENT

In 1906, West Publishing Company began recycling materials left over from the production of books. This began a tradition of efficient and responsible use of resources. Today, up to 95% of our legal books and 70% of our college and school texts are printed on recycled, acid-free stock. West also recycles nearly 22 million pounds of scrap paper annually—the equivalent of 181,717 trees. Since the 1960s, West has devised ways to capture and recycle waste inks, solvents, oils, and vapors created in the printing process. We also recycle plastics of all kinds, wood, glass, corrugated cardboard, and batteries, and have eliminated the use of Styrofoam book packaging. We at West are proud of the longevity and the scope of commitment to the environment.

Production, Prepress, Printing and Binding by West Publishing Company.

CONTENTS

PREFACE

The Instructor's Manual to <u>Entrepreneurship</u>: <u>A Planning Approach</u> is provided to make teaching an entrepreneurship class easier and more effective. Entrepreneurship professors typically come from management, marketing, or finance backgrounds and will have different perspectives regarding how the entrepreneurship course should be taught. This instructor's manual will hopefully fill in some of the gaps instructors may have in the various topics of the entrepreneurship area.

Even though the text is designed to be covered at the rate of approximately one chapter per week, its flexibility will allow those in different disciplines to provide more emphasis on selected areas. For example, instructors coming from a financial background may want to spend more time on financing (Chapter 7), valuation (Chapter 15), and the fisCAL software. Those coming from a planning or strategy background may emphasize the overall planning process and particularly spend time on Chapters 4, 5, 8, 9, 11, 13, and 16. Instructors who want to emphasize marketing aspects of entrepreneurship may want to spend additional time on Chapters 4, 5, 8, 9, 10, and 11.

The cases at the end of the text also provide flexibility in teaching pedagogy. With the cases placed at the end of the text, instructors can assign them at any time throughout the term. Thus, those who prefer heavy use of cases may desire to use all or most of the cases provided. Others may use only a few to illustrate and round out particular topics. Still others may not use cases at all. Further, some of the cases can be used in combination with more than one chapter. This allows the instructor to use a case with several topics rather than with only one and then return to it to illustrate a second or third point.

Videos produced by the Blue Chip Enterprise Institute are provided to adopters. These videos are vignettes about entrepreneurs who made significant changes in their ventures in order to react to or anticipate changes in the environment they face. There are a number of videos on each of the four tapes. The videos can be used as a set in order to illustrate a number of entrepreneurial situations. An alternative method is to combine selected vignettes to illustrate specific points in the course.

Parts of This Instructor's Manual

This manual includes five primary parts. The first part is entitled **Course Design** and includes a number of suggestions for designing an entrepreneurship course. Suggestions for course structure, projects, grading, and course outlines are included. Also included in this section are suggestions for placement of the cases and usage of the Blue Chip Enterprise videos.

The second part of the manual is the **Lecture Guide** portion. It includes suggestions for lecture approaches. In particular, it will indicate how the **Consider This!** segment leading off each chapter and the **Conveniesse, Inc.** continuous case at the end of each chapter can be used to enhance student interest in the course. It will also include an outline for the chapter and suggested answers for the discussion questions, suggestions for use of the exercises, and comments on the **Conveniesse, Inc.** segments.

The third section is the **Case Analysis** section. In this section, teaching notes for each of the text's cases are given. Suggested answers to questions in the cases are provided.

The fourth section discusses the **Blue Chip Enterprise Institute videos**. A summary of each case will be included. In addition, for selected cases a more in-depth summary of the situation facing the firm will be presented. These can be given to the students for analysis before showing the video vignette that discusses how the entrepreneur solved the problem.

The fourth section of the manual consists of **objective and essay test questions**. The objective questions will include at least twenty true/false and twenty-five multiple choice questions. The multiple choice questions have been carefully prepared and have a minimum of the "all of the above/none of the above" variety. The essay questions include both theory and applications.

Finally, **transparency masters** have been selected from the text figures and tables for use as overhead lecture enhancements.

COURSE DESIGN

Entrepreneurship courses have perhaps the most flexibility of any course in the curriculum. This is because there are so many ways of approaching the course. For example, it can be taught simply as a theory based course with few, if any, outside projects. At the opposite extreme, it can be taught as a hands-on applications course with a minimum of lecture and maximum time spent on projects. Midway between the two is a combination of lecture and cases with perhaps a business plan included.

Course Structure

The major aspect of the design of the course revolves around the structure of lectures, cases, exams, business plans, and consulting projects. Following are some suggested course structures. The next section will then focus on alternative outlines and schedules for the course.

Lecture/Exams

The simplest structure for the entrepreneurship course is a combination of lectures with discussion and two, three, or four exams. This structure requires the least effort from both the instructor and the students. It also is the least rewarding from the students' viewpoint. It offers little or no hands-on learning or applications of text material. At the same time, it is realized that some schools' entrepreneurship classes do not lend themselves to projects. Courses taught in large sections or by TA's may not be conducive to a project orientation.

Even if the lecture/exams model is used, some realism can be added by the discussion of a number of the cases. Utilizing one case every other week, for example, breaks the monotony of lectures and gives the students the feeling of applying material to a real situation.

Lecture/Case

Those who teach the Policy/Strategy course are familiar with the case method of teaching. In this structure, a number of cases are discussed in class. Some or all of these may include a written analysis which becomes a significant portion of the grade. In this structure, the text material is important, but primarily so in relationship to the cases. Rather than three or four exams, one or two exams may be sufficient. Alternatively, a series of quizzes or short exams could be given to test text and lecture material, and these could count for perhaps one-half of the course grade.

In the lecture/case scenario, the grades on the cases may be individual, group, or group plus peer evaluation. The grade typically reflects the thoroughness of the analysis and the justification for solutions or strategies. Cases can also be presented orally.

Lectures/Exams plus Business Plans

A third possible structure is to use the lecture/discussion method of presenting material, utilizing perhaps three exams, and requiring a <u>written business plan</u> for a real or hypothetical business. The business plan should count for at least one-third of the total grade. The plan can also be presented to the class as a mock presentation to venture capitalists or lenders.

My experience has been that a significant part of the course should be allocated to the development of actual business plans. My students have consistently concurred that doing the business plan was a difficult but highly rewarding task. At the same time, it must be recognized that those on quarter systems or those with quite large classes simply may not be able to adapt to a structure utilizing a business plan.

The great advantages of requiring a business plan are that it is one of the key factors of entrepreneurship and it forces the students to give careful thought to just exactly what is required to start a venture. I require a plan for a venture of their choice that does not currently exist, that will require from $50,000 to $2 million to start, and that I approve. Having the dollar minimum keeps the students from doing a low thought, low effort project. Having some reasonable upper limit (without special approval) keeps them from reinventing IBM. Requiring instructor approval allows the instructor to make sure the projects are different and to prevent innumerable projects dealing with off-campus bars. I require them to do everything needed to start the venture short of signing on the dotted line. Thus, they have to determine the total costs, the pro forma statements, determine the cost of borrowing, and at least look into locations.

Compressed Lectures with Projects

The final major type of structure is to compress the lecture portion of the course into perhaps seven weeks and use the rest of the term for a major project. This could be a substantial research project or it could be a significant consulting project such as the Small Business Institute program. Approximately 500 schools have the Small Business Institute program. Some of these are done in Policy/Strategy courses, some are done as independent study or honors courses, and some are done as "business consulting" courses. Many, however, are done through small business management or entrepreneurship courses. If the SBI or other significant project is used, the instructor may want to use only two exams and cover two chapters per week. Due to the compressed schedules and focus on small business consulting, some chapters -- perhaps 1, 10, 11, 14, and 16 -- might be eliminated. The loss in topical coverage is overcome by the benefit of the consulting experience.

Alternative Outlines

This section presents a number of alternative outlines. The semester alternatives presented below assume a twice weekly, 75 minute class. Adjustments can be made for a Monday/Wednesday/Friday sequence.

Standard Fifteen Week Semester

OUTLINE

Week 1   Class Objectives/Introduction to Entrepreneurship

Week 2   Nature of Entrepreneurship/The Entrepreneur

Week 3   The Entrepreneur (Continued)/Business Plans and Planning

Week 4   Business Plans (Continued)/Analyzing Entrepreneurial
              Opportunities

Week 5   Exam 1/Discussion of fisCAL

Week 6   Financing (2 classes)

Week 7   Developing Entrepreneurial Strategies (2 classes)

Week 8   Developing Supporting Strategies/Exam 2

Week 9   Franchising Strategies/International Strategies

Week 10   Structuring the Venture/Managing Growth

Week 11   Managing Growth (Continued)/Exam 3

Week 12   Intrapreneurship/Valuing the Venture

Week 13   Valuing the Venture (Continued)/fisCAL Valuation

Week 14   Harvesting the Venture/Concluding Session

Week 15   Final Exam

Fifteen Week Semester with Business Plan Presentations

OUTLINE

Week 1   Introduction to Entrepreneurship/Nature of Entrepreneurship

Week 2   The Entrepreneur (2 classes)

Week 3   Business Plans and Planning (2 classes)

Week 4   Analyzing Opportunities/ Planning the Launch of the Venture

Week 5   Exam 1/Discussion of fisCAL

Week 6   Financing (2 Classes)

Week 7   Developing Entrepreneurial Strategies/Developing Supporting Strategies

Week 8   Franchising Strategies/International Strategies

Week 9   Exam 2/Structuring the Venture

Week 10   Managing Growth/Intrapreneurship

Week 11   Valuing the Venture (2 classes)

Week 12   fisCAL valuation/Harvesting the Venture

Week 13   Exam 3/Concluding Remarks

Week 14   Business Plan Presentations

Week 15   Business Plan Presentations

Fifteen Week Semester with Consulting Project

OUTLINE

Week 1   Introduction to Entrepreneurship/Nature of Entrepreneurship

Week 2   The Entrepreneur/Business Plans and Planning

Week 3   Analyzing Entrepreneurial Opportunities/Planning the Launch
            of the Venture

Week 4   Financing the Venture/Exam 1

Week 5   Franchising Strategies/International Strategies

Week 6   Structuring the Venture/Managing Growth/Intrapreneurship

Week 7   Valuing the Venture/Harvesting the Venture

Week 8   Exam 2/Introduction to Project

Weeks 9 through 15 Consulting Project

Ten Week Quarter

OUTLINE

Week 1   Introduction to Entrepreneurship/Nature of Entrepreneurship

Week 2   The Entrepreneur/Business Plans and Planning

Week 3   Analyzing Entrepreneurial Opportunities/Planning the Launch of the
            Venture

Week 4   Exam 1/Financing the Venture

Week 5   Developing Entrepreneurial Strategies/Developing Supporting
               Strategies

Week 6   Franchising Strategies/International Strategies

Week 7   Exam 2/Structuring the Venture

Week 8   Managing Growth/Intrapreneurship

Week 9   Valuing the Venture/Harvesting the Venture

Week 10   Concluding Remarks/Final Exam

Alternative Ordering of Chapters

Entrepreneurship: A Planning Approach is presented in a chronological order that an individual might consider in the actual entrepreneurial process. After the first section on the nature of entrepreneurship and entrepreneurs, the text focuses on those steps taken prior to launching the venture. In Part II, business plans are covered at the outset because of the importance of a carefully considered plan before the launch of the venture. Then the analysis necessary for the launch decision is covered, and is followed by considerations on the form of launch. Finally, obtaining financing for the launch is covered.

Part III, Planning Venture Strategies covers the strategies and support strategies for the venture. Overall strategies for a number of venture situations are considered, and these are followed by discussion of supporting activities necessary to mesh with the overall venture strategy. Then, two specialty strategies -- franchising and international are added.

Part IV, Planning for Entrepreneurial Management assumes that the business is launched and operating. Structure is considered at this time because it focuses on developmental structures and structures of acquisitions. Further, the classic "strategy, then structure" philosophy is honored by this arrangement. Chapter 13, Managing Growth then focuses on the unique needs in managing the existing growth oriented ventures. The Intrapreneurship chapter then discusses concerns of the well established company.

Finally, Part V, Planning the Entrepreneurial Finale considers two aspects associated with ending a venture. The first is to value the venture, and the second is to consider how to end or harvest the venture. This completes the entrepreneurial cycle.

There are at least three places, however, in which instructors may either philosophically or pragmatically feel the need to rearrange the presentation. These are discussed below.

Business Plan Last

Some instructors feel that the business plan is the culmination of all other planning considerations and should be considered last for emphasis. In this case, moving Chapter 4 to the end of the text is an easy change. This is particularly useful for those who do not use a business plan or project as a major part of the course.

Valuation Earlier

Some of the reviewers of the text suggested moving Chapter 15, Valuing the Venture, next to Chapter 7, Financing. The logic here is that it may be necessary to value the firm before getting capital. This may be true although it may not be necessary before getting capital the first time. I would guess that more valuation goes on during or near the end of the life of the venture rather than at the beginning. Nevertheless, the valuation chapter can easily be covered just before or after the financing chapter. Since Chapter 6, Launching the Venture considers both the starting and buying of ventures, some instructors may want to cover Chapter 15 at that time. Then a logical sequence would then be Chapter 4 - Business Plans and Planning, Chapter 5 - Analyzing Opportunities, Chapter 6 - Launching the Venture, Chapter 15, Valuing the Venture, and then Chapter 7 - Financing the Venture.

Structure Earlier

Chapter 12, Structuring the Venture is placed where it is because of the sequential nature of considering the emerging structure after the venture is launched. Some, however, may desire to move Chapter 12 to immediately after Chapter 6. This would place the organizational structure chapter immediately after the discussion of the legal structure. If the two chapters were covered together, the emerging organizational structure could be correlated with changes in the legal structure. For example, many new ventures are begun as sole proprietorships. As they grow, the legal structure may be changed to add partners or to incorporate. Similarly, growth in the venture may necessitate changing from the basic structure to a functional or divisional structure. Once acquisitions are made, the desirability of incorporation certainly becomes greater.

Suggested Projects

One of the greatest strengths of the Entrepreneurship course is the number of different projects that can be incorporated into the course. The advantage of the projects is that it allows students to delve into the specifics of the entrepreneurship process. These projects include business plans, SBI projects, library research, case writing, or an actual start-up.

Business Plan

The business plan is probably the most relevant project to assign due to the nature of the course. It also provides the greatest learning potential. The business plan forces the students to do research which may include both primary data and secondary data. They must next analyze the data to create a rough sales forecast. The sales forecast then becomes the basis for the business plan. Students must consider the marketing aspects of the venture, the amount and kind of financing that is most appropriate, the human resources needed, the facilities needed, and a host of other issues. In addition, it forces them to actually go out and contact real estate brokers, bankers, and media representatives. They must collect data on the demand for their product/service, determine prices, estimate expenses, and do pro forma financial statements.

I have found that the best way to do this is to create groups of three to five students. Let them choose their business, subject to the instructor's constraints. I put a financial requirement of $50,000 to $2 million on the project in order that they select a project that is doable but challenging. This prevents them from choosing a project that is clearly too simple or choosing one that is so large that it is not realistic.

The grade for the business plan should be significant -- perhaps forty percent. I recommend having the teams present the plan in class as if they were presenting it to loan officers or venture capitalists. Bank loan officers or a panel of entrepreneurs could also be invited to the presentations to add some reality to them. To add even more incentive, there are some business plan competitions in which top plans from a school are submitted to a regional or national panel of judges.

The business plan should be assigned within the first two or three weeks in order to allow sufficient time to complete it. It is also useful to require milestone reports -- such as a market analysis, a sales forecast, and pro forma financial statements -- throughout the semester to prevent a do-or-die project during the last two weeks of class.

In accepting business plan proposals, be careful to prevent too many of the typical student plans -- bars, restaurants, and laundromats -- or proposals that are quite similar to ones done in past years. Also be wary of the proposal that is clearly the brainchild of one team member when other team members are either resistant or are clearly indifferent.

My experience is that students have been pleased with the project even though it is a lot of work. They realize that the process is essentially the same as they may use someday for themselves.

Small Business Institute

The SBI program was discussed earlier. The value of the Small Business Institute program is that it gives the students real world consulting experiences. It forces them to establish rapport with a client, determine the perceived as well as the actual problem, analyze the situation, and recommend a set of solutions. Both a written and an oral presentation is required.

My experience is that students almost universally appreciate the opportunity to do an SBI project. The project can either be assigned very early in a semester or perhaps half-way through the term. If assigned early, then the students will work along on the SBI project while also studying the chapter content of the course. In the other version, the material is compressed into approximately half of the semester. Then attention is turned completely to the SBI project. The first version has the advantage of allowing more total time for the project. However, some teams burn out before the semester is over. In addition, trying to do a project while also listening to lectures and studying for exams is somewhat difficult and confusing. The problem of doing the SBI in the last half is simply the lack of time to do a good job.

Library Research Project

If a class does not lend itself well to group projects, a possible project is to assign a library research project. This project can take different forms. One is to require an in-depth analysis of a particular entrepreneur such as the late Sam Walton, Michael Dell, Ray Speer, or Steve Jobs. The intent here is to study the unique characteristics of significant entrepreneurs. Do they stand out as role models? Are they truly unique? Can others succeed with the same set of characteristics.

A second library assignment is to do an in-depth research paper on some aspect of the entrepreneurial process. Examples could include the characteristics of entrepreneurs, types of financing, the financing process, strategies for potential entrepreneurs with a given product or service, the pros and cons of franchising, passing the firm on to heirs, or valuation methods for closely held firms. This gives the student the opportunity to spend time focusing on some aspect of entrepreneurship that is especially interesting. A side benefit of the process research project is that the <u>instructor</u> gains knowledge of entrepreneurship surreptitiously by reading a number of different research studies.

A third assignment is to have students do either a library-based feasibility study of some opportunity or a statistical analysis of a research hypothesis. The library-based feasibility study would utilize demographic, economic and industry information to assess the feasibility of an idea. The research hypothesis testing could easily be used in graduate courses to determine correlation between given characteristics of an entrepreneurial topic.

Case Writing Project

An assignment that is both interesting and fruitful is to assign students the task of writing one or more cases that could be considered for publication. Cases such as those found in Part VII of <u>Entrepreneurship: A Planning Approach</u> could be prepared by one or more students and should be based on the analysis of a real company situation or problem. It may seem strange to assign case <u>writing</u> as an assignment. However, a significant learning process can occur. First, the case writing must be preceded by some in-depth analysis. A good case must have information on each of the functional areas, so the students must spend considerable time with either an actual client or with written information in order to do the required analysis. Second, the case must have a decision focus. This forces students to think into the future. Third, the case must be written in a professional, yet readable manner thereby giving students an exercise in communicative writing.

Potential cases can come from either the instructor's past consulting, Small Business Institute clients, or from student contacts. This gives an additional learning experience, the establishment of contact and rapport with the focal person for the case. One caveat, however, is that the contact person must understand thoroughly that the information provided will be made public. The person must sign off on the case to prevent any hard feelings later. They must also be made aware that if the case is published, they will likely receive phone calls over the next several years as students try to track down the company for additional information. Disguising the case by changing names and locations can help somewhat but is not always done sufficiently well to avoid later calls. A last very important warning is to allow absolutely no surreptitious gathering of information that could cause later problems when made known.

Actual Start-up

A final project which offers the epitome of realism is to require an actual start-up. Some schools do this routinely and even have a small capital fund dedicated to start-ups. In this situation, students are given the task of actually starting a venture as part of a class project. This works best if either a multiple semester project is used or if the venture is passed on to students the next term. In a few situations, the business is a more or less permanent business which is run each term by a different set of managers. This requires careful guidance of instructors and cooperation of a number of individuals such as bankers, realtors, and the media.

Alternatively, students who have real entrepreneurial interests, such as those who are members of ACE (the Association of Collegiate Entrepreneurs) may start ventures on their own that they may or may not keep after the end of the term. These ventures will vary all the way from one selling balloons and birthday cakes to cleaning businesses to retail clothing stores to computer software or hardware firms.

Suggested Grading Plans

There are as many grading possibilities as there are structures. The following are suggestions, but these are presented only as a starting point. Instructors will surely adapt them to their own personal style.

Four exams @ 100 points each	400 points
Three exams @ 100 points each	
Five quizzes @ 10 points each	
Class discussion - 50 points	400 points
Three exams @ 100 points each	
Two written cases @ 50 points each	
Quizzes - 50 points	
Business plan - 200 points	600 points
Two exams @ 150 points	
Class discussion - 50 points	
Business plan - 200 points	
Business plan presentation - 50 points	600 points
One exam - 200 points	
SBI Project - 200 points	400 points
No exam	
Class discussion - 50 points	
Four written cases @ 50 points	
Business plan - 200 points	
Peer evaluation - 50 points	500 points

No exam
Ten weekly quizzes @ 25 points
Business plan - 200 points   450 points

Three exams @ 100 points
Quizzes - 50 points
Research paper - 100 points   450 points

Two exams @ 150 points
Actual venture results - 400 points   700 points

Suggested Placement of Cases

The cases included in Entrepreneurship: A Planning Approach were selected to illustrate a variety of issues in an entrepreneurship course. They differ dramatically in length, ranging from three to twenty pages. Given the nature of the course, the cases are somewhat heavy on start-ups. But topics also include the entrepreneur, valuation, expansion, the buy/sell decision, financing, family problems, and dealing with conflict between owners. Some cases will have more than one issue involved. Those cases marked with a computer disk logo have been included on the fisCAL key disk accompanying the text. The following charts are intended as a guide in selection and use of cases. Part IV of the manual will discuss the cases in depth based upon the case author's teaching note.

CASE NAME	DIFFICULTY	LENGTH	CHAPTER	TOPICS
A. Artisan's Haven	Moderate	Moderate	6,5	Buy/Sell
B. International Learning Center	Moderate	Long	3,5,8	Start-up, Strategy
C. Doorstep Video	Easy	Medium	3,5	Start-up, Analysis of Opportunity
D. Wisconsin Sealcoating	Moderate	Long	4,5,8	Business Plan, Strategy
E. Southern Cabinet	Moderate	Medium	15,16	Valuation, Harvest
F. Gal-Tech	Moderate	Long	4,5	Business Plan, Analysis of Opportunity
G. Movies R Us	Easy	Short	13,16	Managing, Harvesting
H. Campground for Sale	Easy	Short	5	Analysis of Opportunity
I. Christian's	Moderate	Medium	5,6,15	Buyout, Analysis of Opportunity

J. Martin Enterprise	Difficult	Long	15,16	Valuation, Harvest
K. Mail Order	Moderate	Medium	5,6	Analysis of Opportunity
L. TeleSell	Moderate	Short	5	Analysis of Opportunity
M. Comic Relief	Easy	Short	3,5,6	Entrepreneur, Opportunity Analysis
N. Environmental Systems	Moderate	Short	3,6,13	Problem with Partnership
O. The Fab Lab	Easy	Short	3,5,8,9	Start-up, Strategy
P. Creative Mind	Moderate	Medium	5,8	Start-up, Strategy

Suggestions for Videos

Each of the Blue Chip Enterprise Institute videos is three to five minutes in length and features a company whose entrepreneur overcame adversity in the environment to make the firm successful. The four tapes can either be used as they are or can be shown in groups of selected segments to illustrate key points. Part IV of the manual discusses the videos in more depth.

LECTURE GUIDES

The entrepreneurship class is a relatively easy class to teach once the instructor is familiar with the material. One reason the class is enjoyable is that most of the students want to be there. Typically, two-thirds to three-fourths of the students in an entrepreneurship class have a sincere desire to start their own business. A few others will have an interest in consulting. Because the majority of the students see a direct connection between the class and their career, they have a vested interest in the class. Thus, we can make the assumption that most of the students sincerely want to be in the class.

A second reason the class is an interesting one to teach is that many of the students already have experience in small businesses. Some will already own a business, many will have grown up in a family business, and some of those have plans to return to the business after graduation. Thus, many students have stories to share with the class, it is seldom difficult to elicit discussion on topics.

Lecture Guide Outline

For each of the sixteen chapters, the following will be provided.

1. Teaching Objectives

2. Chapter Outlines

3. Suggestions for "Consider This!" discussion generators

4. Chapter Summary

5.   Teaching Strategy

6.   Suggested answers for Discussion Questions

7.   Suggestions for use of exercises

8.   Comments on Conveniesse, Inc. case

CHAPTER ONE
INTRODUCTION TO ENTREPRENEURSHIP

TEACHING OBJECTIVES

The teaching objectives for this chapter are for students to understand:

1. What needs entrepreneurship can meet for individuals.

2. Why America is turning to entrepreneurship.

3. The significance of entrepreneurship.

4. The nature of the challenges of entrepreneurship.

5. Some examples of America's entrepreneurs.

6. The need for vision in entrepreneurship.

7. The need for ethics in entrepreneurial ventures.

CHAPTER OUTLINE

I. The Trend Toward an Entrepreneurial Society

II. The Significance of Entrepreneurship

III.   The Challenge of Entrepreneurship

IV.   Anyone Can be an Entrepreneur

V.   New Ventures and Survival

VI.   America's Entrepreneurs

     A.   Gustavus Swift

     B.   Richard Sears

     C.   Paul Galvin

     D.   John Johnson

     E.   Sam Walton

     F.   J. W. Marriott

     G.   Mary Kay Ash

     H.   Roy Speer

     I.   Bob Levine

VII.   Entrepreneurial Vision

VIII.   Ethics and Entrepreneurship

IX.   The Plan for the Book

CONSIDER THIS!

The Consider This! comments have, as their sole purpose, the generation of interest in the topics covered in the chapters. The statements or questions may or may not be covered directly in the chapter. They are designed to get the student to thinking about the topic. They also serve well as discussion generators for class. The comments below and in successive chapters are simply suggested replies or responses to the items.

*   Successful entrepreneurs sometimes get folk hero status because their success brings publicity with it that magnifies their accomplishments, their vision, and their willingness to take risks. Further, many entrepreneurs are a touch eccentric and these idiosyncrasies -- good or bad -- become well known. H. Ross Perot is an excellent example and certainly worth discussing. Sam Walton is another. Ray Kroc, Harland Sanders, and Steve Jobs are others.

* There will always be room for successful entrepreneurs. The products or services may be different, but opportunities will always abound.

* This is a good discussion generator. Get the class to speculate on what the next frontiers will be. Electronics? Services? Consulting? Total Quality Management?

* The differences in ethical and unethical entrepreneurs is difficult to determine by looking at someone. Perhaps extended discussion with individuals can give clues to their management philosophies, including their ethical nature. Unfortunately, no precise determination can be made until <u>after</u> an unethical act has been committed.

* Sometimes successful entrepreneurs <u>cannot</u> maintain their charisma after a fall. Still, however, they tend to be remembered for what they gained or created rather than what they lost.

CHAPTER SUMMARY

This chapter sets the stage for the study of entrepreneurship. It sets forth the proposition that entrepreneurship is a challenge, it is significant to the American business scene, and it is part of a growing trend in America. Several examples of classic and successful entrepreneurs are presented. These are discussed as a means of showing how entrepreneurs of the past did, in fact, overcome adversity and competition to make their ventures real growth companies. The value of that is to see that the past sets the stage for the future. There are still frontiers to be conquered in the entrepreneurship area, and there are many opportunities to become the classic entrepreneur of the 21st century. The need for vision in entrepreneurship is noted. As contemporary society becomes more complex, it is important that the entrepreneurial vision be objective and leave room for analysis. Equally important as vision is ethics. An entrepreneur plays a pivotal role in establishing an ethical tone for the venture that can affect actions throughout the entrepreneurial process.

TEACHING STRATEGY

The overall point of this introductory chapter is simply to introduce the concept of entrepreneurship. It hopefully will generate interest in the rest of the book. As such it is good to key on such things as the satisfaction and challenge of entrepreneurship. Discuss why owning one's own business can be good. Get the students to begin thinking now about whether they would like to own their own venture. Get them to realize that it isn't all easy -- that the majority of new ventures do fail. It may not be too early to start asking them what differentiates a successful venture from an unsuccessful venture, although there are no clear answers.

The discussion of historical entrepreneurs is designed primarily to generate interest. You may or may not want to spend time in class on this. If you do, key on what was significant about their venture or their vision or their style that caused the success. Answers such as perseverance, risk taking, the ability to seize an opportunity, and even luck may surface.

The need for vision is a key point. Focus on focus. That is, key on the need for an explicitly directed set of activities to achieve a goal. Key on the ability to analyze an opportunity and exploit it.

Some instructors ignore the discussion of ethics or put it near the end in an obscure fashion. This book hits it here to set the stage and then returns to it in Chapter 13. The need for an early discussion of ethics in an entrepreneurship class cannot be overstated. Entrepreneurs tend to be action oriented, doing whatever is necessary to get what is needed. Some entrepreneurs -- and particularly young ones -- tend to be "wheeler-dealers" who will take advantage of any situation. It is important to establish right up front that ethics in entrepreneurship is both important and doable. Spend several minutes in class emphasizing this point.

This is a good place to show some of the Blue Chip Enterprise Institute videos. In particular, show Kelly Truck Lines.

Discussion Questions

1. Entrepreneurship is challenging both because of the inherent risk and because of the vast amount of effort needed to effectively launch and grow a business. It can be rewarding because of the possible wealth accumulation plus the degree to which it meets psychological needs. It is more rewarding than many occupations in that the entrepreneur is in total control. Thus, both successes and failures are a direct result of the entrepreneur's efforts.

2. The wealth generated by successful entrepreneurial ventures can satisfy virtually all of Maslow's needs, including self-actualization. In McClelland's framework, the wealth can be a symbol of achievement and a means to meet affiliation goals and -- to an extent -- power goals.

3. Evidence of an entrepreneurial society is found in the popular press as the entrepreneur is accorded almost a folk hero status. The number of small ventures increases each year, especially in the high tech fields. Further, large companies are

spinning off (or closing down) divisions. This provides opportunities for experienced entrepreneurs to achieve success on their own.

4.   In a stagnant or recessionary economy, large firms tend to lay off workers instead of hire them. At the same time, there were significant numbers of new firms on the horizons, and many existing ventures were achieving some growth. Thus, the net result is a larger increase in jobs provided by smaller companies.

5.   The entrepreneurs were probably not unique. They did have a vision and a drive to make their product succeed. It is doubtful that they had specific skills that led to their success, and entrepreneurial successes do have their share of luck. We all know, however, that luck often comes to those who work for it. The cliche concerning the relative proportion of inspiration and perspiration is worth discussing.

6.   The answer is a qualified yes for each. Entrepreneurs are not decreed by birth to be so ordained. On the other hand many entrepreneurs were born into entrepreneurial families. Entrepreneurs are partially "made" through education and training. Much of this learning is informal over a period of time. Examples of training would also include the course in which this book is used.

7.   Both Walton and Ash developed unique cultures in their ventures keying on the worth of the individual and the need to give customers what they want. In both cases, their previous employers failed to do that.

8.   Opportunities do not necessarily "just happen," but many entrepreneurs do capitalize on a situation or unmet need. The key is the recognition of the opportunity. This will be discussed more in Chapter 5.

9.   Entrepreneurial vision is a touch hard to define. Call it the ability to recognize an opportunity coupled with a firm grasp on the strategy necessary to capitalize on it. Other parts of the vision could be the ability to analyze developing trends, the ability to analyze and acquire the necessary financial resources, and the ability to attract a management team to help the venture grow. At the same time, it is much easier to discuss a successful entrepreneur's vision than it is to predict how visionary a given person is today.

10. The text mentioned two reasons. First, smaller companies are relatively immune to government watchdogs. Second, however, an exposed unethical act can be terminal. It is quite important to hammer the need for ethics early in the class and every other opportunity during the class. Entrepreneurs -- especially young ones -- are tempted to take advantage of situations and people. It is important to establish the rules of the game. This is all the more important in new ventures because the entrepreneur plays such a crucial role in establishing the culture of the firm.

EXERCISE 1-1

This exercise is a continuation of "America's entrepreneurs." It may be of interest to have students not only guess which entrepreneur goes with which product, but to then have them guess <u>when</u> that product was first introduced. Most will be surprised how far back many of the products go.

Individual	Product/Service	Date of Start-up	Company
William Wrigley	Gum	1892	William Wrigley Co.
John Styth	Soft Drinks	1886	Coca-Cola Co.
F.L. Maytag	Home Appliances	1893	Maytag
Steven Jobs	Personal Computers	1977	Apple Computer
Charles Walgreen	Drug Stores	1901	Walgreen's
W.T. Coleman	Camp Stoves	??	Coleman
Cyrus McCormick	Mechanical Reaper	1831	International Harvester
George Eastman	Cameras	1880	Kodak
William Carrier	Air Conditioners	1914	Carrier
Michael Owens	Glass	1903	Owens-Illinois
Ole Evinrude	Outboard Motors	1909	Evinrude
Cyrus Curtis	Magazine Publishing	1883	Curtis Publishing
Fred Smith	Overnight Delivery	1971	Federal Express
Frank Perdue	Chicken	1940	Perdue
William Proctor	Soap	1837	Proctor & Gamble
David Sarnoff	Broadcasting	1920	RCA

EXERCISE 1-2

This exercise makes a good out of class assignment.

CONVENIESSE, INC.

This is the first installment of Conveniesse, Inc., an upscale convenience store located in an office complex. It is based on an actual business plan prepared for my entrepreneurship class. The unique aspect of the Conveniesse segments is that time passes while being always in the present. That is, the entrepreneurs age, and the chain grows over time. Yet, each segment discusses the venture as if it were in the present. So the assignments that go with the Conveniesse segments are always contemporary. Regardless of whether the focus is on launching the venture, growing it, or eventually considering selling it, the discussion and assignments are as if it were occurring today.

I recommend having the students read the case segment each time. Some days allow time to discuss it, and some won't. You may want to make written assignments or do group discussions in class. None of the assignments require extensive analysis. They are designed to give the students an opportunity to think about how the theory of the chapter could be applied in an actual situation.

In the Chapter 1 segment, the three potential entrepreneurs have just met at a convention, get to know each other, and begin discussing the possibility of an upscale convenience store. This may be the students' first exposure to such a venture. Ask them if they think it will really work. Then key in on whether it will work with these three entrepreneurs. We will come back to these questions in later chapters.

CHAPTER 2

THE NATURE OF ENTREPRENEURSHIP

TEACHING OBJECTIVES

The teaching objectives for this chapter are for students to:

1. Define entrepreneurship and its ingredients.

2. Understand that entrepreneurship is a process.

3. Explain how entrepreneurship differs from corporate management.

4. Explain the five components of a venture launch.

5. Work with the entrepreneurship equation.

6. Recognize that different amounts of entrepreneurship exist in various ventures.

7. Recognize differences in the amount of entrepreneurial activity as venture growth increases.

CHAPTER OUTLINE

I.   What is Entrepreneurship

    A.   Starting a Business

    B.   Creativity and Innovation

    C.   Managing for Growth

    D.   Seeking Financing

    E.   Assuming Risk

    F.   The Essential Ingredients?

II.   Definition of Entrepreneurship

III. Entrepreneurship vs. Corporate Management

    A.   Risk Management vs. Risk Minimization

    B.   Opportunity Driven vs. Resource Driven

    C.   Action vs. Analysis

    D.   Lean Management Team vs. Personnel Heavy

IV.   Intrapreneurship -- the Corporate Compromise

V.   The Components of Entrepreneurial Ventures

    A.   The Entrepreneur

    B.   The Opportunity

    C.   The Structure

    D.   The Resources

    E.   The Strategy

VI.   The Entrepreneurial Process

    A.   The Entrepreneurial Process Illustrated

VII.   The Entrepreneurship Decision

    A.   The Antecedent Factor

    B.   The Triggering Factor

    C.   The Enabling Factor

VIII.   Entrepreneurship and Venture Growth

    A.   The Key Role of the Entrepreneur

    B.   The Low Growth Venture

    C.   The Growth Venture

    D.   The Very High Growth Venture

    E.   The Distribution of Ventures

    F.   Entrepreneurial Activity in the Venture

CONSIDER THIS!

*   Entrepreneurship is a process, not a result. Hence, there is no such thing as "an entrepreneurship." The better question is "Are all start-up ventures entrepreneurial?" This question will probably be debated as long as there are academics teaching entrepreneurship. The position taken in this text is that launching any venture requires at least some entrepreneurial activity, but there is a wide variance in the amount of entrepreneurial activity required.

*   According to this text's view, you were technically an entrepreneur if you had a business when you were growing up. The bigger issue is that these childhood ventures may have set the stage for later ventures.

*   A good idea is far superior to good financial resources. A good idea can generate financial resources. A bad idea will waste whatever financial resources are available.

* Entrepreneurial ventures surely depend somewhat on the potential of the opportunity, and some on the luck of the draw. But entrepreneurship keys on the entrepreneur. An entrepreneurial founder can make a major difference in the growth of a venture.

* Most ventures are not particularly entrepreneurial even though they may be solid businesses. Most will not grow significantly.

* The five components -- the entrepreneur, the opportunity, the structure, the resources, and the strategy.

CHAPTER SUMMARY

Entrepreneurship is the act of starting or growing a business through innovative, risk assuming management. There are several key components that are part of entrepreneurship, although they are present in varying degrees in different entrepreneurial situations. These elements include starting a business, being creative, managing growth, financing a venture, and assuming risks. Although all new ventures contain at least some entrepreneurship, the amount of entrepreneurship varies from venture to venture.

Entrepreneurship is a process, not a result. Entrepreneurship is action oriented. It is not the result of actions but consists of the actions themselves. As such it is a dynamic process. The tasks required for entrepreneurship vary over time, and no one set of actions nor one sequence of actions ensures success.

Entrepreneurship differs from corporate management in many ways. Most notable is the degree of risk assumption, the role of resources and opportunities, the make-up of management, and the tendency toward action rather than analysis. A rare exception to these differences is the intrapreneurial firm which is the larger corporation that adopts entrepreneurial principles.

There are five components in the launch of an entrepreneurial venture. Each is important in the launch and growth of a new venture. The first is the entrepreneur. The skills possessed by the entrepreneur are critical for successful funding and launch of a growth oriented venture. The second factor is the opportunity. Potential entrepreneurs must carefully analyze opportunities to assure that they are real, exploitable opportunities. Financing is the third factor. Most new ventures are undercapitalized. Financing is important to the future growth of the venture. The fourth factor is the structure which refers to the type of legal organization used and the general method of competing, such as franchises, manufacturers, distributorships, or retailers. The final factor is the strategy. This is important in determining how the venture will compete.

Three sets of variables help determine whether or not a venture is likely to be launched. The antecedent factor consists of variables in a person's background or current job that make entrepreneurship appealing. The precipitating or triggering factor consists of variables that encourage the individual to take the steps necessary to actually launch the venture. These include being laid off from a job, moving to a new location, discovering or developing a new product, or a change in lifestyle. The enabling factor consists of those variables which allow a venture to be launched. These primarily include an opportunity and necessary resources. The greater the number or strength of variables present in any of the three factors, the greater will be the likelihood that the venture will be launched.

Two broad types of ventures exist. The first is the typical small business venture which is started small with the intention of remaining small. The second type is the growth oriented venture which is started with the intention of achieving sustained growth. The growth venture will be better capitalized and will typically have a developed competitive strategy. A small number of ventures are very high growth ventures. These require major financing, a strong management team, and actions necessary to increase and maintain growth.

The amount of entrepreneurial activity a venture exhibits will be a function of the entrepreneur's desires and skills. This amount of activity will increase over time for growth ventures and will be much lower for low growth ventures.

TEACHING STRATEGY

This chapter begins the meat of the discussion of entrepreneurship. This is the time to fully differentiate between entrepreneurship and management. Students may not recognize that entrepreneurship is not just "good management." They need to understand that the nature of starting and growing an entrepreneurial venture includes a different set of actions and a different philosophy than corporate management does. While some will argue that good managers will also take risks, note for them that entrepreneurs invest their own capital, have limited staff and resources, and typically have short time horizons.

Entrepreneurship is, indeed, action oriented. In fact, this text constantly entreats students and entrepreneurs to be <u>less</u> action oriented and to take time to analyze and plan. On the one hand, it is recognized that entrepreneurs <u>must</u> be action oriented while on the other, we are all aware that many entrepreneurs are too action oriented and shoot from the hip. Entrepreneurs must deal with both a short and long time horizon. Opportunity windows are frequently quite short and require quick reaction. Sometimes, however, an extended length of time is required before success is realized. New ventures are almost always understaffed and undercapitalized. Point out that this is what makes entrepreneurship interesting -- the challenge of doing more with less.

The five components of entrepreneurial ventures is fairly straightforward but is worth discussing. The entrepreneur is the force behind the venture. The opportunity must be real and not an illusion. Gaining financing for the venture may be the most difficult task. The structure chosen for the venture may be a key to success. Finally, the strategy developed provides the actions necessary to achieve venture goals.

A significant amount of time can be spent on the topic of entrepreneurship versus small business. In particular, discuss the relative amounts of entrepreneurial behavior required to start various types of ventures. What is the difference, for example, in the launch of Apple Computer as compared with a corner restaurant or craft store? Both required some amount of entrepreneurial behavior, but Apple obviously required far more than the small business. An interesting discussion is to get students involved in the debate regarding whether the small business really is an entrepreneurial venture.

The final topic in the chapter deals with the entrepreneurial equation. This is a lead-in to the next chapter on the entrepreneur. The equation states that the likelihood of launching a venture is a function of the potential entrepreneur's background, triggering events, and the ability to launch the venture. This should generate discussion. Students may suggest that they are an exception one direction or the other. That is, they may desire to start a venture, but not have high "scores" on any of the factors. Conversely, a person may have high scores but not want to start a business. Discuss whether these are exceptions to the rule or whether the equation is too broad or too narrow.

DISCUSSION QUESTIONS

1.   The definition used in this text is: Entrepreneurship is the launch and/or growth of a venture using innovative management. Some sources key on the launch while others focus on innovation and growth.

2.   The ingredients in entrepreneurship include innovation, launch, growth, financing, and the acceptance of risk. Risk is inherent in any venture. Perhaps most important for continued growth is innovation. Unless the entrepreneurial team continues to innovate and capitalize on the innovation, it will be overtaken by competitors.

3.   Entrepreneurship is something you do, not something you have. It is a set of actions, not a set of results. Thus, one venture can be more entrepreneurial than another because its owners exhibit a higher level of entrepreneurial behavior.

4.   The text suggests that the first step is to analyze the opportunity. This is most critical and should be done first. The remaining steps would not have to be in that order. Perhaps the entrepreneur should identify resources before determining the structure. And perhaps a strategy should be developed first in order to know what resources are necessary. Thus, the last three are somewhat arbitrary after the opportunity analysis.

5.   Antecedent refers to coming before or pre-existing. Thus, antecedent variables are those that already exist in an individual's background. Although there are exceptions to everything, most researchers feel that the greater the strength or number of antecedent variables, the greater will be the motivation to start a venture.

6.   College students are likely unaware that precipitating or triggering variables may be encountered relatively soon. Graduation is one. An undesirable first job after graduation occurs more often than they realize. College friends also stay in touch and may provide a trigger in the form of a partnership offer.

7.   A low growth venture will have a smaller management team. It will typically have less experienced managers. It will require less analysis -- sometimes very little. Many low growth ventures will require little, if any, outside funding. A low growth venture may be somewhat less likely to exist five years into the future simply because it may be undercapitalized and have a limited management team. The growth oriented venture may be more likely to survive because of a more experienced team and a more in-depth analysis prior to start-up.

8.   A low growth venture is clearly easier to start than a growth oriented venture because it requires less financing, less other resources, less marketing, and less commitment.

9. Answers will vary, but students should be able to identify businesses that fit in either category.

10.   In many cases, the two types of firms are identifiable in an unscientific manner by looking at the knowledge and aggressiveness of the entrepreneur, the amount and types of financing, and the degree to which a strategy has been developed.

Exercise 2-1

This is a simple and unscientific exercise to get students to think about their own backgrounds and future plans. It can be either assigned for an outside project or partially done in class. Students may note an inability to quantify some of their variables. A subjective weighting may be required in order to get a comparison. The idea here is not to reach a definitive number, but to point toward tendencies.

Conveniesse, Inc.

In this segment, the three potential entrepreneurs take turns telling about their backgrounds, their current jobs, and their plans for the future. Looking at their entrepreneurial equation scores, we can see that Sarah already owns a venture and is considering selling out. This suggests high scores on all three factors, including the enabling factor. Jason grew up in an entrepreneurial family, wanted to reject those experiences, but found a recurring tug to do something on his own. He also did not seem tied forever to his job. Yolanda does not seem to have much of a tendency on any of the three factors.

CHAPTER 3

THE ENTREPRENEUR

TEACHING OBJECTIVES

The teaching objectives for this chapter are for students to:

1. Define the term <u>entrepreneur</u>.

2. Recognize typical characteristics of entrepreneurs.

3. Understand the traits which constitute the entrepreneurial personality.

4. Understand similarities between male and female entrepreneurs, minority and non-minority entrepreneurs, and successful and unsuccessful entrepreneurs.

5. Understand the unique problems facing women entrepreneurs, minority entrepreneurs, and family business entrepreneurs.

6. Differentiate between entrepreneurs who own low growth ventures and those who own higher growth firms.

7. Understand the need for carefully developing an entrepreneurial team and advisory team.

CHAPTER OUTLINE

I.   Definitions of Entrepreneurship

II. Characteristics of Entrepreneurs

    A.   Entrepreneurial Backgrounds

    B.   Age

    C.   Education Level

    D.   Motivation for Starting the Venture

III. The Entrepreneurial Personality

    A.   Risk-taking Propensity

    B.   Autonomy and Locus of Control

    C.   Need for Achievement

    D.   Tolerance for Ambiguity

IV. Successful vs. Unsuccessful Entrepreneurs

V.   Low vs. High Growth Entrepreneurs

    A.   The Small Business Entrepreneur

    B.   The Growth Entrepreneur

    C.   The High Growth Entrepreneur

VI. Women, Minorities, and Family Business Entrepreneurs

    A.   Women Entrepreneurs

    B.   Minority Entrepreneurs

    C.   Family Business Entrepreneurs

VII.   Assembling the Entrepreneurial Team

VIII.   Assembling an Advisory Board

CONSIDER THIS!

*   Entrepreneurs vary greatly, so there can be no one combination that is "the right stuff" for entrepreneurs. However, research does suggest that a need for achievement, need for autonomy, an internal locus of control, and a moderate risk-taking propensity are key characteristics.

*   Because of the variation among entrepreneurs, there are many exceptions to the rules. Thus, some students will identify entrepreneurs who are counter to much of what is suggested here. My experience, however, is that students will generally agree with the above. The entrepreneurial personality is quite pervasive.

*   The answer is a qualified yes to both of these. Evidence suggests that many entrepreneurs did have those tendencies at a young age although socialization may be stronger than heredity. At the same time, evidence also suggests that entrepreneurial characteristics can be developed. Certainly entrepreneurial skills can be taught.

*   Entrepreneurial role models are frequently a parent. But they could also be friends, other relatives, or neighbors. The key is not the particular relationship, but rather that the budding entrepreneur spent quality time with or near the role model.

*   Many entrepreneurs are adamant in their unwillingness to work for others. They clearly have a strong need for autonomy. This transcends their need for success.

*   This certainly is true -- to the extent that some authors and/or instructors resist the temptation to pigeonhole entrepreneurs as a group. Still, the entrepreneurial personality and other characteristics are strong antecedents for entrepreneurship.

CHAPTER SUMMARY

This chapter presents the entrepreneur as a relatively independent, achievement motivated individual who is a moderate or calculated risk taker. Entrepreneurs often begin their first venture while they are in their 20s or 30s although a number begin later in life. Most entrepreneurs are inner directed; that is, they feel in command of their fate. They are achievement motivated, have a high need for autonomy, and have high tolerance for ambiguity or uncertainty. They are increasingly higher educated, especially if they start high-tech related firms.

Some entrepreneurs are "pushed" into starting a venture either because they were fired or laid off from their jobs, because of geographic move, or other reasons that form a negative encouragement to start a venture. Dissatisfaction with jobs or the role of homemaker cause many women to launch their first venture. Other entrepreneurs are "pulled" into starting a venture by a potential opportunity. Many high-tech entrepreneurs were attracted to their venture by the opportunities of the fast growth computer-related industry.

Differentiating successful entrepreneurs from unsuccessful entrepreneurs is difficult because of the inability to unequivocally define the term "successful." However, there are salient differences in high growth versus low growth entrepreneurs.

Small business entrepreneurs typically start small ventures that remain relatively small. The business is seen as a means of earning a comfortable living, and growth of the business is neither planned nor desired. Growth entrepreneurs are far more growth oriented and take the necessary planning steps to achieve that growth. Low growth entrepreneurs have different philosophies regarding delegation of authority, financing, risk, and their definition of success.

Women and minority entrepreneurs tend to be more like their white male entrepreneurial counterparts than they are like other women or minorities, and they tend to start ventures for the same reasons. They sometimes have trouble gaining financing and other assistance because of discrimination, inadequate training, or the type of venture they start.

Family business entrepreneurs, though little different from non-family entrepreneurs face added challenges because of the interface between the family and the business. Copreneurs -- husband/wife combinations -- are increasing in numbers. These combinations offer substantial advantages if the work/home responsibilities can be kept separate.

Entrepreneurs must consider the makeup of their venture team as part of the pre-launch planning. Growth ventures require experienced team members who can make significant contributions to the success of the venture. The lead entrepreneur must determine exactly which managerial positions are necessary and what skills are needed to balance the strengths and weaknesses of other team members. Finally, every venture should have an advisory board of some type to give objective advice to the owner and to provide contacts with others.

TEACHING STRATEGY

The key to this chapter is to get the students to determine whether they think there is such a thing as a set of characteristics that defines an entrepreneur. It is important to establish up front that the characteristics are tendencies and not cast in stone.

This chapter is an exciting one to teach because of the makeup of the class. In most sections, over 2/3 of the students will have an interest in starting their own venture. Thus, they are interested in seeing how well they fit the entrepreneurial model. (Interestingly, I have found that the percentage who want to start their own venture goes up as the desirability of the class time goes down, since budding entrepreneurs will seek out the section regardless of the time slot.)

I like to ask one of our testing counselors to come to class and administer the Myers-Briggs Personality Inventory. I usually do this on the first or second day of class so the results can be back by the time I get to Chapter 3. Bradley's counselor does a good job of identifying the different personality types that are relevant. Typically the ESTJ, ENTJ, and ENTP groupings are identified. Some research suggests that the STJs tend to make good small business entrepreneurs while the NTPs make better growth entrepreneurs. If the counselor is well trained and knows entrepreneurship (You may have to assist here.) she or he should indicate the need for a combination of personalities to balance the entrepreneurial team. The NTP tends to be the visionary while the STJs tend to be better managers. Other tests could be used to elicit thought on the entrepreneurial personality. The value is to get the students to think about their own characteristics as they apply.

This is also a good opportunity to get student involvement in discussion. Ask those students who grew up in a family venture to share their experiences. Some are fascinating.

Discuss low-growth versus growth-oriented entrepreneurs. Some may debate the model suggesting differences in backgrounds between the small business entrepreneur and growth entrepreneur even though research supports the position presented. Ask the class whether this is changing. For example, with more high-tech related ventures and service ventures, could there be a trend toward a new category of low-growth, but professional businesses whose entrepreneurs share characteristics of both the low-growth and growth oriented entrepreneurs?

Spend some time discussing entrepreneurial teams and advisory boards. Note to the class that very few small businesses have advisory boards. Ask for suggestions as to why this occurs (need for autonomy, unwillingness to share power). Does this account for some failures?

DISCUSSION QUESTIONS

1.   Entrepreneurs appear to have similar personality types because they have similar values. For example, virtually any entrepreneur and many entrepreneurship students will tell you that they simply do not want to work for someone else. Most will say that they don't mind taking the risk associated with launching a venture. And many, but not all, will say that success is measured not by dollars but by a sense of achievement.

2.   A role model is more relevant for entrepreneurs than for many other occupations because of the intensity of the experience. In no other occupation except perhaps the ministry or farming are the children so closely involved with either day to day operation of the business or hear so much about it discussed at the dinner table. Thus, the experience is very pervasive throughout the younger person's formative years.

3.   The entrepreneurial window, primarily between 30 and 45, is significant. Before that age, most do not have sufficient capital or experience. After age 45, most are tied to a company. With early retirements a second window may be the 55 to 65 range. In response to someone saying they want to start a business at some other age, the answer should be cautious encouragement. A younger person should understand the need for capital, and the older person should understand the concept of investing one's retirement income. Aside from that, however, there certainly is nothing to prevent someone outside the window from launching a venture.

4.   "Successful" is a relative term because different people define it differently. One may assert that being successful means having a comfortable living. Another may insist that substantial wealth is the minimum acceptable definition. Still another may define it as the successful harvest of the venture. One highly successful entrepreneur questioned the meaning from the opposite viewpoint. Even though he is worth millions now, he mused that he sometimes wondered if it was worth all the sacrifice of his personal time. His significant comment was, "There is a limit to how many suits a person needs." The importance of this definitional problem is that outsiders may have inappropriate expectations of a given entrepreneur who may or may not be successful from someone else's perspective.

5.   Most launches will have elements of both a push and a pull. Usually some amount of dissatisfaction with the status quo is necessary to start the entrepreneurial juices flowing. An interesting exercise to is compare the push/pull hypothesis with the antecedent and triggering variables discussed in Chapter 2. They are not the same, but there are some similarities.

6.   Women have, in the past, had a tougher time because lenders, suppliers, and customers -- many of whom were male -- did not take them seriously. Fortunately, this is changing. Exacerbating the problem is that many women start service businesses, and

these are by nature more difficult to finance externally. This should continue to change as more and more women receive business degrees, hold managerial jobs, and operate successful ventures.

7.   An interesting exercise.

8.   Typically, an entrepreneur would not make a good manager in a large corporation over time because they would not have the patience needed in a large organization and because they would not be happy working within a multi-layered bureaucracy. They also may not be successful in a large business because they may appear to be somewhat of a maverick.

9.   This chapter suggested that low growth entrepreneurs tended to have a narrower education that is somewhat more trades related. Growth oriented entrepreneurs are thought to have a broader education perhaps including college and graduate degrees. Certainly exceptions to this can be found, especially among service businesses. It isn't clear why the low growth entrepreneurs are more risk averse.

10.   A growth oriented entrepreneur would likely not be content in a low growth business for long. One of two things will likely happen. First, the entrepreneur might exit the venture because of lack of challenge. The second alternative is that the growth oriented entrepreneur might transform the low growth venture into a growth oriented venture.

11.   I know of no research that clearly shows the relationship between motivation to start a venture and its subsequent growth. However, the relationship is a logical one.

12.   In a word -- balance. A team should have a visionary and a control oriented person. A growth oriented venture should have a financial expert. Aside from that, adding team members that fill voids is wise. It is good advice to determine the needs first and then find the team members rather than the opposite.

13.   An advisory team can serve as a sounding board. The advisory board can differentiate between the forest and the trees. It can keep the entrepreneur "honest" and encourage necessary analysis before taking action. An advisory board can also serve a pragmatic function of providing contacts. It is not necessary that all advisory board members be from outside the company, but at least some should be.

EXERCISE 3-1

I strongly recommend use of personality assessments in the entrepreneurship class. They give students an aid in determining their career path regardless of whether they become entrepreneurs or not.

EXERCISE 3-2

Since the text went to press, word has been received that ACE is no longer at Wichita State. It is now headquartered in New York. If your college or university encourages organizations, ACE is a good addition to student organizations. A word of caution: Be aware of the consequences of getting entrepreneurial students together in an organization. It can have interesting results.

EXERCISE 3-3

An interesting in-class project. It should generate some interesting interchange among the students.

CONVENIESSE, INC.

In this vignette, the three entrepreneurs are beginning to get serious about starting a venture together. Wisely, they decide to discuss their similarities and differences. Have the students discuss the three individuals' personality and background differences. Ask the question, "Even if the idea is good, are these three the best choices for an entrepreneurial team?" Do they balance each other? Who would the students guess will rise as the lead entrepreneur over time?

Jason seemed to be creative, but somewhat disorganized and not too analytical. Yolanda scored high on internal locus of control and self-confidence. Sarah scored quite high on risk-taking even though she seemed to have a more external locus of control. Ask students to discuss each of these and compare them with the information from Chapter 2. Sarah, for example, may have scored high in risk-taking because she was disillusioned with her own business and was ready for a change. Yolanda seemed to be the organized, self-confident and "take-charge" type. Yet, she also was happy in her job and was quite successful in it. Jason seemed to offer the least in terms of the needs for a convenience store. He admitted being disorganized and seemed to reject his own earlier experiences of growing up in a small business. Summarizing, each had some strengths and some weaknesses -- not atypical of any three entrepreneurs. Could they work together? Ask students to discuss whether they would make good <u>team</u> <u>members</u> regardless of whether they were starting a business or on a bowling league.

CHAPTER FOUR

BUSINESS PLANS AND PLANNING

TEACHING OBJECTIVES

The teaching objectives for this chapter are for students to understand:

1. The strategic planning process.

2. The use of business plans.

3. The difference between a strategic plan and a financial plan.

4. The benefits derived from developing business plans.

5. Important considerations in developing plans.

6. Formats of strategic plans and financial plans.

7. How to do a rough estimate of sales for new and existing firms.

CHAPTER OUTLINE

I.   The Nature of Business Plans

      A.   Strategic Plans

      B.   Financial Plans

II.   Benefits of Plans and Planning

III.   The Strategic Planning Process

      A.   Determining the Nature of the Venture

      B.   Assessing Entrepreneurial Opportunities

      C.   Analyzing the Venture's Capabilities

      D.   Identifying Distinctive Competencies

      E.   Developing Venture Strategies

      F.   Developing Supporting Strategies

          1. Marketing Strategies
          2. Operations Strategies
          3. Financial Strategies
          4. Human Resource Strategies
          5. Community Involvement Strategies

      G.   Implementation of Strategies

IV.   Writing the Strategic Plan

V.   Writing the Financial Plan

VI.   The Financial Plan Format

VII.   Developing the Sales Forecast

      A.   Forecasting for Existing Firms

      B.   Forecasting for Start-up Ventures

VIII.   A Concluding Note

IX.   Summary

CONSIDER THIS!

* The popular press is replete with examples of successful ventures whose entrepreneurs did not do formal planning. One can only question whether the entrepreneur was an astute intuitive planner and simply did not commit the plans to paper. Further, would there be even more successful firms if more had planned?

* The resulting documents may be used only once. They may also be out of date in a very few months as the situation changes. The <u>process</u> is the important aspect. The process is what encourages the entrepreneur to do objective analysis and carefully craft a strategy.

* A generic plan can be used if the funding sources are similar, such as one taken to two or three different banks. A distinct plan must be created for each distinct type of investor. Much of the plans will be the same regardless of differences.

* If something can't be said well in forty pages, it won't be said well in eighty pages. If a plan rambles on and on, investors will surely be concerned whether the entrepreneur would be sufficiently organized to operate the venture.

* Both of these sentences are true. Certainly planning and plans are most critical at the time of start-up. However, a start-up has no track record or history. Thus, developing a plan is a very difficult task.

CHAPTER SUMMARY

This chapter presents the value and nature of business plans. The benefits of developing a plan come both from the future use of the plan itself and the planning process which leads to the actual written plan.

The strategic planning process is a critically important prelude to writing either a strategic plan or a financial plan. The planning process includes determining the basic nature of the firm, analyzing opportunities and capabilities, identifying distinctive competencies, developing the venture strategy and supporting strategies, acquiring resources for the venture, and implementing the strategy.

Strategic plans are guides to the operation of the venture over the next year or years. They are internal documents designed to present the strengths and weaknesses of the venture compared with the opportunities facing the venture team. This plan should be developed with the help of key people in the organization and should be communicated to others within the venture.

The format of a strategic plan is not critical. However, several elements are important. It should include the venture mission statement, which states the nature of the venture and its philosophy. It should include a significant assessment of the venture's environment. This should be followed by an analysis of the firm's strengths and weaknesses. The major part of the plan should be the venture strategies. The plan should include both one-year and five-year goals, and it should end with carefully determined financial projections.

Financial plans are generally written to obtain funding for the venture. They must be done carefully and in such a way as to convince lenders or investors to underwrite the venture. The plan must be succinct, yet thorough. It must be objective and include substantial financial analyses and projections. The parts of the plan include the all-important executive summary, the nature of the venture, a description of the market, an explanation of the product or service being proposed, resumes of the management team, objectives and strategies for the venture, and financial statements and projections.

TEACHING STRATEGY

The key to this chapter is to get the students to understand the critical importance of the strategic planning process and the two types of plans. Entrepreneurship theory, how-to books, and popular magazines all point out the difference that planning can make in the success of a venture. Lack of planning is usually cited as one of the top three reasons for the failure of new businesses. Thus, it is very important to hammer this fact home at every opportunity.

The strategic planning model presented here is essentially the same as found in strategic management text books. It is adapted in Entrepreneurship: A Planning Approach to fit emerging ventures better. In particular, it includes the identification of distinctive competencies, the development of supporting strategies, and the acquisition of resources. It is important to key on the analysis stage of the planning process. Encourage students to differentiate between viable opportunities that have been carefully researched and those off-the-wall ideas that many potential entrepreneurs have. The analysis of opportunities will be covered in depth in Chapter 5.

In order to get students to focus on the planning model, utilize one of the start-up cases in the text, such as International Learning Centers, Doorstep Video, Campground for Sale -- Sold!, or Christians. The Campground case is brief and relatively easy to use for this purpose. Doorstep Video is even better since it can be used as of the time the case was written and then repositioned to current time and situation facing the video industry.

The strategic plan should be emphasized, especially for the start-up venture. Emphasize the need to do a strategic plan at the time of start-up. This plan then becomes the baseline for comparison with actual performance at the end of the year. Emphasize the need to review and update the plan. Suggest having a one-year and five-year plan. The five-year plan will be broad, but it points the direction for the firm.

Many people feel that the financial plan is the more important of the two types of plans. This is, of course, debatable. Regardless, the financial plan is important for venture funding and must be done well. Remind the students that they have only one chance with each potential funding source. Thus, they must do a good job the first time.

The format for the financial plan does not have to be precisely as presented in this chapter, but it should contain all the important ingredients. Key on the Executive Summary and its importance. Note to the students that venture capitalists see up to three or four hundred plans a year and fund only about one percent. Thus, the need for a good first impression is critical.

Financial data and projections are also very important. Income statements, balance sheets, and cash flow states should be presented and pro formas should be developed for at least three years into the future. My personal recommendation is that pro formas should be monthly for eighteen months to show a complete yearly cycle after the venture has stabilized. Then quarterly pro formas for three more years will show future trends.

Have the students read the Kryos, Inc. plan through. It is a lengthy plan, and some portions are omitted for space reasons. It is a good example, however, of thorough, objective analysis in support of the plan. It carefully lays out the size of the market for each kind of organ and bases those figures on government data. It suggests the benefits of vitrification in terms of money and lives saved. And it lays out very clear milestones. Compare it with the Conveniesse, Inc. plan which was "quickly put together" for the three entrepreneurs. It is an acceptable plan for the purposes for which it was designed, but is clearly not the quality of Kryos. The Gal-Tech and Melanin case also presents a set of facts and then a business plan prepared by the case authors. It is also well done and worthy of study.

The chapter ends with a discussion of developing a sales forecast. The sales forecast is, of course, the key to the pro formas. The forecast must be realistic and must be documented. This is a difficult task for any venture and nearly impossible to do well for a start-up. Key on the need for market research. Discuss ways to collect data for start-up or existing ventures. Have the students pick a particular idea for a venture, and then discuss how and where to find information on that particular idea.

DISCUSSION QUESTIONS

1. Entrepreneurs do not plan for a variety of reasons. They often do not know how to plan. More likely, they are too busy. They may also not see a real need for planning, being convinced that they already know everything they need to know.

2. These are summarized in Figure 4-1 in the text. The two types have many similarities -- market analysis, management team, strategies, financial projections. The differences are primarily in the uses of the plans, and hence, the differences in who prepares them and how they are prepared.

3. The differences in tone are a function of their usage and the intended readers. Thus, the strategic plan is forthright and candid. It is used for internal purposes, so it is written by and for key people inside the firm. The financial plan, on the other hand, is written for outsiders. Although it must be objective and well documented, it is still written in an optimistic tone in order to convince investors that the venture is worthy of their involvement.

4. Key employees should be consulted for two reasons. First, the motivating effects of including key workers is significant. Second, these employees will have valuable inputs for the strategy. Third, they are the ones who will be tasked with implementing the plan, so it makes sense that they are involved in its development.

5. A separate plan must be used for each type of funding desired because the investors will have different goals. For example, lenders will have different perspectives than venture capitalists. Informal investors will be still different. If a venture will need multiple sources of financing, then each must be addressed in a single plan. One reason for this is that each investor must be able to see how its involvement fits in with the other investors. If, for example, an entrepreneur will use a combination of informal investors, bank loans, SBA loans, and state economic development money, the entrepreneur must be able to show in a single plan how the informal investor will receive an adequate return while the two lending agencies receive continuing interest payments. The plan may also need to address job creation or other impact for the state agency. Thus, the plan will be somewhat more complex in order to address each of the constituent's needs.

6. This is an interesting assignment. If it is too much trouble to have students go out into the community, ask those in class who grew up in family businesses to report on their parents' ventures.

7. It is not critically important that a CPA be involved, although they can be helpful in generating the numbers. The more important issue is that the entrepreneur must be intimately involved in the process. Unfortunately, there are private businesses and economic development agencies who sell the service of developing business plans for

entrepreneurs. The problem is that the entrepreneur is not sufficiently involved to fully understand either the numbers or the concepts presented in the plan.

8.   Various answers could be given. A rule of thumb might be "at least annually or when the venture or its environment change significantly." Reviewing plans quarterly is a good idea for benchmarking purposes.

9.   Yes. Low growth ventures also need a strategic plan. The environment some low growth entrepreneurs face may not change as rapidly, but it changes more rapidly for others. In either case, a plan should be developed to assure that the venture is headed where the entrepreneur wants it to go. And, as in Question 8, the plan should be written for benchmarking purposes.

10.   The formats for the two types of plans really do not differ significantly. The primary difference is in the tone and, hence, how the information is presented.

11.   The Kryos, Inc. plan stays pretty close to the information in the chapter. As a bio-tech firm, it will necessarily emphasize the technical developments more than a plan for a craft store would.

EXERCISE 4-1

This exercise is fairly involved, but worth the effort. It will take either an out-of-class assignment or most of an hour in class to prepare. An interesting part of it is to notice the differences in the two groups' reports. Have the "entrepreneurs" go first. Then note their responses to the "venture capitalists." Then open the class to general discussion on research and presentation of plans to investors.

EXERCISE 4-2

The fisCAL software does a good job of developing pro formas, although students must think carefully about their assumptions. The case data is already on the student key disk, so that will make the task easier. This is an excellent exercise to use during the early part of the semester if the students are also assigned a business plan to do later in the term.

CONVENIESSE, INC.

Writing a rough draft strategic plan for Conveniesse, Inc. is a valuable exercise because it forces students to assemble information into a format. This could be a graded assignment, or it could be an in-class exercise. This works quite well if your university has case study labs complete with computers and word processors. Teams of three to five students can huddle around a computer, putting together the plan section by section. They then can print off a final copy and report on it late in the hour or the next class period.

CHAPTER FIVE

ANALYZING ENTREPRENEURIAL OPPORTUNITIES

TEACHING OBJECTIVES

The teaching objectives for this chapter are for students to understand:

1. How to find or develop opportunities.

2. How to evaluate opportunities, both informally and formally.

3. Common sources of opportunities.

4. Characteristics of opportunity windows.

5. Components of marketing, financial, and technological feasibility analyses.

6. How to match opportunities with capabilities.

CHAPTER OUTLINE

I.   Venture Opportunities

II.   Sources of Venture Opportunities

      A.   Identifying Trends

            1. Demographic Trends
            2. Social Trends
            3. Technological Trends
            4. Business Trends

      B.   Information Sources

      C.   Other Sources of Opportunities

            1. Launchpad Jobs
            2. Moonlighting
            3. Invention Related Opportunities

III.   Recognizing Opportunities

IV.   The Need for Opportunity Analysis

V.   Criteria for Analysis

      A.   The Window of Opportunity

      B.   Depth and Breadth of the Market

      C.   Size of Total Market

      D.   Protection from Competitors

      E.   Investment Requirements

      F.   Return on Investment

      G.   Ability to Spread Risks

VI.   The Opportunity Evaluation Process

      A.   Stage I -- The Informal Analysis

      B.   Stage II -- The Formal Analysis

            1. Marketing Feasibility
            2. Financial Feasibility

CONSIDER THIS!

* In the vast majority of cases, the opportunity exists, at least latently, in the environment. The job of the entrepreneur is to recognize the opportunity and develop it.

* The entrepreneur differentiates between the real opportunity and the mirage by doing careful, objective analysis. The mirage will disappear under analysis; the real opportunity will surface.

* In many cases, significant products that seem routine today could not have been developed at all thirty or even fifteen years ago. Thirty years ago, a computer filled a room. Today it sits on a lap. Many opportunities surface because of increasing technology.

* Technology or some dramatic event may suddenly open up a host of opportunities. More likely, however, opportunities develop over time as society slowly changes.

* Some products are fads (the pet rock?) and some products are eliminated by increasing technology (the 286 computer). Others have an extended life cycle (basic foods, undergarments, etc.). One reason for the difference is the speed at which a better product is introduced into the market.

CHAPTER SUMMARY

Opportunities for entrepreneurial ventures must be carefully considered in order to prevent unnecessary failures and inefficient use of resources. Some opportunities are either developed by the entrepreneur or are presented to an entrepreneur for analysis. In other situations, the entrepreneur must search for the opportunity. In either case, the opportunity must be studied for its feasibility.

Societal trends are the source of many opportunities for new ventures. Demographic and social trends are particularly ripe sources of entrepreneurial opportunities. Business and technological trends are also frequent sources of ideas. Opportunities may also be found through current experiences on the job. Some jobs lend themselves naturally to the launch of new opportunities. Other opportunities may be found through casual contacts, inventions, hobbies, or part-time jobs.

Some opportunities are not obvious. Entrepreneurs may have to be innovative in analyzing markets, products, trends, and target populations to uncover opportunities that could become the basis for real entrepreneurial ventures.

Once an opportunity is identified, then the entrepreneur must evaluate the opportunity. A suggested format is to first do an informal analysis followed by a formal, objective analysis. The objective analysis should include a determination of the marketing feasibility, the financial feasibility, and the technical feasibility. The marketing feasibility study considers whether the opportunity is trend based, the size of the total market, the number and type of competitors, and the timing of the window of opportunity. The financial feasibility must consider the start-up costs, the break-even point in both quantity and time, the overall return on investment predicted, and the projected cash flows. Finally, the technical feasibility should address concerns of necessary equipment, lead times, the possibility of sub-contracting, and design requirements.

A final step in the analysis of opportunities is the consideration of fatal flaws. These are conditions that may kill the project regardless of the other aspects of the feasibility analyses. These fatal flaws may include extremely high start-up cost relative to projected returns, a quite small market, significant competition, and the inability to successfully grow or harvest the venture.

Finally, the feasibility of the venture must be matched with the capabilities of the entrepreneurial team. The entrepreneurial capabilities must not only be acceptable in general, they must also be acceptable for the specific venture being considered.

TEACHING STRATEGY

This chapter has two rather distinct parts. The first is the creation of or the search for and recognition of opportunities. The important thing for students to recognize here is that creativity and innovation is important, but most new products do not arise from a creativity exercise or staring out a clean window. Most opportunities arise from some source -- a trend, a similar product, a problem that begs for a solution, or some void that is left by others.

The second, and probably more important, part of the chapter is the discussion of methods of analyzing opportunities. This is the part that differentiates the opportunity from the mirage, the real opportunity from the pipe dream. The importance of this part is to instill in the student the need for objective analysis. This includes the collection of objective information, the careful analysis of that information, and the reaching of conclusions based on the analysis.

Emphasize trends. For example, a discussion of baby boomers is always of interest and importance. Get students to visualize products that are really appropriate for baby boomers at different ages. Note how many think the baby boomers (now 30-45) are ready for retirement. An approach is to ask the questions "What products or services would be in high demand in 1970? in 1980? in the year 2000? in 2020?" This could take several minutes if you list the products as you go.

Then turn the focus more towards criteria. Trends, size of market, potential returns, investment requirements, depth and breadth of market, competition, and others can be used as either objective or subjective requirements. It is important to note that criteria typically are not of a yes/no variety. Most will be somewhat subjective in nature. Discuss with the students such things as "How big must a market be? What market share is acceptable? How much growth in a given trend must there be? How small or large can a niche be and still be profitable?" This may be disconcerting for students who may wish for black and white answers.

The concept of fatal flaws should be discussed in some depth. In the case of many of the criteria, a shortfall may be disappointing but not disastrous. If a fatal flaw surfaces, however, the project is doomed. Typical of this is the potential entrepreneur who wants to start a business needing perhaps $100,000 and expecting to borrow $98,000. The lack of financing here is a fatal flaw unless the entrepreneur can somehow identify a source of equity capital.

The final section of the chapter briefly discusses the capabilities of the firm or entrepreneur. This is the final test. Prior to this, opportunities were analyzed without regard to how a particular entrepreneur could capitalize on them. Some opportunities are excellent if a person with appropriate skills develops them. For others, however, the entrepreneur may have insufficient skills to make the opportunity reach its full potential. This section puts Chapter 3 and Chapter 5 together. Spend some time getting the students to visualize themselves developing a selected opportunity. Is there a match? Will the entrepreneur's weaknesses be fatal flaws?

DISCUSSION QUESTIONS

1. Some ideas are quite obviously ill-conceived and have no chance of success. Common sense is sufficient to eliminate these. A few ideas are quite good. The tougher choices are those which probably have a relatively small chance of success but are not clearly bad. These may have a small market or the match between the entrepreneur and the opportunity is not good. If there is a good answer, it must come from a careful analysis of the environment, competitors, the size of the market, and financing considerations. Caution should be emphasized.

2. Going with a naturally developing opportunity is far superior to the seek and find strategy. Searching for an opportunity may lead to investment in the first marginally acceptable opportunity. The exception to this is an experienced entrepreneur looking for a venture to buy.

3. Sources of opportunities for a recent college graduate may revolve around the university itself. The entrepreneur will have just finished four or five years of involvement in a university environment and will know the likes and dislikes of college students. Unless the student is independently wealthy or has financial contacts back home, most ventures will be of relatively small scale. An obvious exception to that is Michael Dell, founder of Dell computers.

4. The primary reason for doing the informal analysis first is that it will eliminate the vast majority of ideas before investing money into the formal analysis. The informal analysis is relatively cost-free. A formal analysis will be more expensive and more time consuming. The second reason is that doing the informal analysis first will set the tone and direction for formal analysis. It may help identify sources of information as well as giving a general idea of the probability of success.

5. The basic analysis techniques would be the same regardless of whether the venture is intended as low or high growth. The difference will be in the scope of the analysis. A low growth venture will typically be restricted to a single location in a single community. A higher growth venture may quickly move beyond a single community, and it may be designed as a regional or national venture from the start. Thus, the market research must include those target markets throughout the intended market area. This is one reason why the launch of a growth venture takes longer than the launch of a low growth venture.

6.   A good exercise for in class or a short written exercise. I have used essentially this question on an essay exam since it forces the student to think through the process for an actual venture.

7.   The opportunity/capability match refers to the entrepreneur's skills or the venture's strengths as they relate to the specific venture. An individual may have basic entrepreneurial skills, but if they are not appropriate for the specific opportunity being considered, then considerable caution should be used in deciding to go forward.

8.   The results of the opportunity analysis should be written into the section on the nature of the product and the nature of the market. In addition, the discussion of the management team should be a result of objective analysis and the opportunity/capability match.

9.   Different schools of thought exist here. On the one hand, the entrepreneur is likely to be the one most knowledgeable about the opportunity as it relates to the proposed venture. On the other hand, an entrepreneur's objectivity may be clouded because of an innate desire to capture the opportunity. An outside consultant can bring objectivity to the analysis.

10.   The analysis will differ for service ventures versus manufacturing ventures only in the assessment of the necessary production facilities and in the distribution of the product. The market will still have to be researched.

EXERCISE 5-1

 This is an excellent exercise to illustrate two things. First it illustrates that creativity can be enhanced. I have students do this for a couple items, and then put them into groups. As would be expected, the number of items increases significantly as the students key off each other. Second, it can illustrate how opportunities can be developed by considering alternative uses of common products. A third benefit of using this exercise is to excite the class into one of key aspects of entrepreneurship -- identification of opportunities.

EXERCISE 5-2

This exercise is used to illustrate how successive refinement of a target market can begin to give a rough idea of how well a product or service might do. This is not intended as a scientific exercise, but rather as an exercise in decision making. One note: Caution students against being overly optimistic. It is unrealistic to expect a new retail store to immediately pick up 20% market share if there are four or five other direct competitors.

CONVENIESSE, INC.

This segment of Conveniesse shows the three entrepreneurs beginning to research the possibilities for the upscale convenience store. Yolanda begins by researching the secondary data and talking to her industry contacts to get production selection and cost data. This is a good example of market research. Sarah was going to do local area research and consult Census data. Again, this is a good move. The excitable Jason then calls with the news that someone who has a similar store is willing to talk. This, too, should yield excellent bits of information if the discussion goes well.

The assignment is to develop questions to ask the person in Detroit. This is important to get the students to think about what questions actually should be asked and how they should be asked. It is getting the students to move from the theory into practice. This is a useful skill -- knowing what questions to ask and how to draw out a person who is willing to share information. Caution: Make sure students understand the difference between ethical and unethical research.

CHAPTER SIX

PLANNING THE LAUNCH OF THE VENTURE

TEACHING OBJECTIVES

The teaching objectives for this chapter are for students to understand:

1. The advantages of a start-up compared to a buyout.

2. The nature of leveraged buyouts.

3. The differences between a sole proprietorship, a partnership and a corporation.

4. The uniqueness of a family venture.

5. The nature of incubators.

CHAPTER OUTLINE

I. The Start-up

    A. Advantages of Start-ups

        1. Flexibility

      2. Image
      3. Staffing
      4. Cost

   B. Disadvantages of Start-ups

      1. Time to Launch
      2. Credibility
      3. Difficulty in Financing

II. The Buyout

   A. Advantages of Buyouts

      1. Continuity
      2. Name
      3. Employees
      4. Competition
      5. Location
      6. Availability of Financing
      7. Availability

   B. Disadvantages of Buyouts

      1. Lack of Availability
      2. Initial Cost
      3. Poor Image

III. The Buyout Search Process

   A. Industry Searches

   B. Location-based Searches

   C. Third Party Searches

   D. Advertised Intentions

IV. Special Launch Situations

   A. The Leveraged Buyout

      1. The Leveraged Buyout Process

B. The Franchise

C. The Incubator Start-up

    1. Types of Incubators
    2. The Impact of Incubators

D. The Family Business

    1. The New Family Business
    2. The Old Family Business

V. Determining the Legal Form of the Venture

A. The Sole Proprietorship

    1. Advantages of Sole Proprietorships
    2. Disadvantages of Sole Proprietorships

B. The Partnership

    1. Advantages of Partnerships
    2. Disadvantages of Partnerships
    3. The Limited Partnership
    4. The Need for a Partnership Agreement

C. The Corporation

    1. Advantages of Corporations
    2. Disadvantages of Corporations
    3. The Sub-Chapter S Corporation

VI. Summary

CONSIDER THIS!

*   The key question here is "Who would you like as a partner?" But the answer is not as easy as it seems. Many lost friendships (and some divorces) have been because of a partnership in a new venture. Just because two people are friends does not mean that they would make good partners. Similarly, parents can certainly provide support and wisdom to young entrepreneurs, but one must ask how stable the

relationship is. Parents must remember that in a business situation they are partners, not parents.

* Low growth ventures will tend to have less cushion than growth ventures and cannot withstand a downturn or competition as well. They are also sometimes started by less skilled entrepreneurs. The eighteen months to three years is suggested because it often takes an entrepreneur that long before realizing that funds are dried up and that there is little future in the business. If a business can last three years, the probability is on the side of success.

* Ventures that are started with growth in mind should be started as corporations in order to ease the funding process and to provide personal protection in the case of failure. Most ventures that start out as proprietorships and partnerships convert to corporations when growth begins.

* There really should not be significant differences, except that when two or more families are involved -- either two generations or two or more siblings -- the business has to support those families. Hence, there may be pressure to take money out of the venture rather than reinvesting it for growth purposes.

* This may depend on the definition of fostering entrepreneurship. If this means increasing the number of ventures that are launched, the impact is quite small. Most ventures that are started in an incubator would start without the incubator. On the other hand, incubators do either directly or indirectly foster entrepreneurship through improving the success rate of the ventures.

CHAPTER SUMMARY

Launching a venture entails major decisions simply to determine how to launch the venture. Each of these major decisions then leads to a myriad of smaller, administrative decisions that must be made in order to achieve a successful launch. This chapter illustrates some of the key planning issues that are included in the decision process.

The start-up venture has advantages revolving around the flexibility of starting the venture according to the specific desires of the entrepreneur. Issues to consider here include the ability to create the desired image, the ability to choose employees, the possibly lower cost, and the ability to locate the venture in a desired location. The start-up may be the only method available to launch some ventures.

The buyout has many advantages, and it is a more desirable method if a firm is available and certain conditions are met. Nevertheless, there are some disadvantages to buying a venture. These may include the existing poor image, resistant employees, and the condition of the firm.

Specialized situations also exist. The leveraged buyout is a form of buyout with the extensive debt necessary to purchase the firm being applied to the purchased firm's balance sheet. The family firm is often passed from generation to generation. It presents both opportunities and concerns that should be considered. Franchises offer extensive management training, structured operations, and a nationally known name but at a substantial cost and restricted flexibility. Incubators are a new method of starting ventures in a sheltered environment. Incubators offer substantial services to fledgling ventures when they are most at risk.

A final decision to be made is to determine the legal structure of the firm. The proprietorship, the partnership, and the corporation all have advantages that make them worthy of consideration during the launch phase.

TEACHING STRATEGY

This chapter discusses two aspects of the venture launch. The first is the type of launch. The second is the legal form of the launch.

The start-up and buyout are the two options in launching a venture. Each has its advantages and disadvantages. The buyout is probably more desirable if one is available for an appropriate price. The Shannons in the Entrepreneurial Profile chose the buyout because of the lower failure rate, and this makes sense if one is affordable. On the other hand, more launches are start-ups simply because of lack of availability of buyouts. Further some start-up ventures are new concepts or products and therefore must be start-ups. It is not important to convince students that one is innately better than the other. Rather the key is to let them know the pros and cons of each.

Discuss the advantages and disadvantages of leveraged buyouts. Most will never be exposed to that opportunity, particularly as a first time entrepreneur. Yet, the activities required to put a leveraged buyout together certainly put it within the realm of entrepreneurship. Let the students know the downside of LBOs. That is that they are so heavily leveraged that their strategy is severely restricted. Further, a downturn in revenues makes servicing the debt extremely difficult.

The incubator is a relatively new phenomena, circa 1985. Most are at least partially state funded and many are located on or near university campuses. If an incubator is on your campus, ask the director to speak to your class. Most are quite willing, and students are typically interested in these unique organizations.

Most students have heard of sole proprietorships, partnerships, and corporations at least two or three times and perhaps in a half dozen different classes. The approach that works well here is to not try to explain each of these, but rather to discuss the pros and cons of each in a <u>start-up</u> situation.

DISCUSSION QUESTIONS

1. Clearly there is a relationship between legal form and growth although this may be one of correlation more than causality. Growth oriented ventures may have to adopt the corporate form in order to ease the fund raising. Low growth ventures typically do not require a corporation, so this is one of personal choice.

2. The responses to the examples could certainly be debated. Other reasons than those given could change the decision.

A. A small shop selling motorcycles could be any of the three. Having two working partners -- one in sales and one in service -- is desirable. A Sub-Chapter S corporation is also a possibility, giving somewhat more protection while allowing the income taxes to be paid on the individual 1040s.

B. Manufacturing high-tech equipment probably requires significant capital. Go with a corporation.

C. A consulting business is a low investment business. A proprietorship or partnership should be acceptable.

D. There is no particular need for a corporation here unless desired. The corporation provides more protection against liabilities, but a good insurance policy could take some of that risk away.

3. A partnership certainly is desirable here, but a partnership agreement is critical if one partnership has capital and the other contributes skill. A case could also be made for a corporation. Since the person has capital but no expertise, becoming a silent partner or a limited partner might be appropriate. Otherwise, finding someone with the requisite skills and opportunity is necessary. If someone has skills, then the task is to find a place to utilize the skills. Perhaps joining an existing venture would be best.

4. An LBO is extremely dangerous for a small venture. Small companies often have a tough time with financing under normal situations. Adding the substantial debt required in LBOs would seriously hamper chances for survival, especially if the economy or industry turned down.

5. Family ventures are of interest because they can have problems that are similar to most other family ventures but different from non-family ventures. Thus, they are interesting to work with, good candidates for research, and can often be helped with similar types of solutions. The interest in family ventures is also part of the overall interest in small and growing ventures.

6. The value of incubators is not in the increased number of ventures <u>started</u>, but increasing the probability that they will survive. With the shared services, often low rent, and access to management assistance, the odds of success are increased considerably. And this is of interest to state and local economic development centers.

7. This will be discussed in more depth in Chapter 10. But key questions should address the amount and kind of assistance provided, the initial and ongoing cost, the problems likely to be encountered, and the success rate of average franchisees.

8. A venture should be launched as a corporation if it will require frequent or significant additions of equity capital. The corporate form should also be used if the venture will be risky from either a financial standpoint or a liability perspective.

9. The Sub-Chapter S corporation is restricted to 35 stockholders. If more capital is needed than can be provided by the 35 investors, then the regular corporation will be required.

10. Spending considerable time together in frank discussions is a good start. Taking personality tests or inventories with the help of qualified counselors is also well advised. Visiting with attorneys regarding partnership agreements is also quite important and should be done before any of the parties commit to the partnership.

EXERCISE 6-1

I would want to know more detail about the market for its products. If it only makes defense equipment and is only a subcontractor for those products, the venture could be risky. With the break-up of the Soviet Union, the growing national debt, and possible Democrat president, the defense budget is sure to be cut or held to modest increases. Thus, I would want to know if there are other markets for the products or if there are other products that could be made given the firm's technology capabilities. The legal form of the business should not be significantly affected by the particular product market.

CONVENIESSE, INC.

In this segment, the group has gathered more information that seems favorable, including the availability of a location in about six months. They determine that the start-up costs will be significant although they have not determined just how high it will be. Nor have they determined at this time how much each partner will contribute. The assignment is to determine the legal structure. The choices would be either a partnership, a corporation, or a Sub-Chapter S corporation. A case could be made for any of the three. The best seems to be the Sub-S corporation. This would protect them from liability in the event of an injury on their premises and perhaps liabilities from problems in their business arrangements. If we expect the total start-up capital to be less than $500,000 and if they have at least some of their own to invest, they should be able to fund it with debt and perhaps a limited number of investors. This suggests the Sub-S corporation since they would have the ease of taxes with the benefits of the corporation.

CHAPTER SEVEN

FINANCING THE VENTURE

TEACHING OBJECTIVES

The teaching objectives for this chapter are for students to understand:

1. The need to adequately finance a venture.

2. The need to carefully analyze the amounts and kinds of financing that are best for a particular venture.

3. The nature of equity financing.

4. The different kinds of debt financing.

5. Venture capital and initial public stock offerings, their nature and use.

6. Considerations in developing a financial package.

CHAPTER OUTLINE

I.   The Need for Financing

II. Equity Financing

    A. Personal Funds

    B.   Friends and Family

    C.   Informal Investors

    D.   Venture Capital Firms

        1. Private Venture Capital Firms
        2. Small Business Investment Companies
        3. Corporate Sponsored Venture Capital Firms

    E.   Investment Bankers

    F.   Public Offerings

III.   Debt Financing

    A. Borrowing from Friends and Family

    B.   Banks

    C.   Small Business Administration

IV.   Other Capital Sources

    A.   Supplier Capital

    B.   Customer Capital

    C.   Economic Development Funding

    D.   Relationships With Other Companies

    E.   Internal Cash Management

V.   Matching Financing to Venture Development

    A.   Stage of Development

    B.   Growth Rates

VI.   Developing the Financial Package

VII.   Summary

CONSIDER THIS!

*   Most new and/or small ventures are under-capitalized, and this is one of the prime causes of business failures.

*   It may not be true that it is easier to get a $100,000 loan than a $10,000 loan, but typically the entrepreneur asking for $100,000 has done the necessary homework, has a better idea, and has more collateral than the person requesting only $10,000.

*   It definitely takes enough money to survive until the cash flow becomes positive.

*   The availability of financing depends on many factors -- the entrepreneur, the industry, the size of the business, whether it is a start-up, buyout, or franchise, and others.

*   This is true, although the ratio of ownership given up to the amount of financing acquired will vary greatly.

*   The cost of public offerings is often well over $500,000.

CHAPTER SUMMARY

Capital is the lifeblood of any business venture. Few ventures and virtually no new ventures have enough capital to begin life and grow without an infusion from external sources. This chapter discusses the various needs for capital, the sources of equity and debt capital, and the relationships between growth rates of ventures, stages in venture development, and the types of capital that are most appropriate.

Equity capital is that capital which provides ownership to the investors. Some amount of equity capital will be required regardless of the type or level of the venture. Equity capital includes personal funds of the entrepreneurs, partners, private stockholders, informal investors, venture capitalists, or public stockholders. Debt capital does not provide ownership, but provides a return to the investor in the form of interest on capital supplied. The most common form of debt capital is loans from banks. The Small Business Administration also provides money to those whom banks will not lend to unassisted. In addition to traditional debt and equity, entrepreneurs can also obtain the use of capital from suppliers, customers, and efficient use of their own internal policies.

Some forms of financing are more viable for some types and levels of ventures than others. Small business ventures are, by their nature, restricted to their own personal funds for pre-launch financing. They may utilize banks and the SBA for later stage financing. Moderate growth ventures will make extensive use of bank financing, and some of these may go public after several years of sustained growth. Venture capital and IPOs are more applicable for rapid growth ventures, and they will more likely be used for later stage financing than for start-ups and pre-launch financing.

Regardless of the type of financing used, substantial planning must be done to insure that funding can be generated. A business plan is necessary for virtually all types of funding, and a carefully written plan is a must for anything other than the most simple financing sources.

TEACHING STRATEGY

This chapter is a fairly straightforward discussion of the forms of capital with specific emphasis on equity and debt capital. There are two places where this text differs from competing texts. First is the relatively lower emphasis placed on IPOs and, to an extent, venture capital. Although these are the glamour sources of stock, we all know that only one or two percent of new ventures will ever have occasion to use them. It is more useful to key on the traditional forms of capital, which to use when, and how to put together the package.

The second differentiating aspect of the treatment of financing is the matching of sources of funding with needs for funding. This should be a key part of the lecture. Students need to realize not only what sources there are, but when each should be used, and what the impact of it will be on current and future strategies. They should understand that if an entrepreneur chooses to use exclusively debt, that there will be a limit on how much debt provided. Further, the cost of the debt will increase. Similarly, exclusive use of equity may dilute ownership too much or limit growth. Spend considerable time on Table 7-3 which matches funding sources with stages of development and rate of growth. This could easily take up an entire class period.

Students should also understand that good cash management is a key in the financing strategy. Although the actual financial strategy is discussed more in Chapter 9, it is important for the students to understand the need for planning for the financial needs of the venture.

DISCUSSION QUESTIONS

1. In start-up situations, the venture may be too risky for any investor, thereby forcing the entrepreneur to use personal funds. In addition, bankers will insist that the owner invest personal funds in order to insure a personal stake in the business. Otherwise, the entrepreneur might simply skip town at the first sign of trouble.

2. A good business plan will be extremely useful. Remember that banks are relatively conservative and are there to make money. If they lend to a pre-launch situation, the venture might never get started, and they would have trouble collecting personally from the entrepreneur.

3. Find out as much as possible about the business, the amount of personal capital (in cash) that is available, how long the person wants to keep the business, how much growth is desired, and who else will be involved with the business. In particular, who will be on the management team?

4. Interest rates for specific ventures are primarily a function of the risk involved. Hence, start-up entrepreneurs will pay more than owners with a history of dealing with the bank. Rates might also differ for service ventures compared with manufacturing firms because of the difference in the amount of identifiable assets.

5. Venture capital is high risk capital. Venture capitalists will fund only a small percentage of those business plans presented to them. Hence, they are extremely careful regarding which ones they pick. Venture capitalists also have specific criteria that are unique to their particular company, such as location of funded venture, the industry it is in, and the stage of development funded. It will only be appropriate when there is a real chance of high growth and when the entrepreneur is willing to give up substantial ownership just to get the funding.

6. See Question 5. No, they should not be less restrictive. Remember that they, too, are in business to make money. Given the success rate of the ventures they do fund, consider what it would be if they funded less quality plans.

7. Investment bankers are necessary because of the expertise they have, the contacts they have, and the amount of dollars that is required to do the IPO.

8. An interesting assignment.

9. Consider assigning this as an outside project or even for a research paper topic. Students may be surprised how different bankers are even though they all profess to be interested in small businesses.

10. For a small loan of, say $10,000, a limited amount of effort will be required. A loan application will be required, and supporting documents may be prepared. For larger ventures, informal investors and venture capitalists will want to know the value of the venture, specific projects of revenues and incomes, details regarding when and how much return will be provided. These required major amounts of effort and will often require the assistance of a consultant.

EXERCISE 7-1

This would make a good in-class exercise or exam question.

EXERCISE 7-2

Venture and Development Stage	Type of Financing Most Logical
Baskin-Robbins start-up	Personal equity, bank loan
Bio-tech pre-start-up	Venture capital, informal investors
Retail, seasonal financing	Cash flows, bank loans, supplier credit
Auto repair pre-start-up	Personal funds
Computer producer, growth	Public Offering

CONVENIESSE, INC.

This is a good place for an in-class assignment. The three entrepreneurs have pooled their funds and know that they still need considerably more. But this venture could lend itself to a number of different alternatives. Perhaps a bank would loan them the entire amount, but that is not probable. Issuing stock doesn't make sense except to some informal investors. Don't underestimate borrowing or selling stock to the developer. If he wants them in badly, he might be more than willing to accept this kind of a deal. This is also a good time to have students look at the Conveniesse, Inc. Business Plan.

CHAPTER EIGHT

DEVELOPING ENTREPRENEURIAL STRATEGIES

TEACHING OBJECTIVES

The teaching objectives for this chapter are that students understand:

1. The strategic planning process.

2. Generic strategies for entrepreneurial ventures.

3. Entry wedges for new ventures.

4. How new products are introduced.

5. The advantages and disadvantages of niche strategies.

6. Ways to exploit competency based strategies.

7. Captive supplier strategies.

8. Key factors in retail strategies.

9. Considerations in developing service venture strategies.

CHAPTER OUTLINE

I.   The Strategic Planning Process

II. Generic Strategy Types

    A. Differentiation Strategies

    B. Low Cost Leadership

    C. Focus Strategies

III. Entry Wedges

IV. Strategies for Unique Situations

    A. Strategies for High-Tech Manufacturers

        1. New Product Innovation Strategy
        2. Derivative Product Strategy
        3. Product Variation Strategy
        4. High-Tech Differentiation Strategy
        5. Support Product Strategies

    B. Strategies for Low-Tech Manufacturers

    C. Niche Strategies

    D. Competency Based Strategies

    E. Captive Supplier Strategies

    F. Strategies for Retailers

    G. Strategies for Service Ventures

    H. Strategies for Direct Marketing Ventures

        1. Mass Media Advertising
        2. Direct Mail
        3. The Electronic Market Place

V. Summary

CONSIDER THIS!

*   Once a venture is launched and stabilized, most strategic changes are incremental rather than revolutionary. Only when new breakthroughs in the market occur, the CEO changes, or the success of the venture is in question does the entrepreneur consider major changes. On the other hand, this will likely occur with more frequency in entrepreneurial ventures than in larger, traditional ventures.

*   The overall venture strategy points the direction and gives general guidance for the firm. Supporting strategies are necessary to refine the venture strategy into more easily implemented and controlled segments.

*   Ventures change. Situations change. Entrepreneurs change. Thus, there is no one best strategy for a given combination. Further, more than one strategy might work in some cases. None may work in others. The object is to carefully analyze all aspects of the situation and develop that strategy which appears to be best.

*   High-technology situations may offer the greatest number of strategies because of the rapid developments within the market. However, the strategies may also be most risky.

*   The danger of the niche strategy is that if the niche is not large enough, the entrepreneur cannot survive. If it is too large, and the venture is too successful, larger firms will move in. Donald Burr of People Express Airline found this out when the majors moved in on his niche.

*   The captive supplier strategy is desirable for many small companies who feel that dealing with a single customer is better than constantly trying to develop and keep many customers. On the other hand, "putting all the eggs in one basket" is not appealing to many who fear that the single customer could put them out of business in the event of a strike, a change in demand, or some arbitrary decision by the customer.

*   The largest failure rate is in retail partially because some retail is quite susceptible to the economy, retail requires substantial capital for the start-up, and because operating a retail business is more difficult than it looks.

CHAPTER SUMMARY

Key to the success of a new or emerging venture is the development of a definitive entrepreneurial strategy. The strategic planning process, discussed in Chapter 4, consists of analyzing the new venture and its environment in order to develop a viable strategy.

With the strategy and its support strategies in mind, attention then turns to obtaining necessary resources and implementing the strategy.

Strategies tend to fall into one of three broad categories. Differentiation strategies are those which provide value to a product beyond what competing products give. Low cost leadership strategies concentrate on providing competing products at the lowest possible cost. Focus strategies may be either differentiation or low cost, but they focus on specific target markets.

Karl Vesper suggested fourteen "entry wedges" for new ventures. These include new products or services, parallel competition, franchising, geographical transfer, supply shortage, tapping unutilized resources, customer contract, becoming a second source, joint ventures, licensing, market relinquishment, selloff of a division, favored purchasing, or rule changes.

There are a myriad of specific entrepreneurial strategies available to ventures and no one strategy will be successful in a given situation. High-tech strategies typically revolve around a product. That product can be either a brand new product, a derivative product, or a variation of an existing product. It can be a support product that is related to the existing product. In high-tech industries, new products have a relatively short window before competitors bring similar or superior products to the market. Ironically, low-tech products face many of the same problems as high-tech products except for the fact that they are not produced by or for high technology industries. They still face the problems of obsolescence or competing with other newer or superior products.

Niche strategies are those strategies in which the entrepreneur attempts to serve a small segment of a larger market. The advantage of a niche strategy is that the entrepreneur can become an expert within the narrow scope of the market. The problems with niche strategies are that the niche may be too small or that large companies may move into the niche and squeeze out the entrepreneurial firm.

Rather than focusing on a particular market, competency based strategies build upon special skills, products, or processes unique to the venture. The entrepreneur then exploits the strength through effective marketing and continued development of the competency. In the captive supplier strategy, the entrepreneur provides a product or service to one customer only. Once the arrangement is complete, the small venture has to do no marketing and simply produces the product in the amounts and specifications demanded by the larger customer.

Most new and small ventures are retail or service. In either case, launching the venture may be risky because of the intense competition from other small ventures and from larger chains and franchises. Keys to success revolve around the effective design and location of facilities, effective merchandising, promotion, and pricing strategies, and the provision of appropriate services to the customer. In both cases, the need is to provide a product or service that provides a sufficient price/value ratio to attract customers away from competitors.

Direct marketing is a broad category that includes advertising in mass media for direct response, direct mail, electronic shopping, and advertising through catalogs. Direct marketing has the advantage of targeting specific markets and not requiring retail showrooms. The disadvantage is that customers cannot see or test the product without ordering it first.

TEACHING STRATEGY

This chapter allows a variety of teaching methods. One is to focus on the many strategies as they are grouped in the categories -- generic, entry wedges, high-tech, low-tech, niche, and so on. This can easily take two class periods to work through the litany of strategies. Teaching the chapter as a strategy theory lecture allows one to compare Porter's strategies with Vesper's entry wedges, and to then look at the strategies presented in the remainder of the chapter to discuss how they fit within the two classic strategy sets.

Another option is to consider various competitive situations, add a new product and an entrepreneur with some set of strengths and weaknesses, and then spend time working through which might be the best strategies. This situational approach to developing strategies is appealing to some since it forces the student to look at situations and find strategies to match.

A third option is to make use of some of the cases. Using some of the start-up related cases -- Doorstep Video, Christians, Campground for Sale, International Learning Center, or others that have strategic emphases to them -- and discuss them in terms of the strategies presented in the chapter. Ask questions such as "Which generic strategy or entry wedge is being used?" "Is Doorstep Video's niche strategy sufficient over the long run?" "Describe the International Learning Center strategy in terms of Vesper's entry wedges." "Analyze the proposed strategy for Conveniesse, Inc. in terms of its strengths and weaknesses." Any of the above cases can generate substantial discussion.

The object of the discussion, regardless of which approach is used, is to get the students to think through the vast possibilities of strategies that may be appropriate to a venture situation. They should realize that a given strategy or type of strategy may be appropriate in a number of situations. Conversely, a given opportunity may be captured by a number of different strategies.

A final task might be to get the students to think through which strategies are most appropriate for a venture as it moves along its growth path. Ask the question, "If a niche strategy is appropriate for a start-up company, will it still be appropriate five years from now? If not, how does the company move from one to the other smoothly?

DISCUSSION QUESTIONS

1. Most instructors are aware that while there may not be any "right" answers, there certainly are many "wrong" answers. The object of the chapter is not to delineate the right strategies, but to highlight some of the possible strategies and situations in which they might be appropriate.

2. Porter's generic strategies -- differentiation, low cost leadership, and focus strategies -- are perhaps _more_ important for new and emerging ventures than for large companies because of the entrepreneurial venture's ability to adapt. Smaller companies, in particular, may want to use the differentiation strategy when competing against larger firms. Low cost strategies may or may not be successful depending on the dynamics of the environment. The focus strategy may also be appropriate for new and smaller companies rather than trying to do something for everyone.

3. Vesper's entry wedges are not intended as parallels to Porter's generic strategies. The new product wedge, parallel competition, and contracting could fit the differentiation strategy, a number of them could fit the low cost leadership depending on how they are done, and some such as joint ventures might fit the focus strategy. But the two paradigms are, in general, unrelated. Each should be considered on its own merits.

4. Parent sponsored entry wedges are those where a venture works closely with either a parent firm or a large, friendly, firm for a specific purpose. These include licensing, joint ventures, market relinquishment, or selloff of a division. None of these would be possible without the assistance of a larger firm.

5. A government sponsored entry wedge is certainly viable for new ventures. Contracting or subcontracting with the government can be lucrative if the venture can meet the contract requirements.

6. The derivative product strategy suggests making a new or similar product for a market use that is different from the original product. Innovative entrepreneurs can sometimes be quite successful by modifying an existing product for a completely different use. The product variation strategy is simply producing a slightly different version of the original in hopes of attracting customers from the original product market. The derivative product strategy would typically be more useful since it addresses new markets.

7. "Low-tech" may initially have a derogatory image. However, closer study reveals that low technology products can be quite high quality. Further, virtually all franchises would be considered low-tech.

8. A niche strategy is market focused whereas a competency based strategy is venture focused. A niche strategy, by nature, can be quite risky. A competency based strategy is less risky once it is successfully launched.

9. The captive supplier strategy seems boring because the venture only has to meet the needs of the single customer, and does not have to consistently worry about marketing, distribution, plant capacity, or pricing. It can, however, be a successful and reasonably profitable strategy because of the reduced selling and overhead expenses.

10. The retail success factors will be either more or less prevalent based on the competitive dynamics of the market and the nature of the product. The aesthetics of physical facilities would be much more important for the dress shop than the auto parts shop. Merchandise is critical for specialty stores. Pricing is based on the price elasticity of the product as well as the nature of the store. For example, the corner grocery store should be expected to charge higher prices than the supermarket, but will compensate by providing better service. Similarly, promotion and are based on the competitive dynamics. Large discount stores have to be price conscious, but must also be aware of the impact of the facilities, promotion, and merchandise selection.

11. Many inventors start selling their product via direct marketing until it gets enough acceptance to be attractive to national chain stores and their purchasers. Thus, when Paraguage was first introduced, it probably was not sufficiently well-known to be of interest to major retailers.

12. A good out of class assignment.

EXERCISE 8-1

The personal pulse and blood pressure monitor appears to be excellent for marketing in running and other sports magazines. The direct marketing approach can be useful since it is a specialty product. Consideration might also be given to buying a mailing list from a running magazine, since this would also target a very specific market. The remote control device is also a specialty product, but the market for it might be harder to tap directly since older customers are less mobile and more conservative regarding new products. Marketing through service agencies catering to the seeing impaired and through retailers specializing in medical equipment might be useful. The decision whether to have a single venture or not is of no particular significance either way.

EXERCISE 8-2

This may be a difficult assignment unless assistance can be given in identifying specific companies. If it can be done, the results should match the two-edged sword problems discussed in the chapter.

EXERCISE 8-3

Any strategies dealing with new products, new processes, or new markets will be more risky. Those dealing with existing products and markets will be less risky unless the market itself is highly dynamic.

CONVENIESSE, INC.

The task is to develop a strategic plan. The benefit is not to grade a good or bad plan, but to get the students to begin looking at the situation and determine what the strategy should be. Thus, the process is more important than the results.

CHAPTER NINE

DEVELOPING SUPPORTING STRATEGIES

TEACHING OBJECTIVES

The teaching objectives for this chapter are that students understand:

1.   The importance of developing functional strategies to support the overall venture strategy.

2.   The need to do analysis and research before developing functional strategies.

3.   The need to insure that functional strategies mesh with the overall venture strategy.

4.   The ingredients in a marketing plan.

5.   The financial planning process.

6.   The most important financial ratios for emerging ventures.

7.   The different possible human resource strategies.

8.   The importance of an ethics strategy.

CHAPTER OUTLINE

I. Developing the Marketing Strategy

    A. Conducting Market Research

    B. Developing the Overall Marketing Strategy

    C. The Product/Service Strategy

    D. The Promotional Strategy

    E. The Pricing Strategy

    F. The Distribution Strategy

    G. The Need for Consistency

II. Financial Strategies

    A. The Financial Strategy Process

    B. Analyzing the Current Financial Condition

        1. Budget Analysis
        2. Ratio Analysis

    C. Developing the Financial Strategy

III. Developing Human Resource Strategies

    A. Analyzing the Current Condition

    B. Projecting Needs

    C. Developing the Human Resources Strategy

IV. Developing an Ethics Strategy

    A. Areas of Ethical Concerns

CONSIDER THIS!

* Some entrepreneurs do have either the big picture without the small picture or vice versa. Successful entrepreneurs have both.

* The reason functional strategies require the time is because there are more of them and their specificity is greater.

* Mis-allocating too much to the grand opening prevents the continued use of advertising throughout the initial year.

* It is not uncommon for a venture to use personal funds at the outset, bank funding early months or years, and equity capital or a combination of equity and debt to underwrite growth.

* In large companies a few bad HR decisions can be overcome. In small firms, each person plays a more critical role. Thus, the impact of a bad hiring decision can be devastating.

* Having highly trained workers in a new venture can ease many problems for an entrepreneur. Caution must be used, however, to make sure that the experienced workers accept direction from the entrepreneur.

* Being ethical is an attitude. It does not mean that an entrepreneur cannot be a fierce competitor. It simply means that ethics is more important than profits.

CHAPTER SUMMARY

This chapter considers the development of support strategies for the entrepreneurial venture. The functional strategies of marketing, finance, and human resources were discussed. Then attention turns to the important topic of the role of ethics in the venture's strategies.

The marketing strategy delineates the actions necessary to get the venture's products or services to the customer. Included in the strategy should be a product/service strategy, a promotion strategy, a pricing strategy, and a distribution strategy. Important within the promotion strategy is the advertising plan. Throughout the marketing strategy development process, the entrepreneur should consider the need for consistency among the components.

The financial strategy process begins with an analysis of the venture strategy, the firm's current condition, the external situation, and the overall goals of the entrepreneur. The entrepreneur should analyze the venture's condition through budget analysis and ratio analysis. The financial strategy should include the total amount of capital needed, the mix between equity and debt, and the sources of both debt and equity.

Entrepreneurs should develop a human resource strategy that will guide them over time. Like the other functional areas, the human resource strategy process should begin with an analysis of the current venture team along with the plans for the future. The human resources strategy should include a hiring strategy both for managers and for lower level workers, a compensation strategy, a training strategy, and a promotion strategy.

Ethics is critically important to the entrepreneur because of the relatively greater freedom a small business has and because of the deleterious effects that an unethical act could have on the venture. The need for an ethics strategy as well as an ethical decision making process were discussed. It is important that the entrepreneur set an ethical tone or philosophy for the venture.

TEACHING STRATEGY

The supporting strategies reduce the overall venture strategy into doable parts. Each segment is more specific, more short run, and more encapsulated than the overall strategy is. Functional management includes marketing, finance, human resources, operations, accounting, and, depending on how one defines it, public affairs, research and development, and the computer aspects of the venture. This chapter covers only three of these -- marketing, finance, and human resources. The remainder are important but to a lesser extent than the three presented here.

The key to teaching this chapter is to get the students to "think small." That is, they must be encouraged to zero in on a particular aspect of a strategy and delineate specific tasks that must be done to make the strategy work. A good example of this is illustrated by Figure 9-1 in the text. Each of the steps is integral to the overall marketing strategy, and the overall marketing strategy is a key part of the entire venture strategy.

Again keying on Figure 9-1, encourage the students to refine the steps even more. In other words, have them break the promotional aspect into its component parts or break the pricing strategy into more specific tactics. Then do the same for the human resource strategy. The end result is that students understand the links among the overall strategy, the supporting strategies, and the components of the supporting strategies.

Another aspect of this chapter is to get students to think through the <u>planning</u> process at the support strategy level. As shown in Figures 9-4 and 9-5, these are similar to the overall process discussed in Chapter 4 and again in Chapter 8. The level within the firm is different, but the process is similar.

The final part of this chapter deals with entrepreneurial ethics. I have found that the more entrepreneurial some of my students are, the more disregard some have for playing by the straight and narrow rules. Thus, I find that it is important to stress that the only thing more important than entrepreneurship is <u>ethical</u> entrepreneurship. Encourage them to develop a clear view of ethics and how ethics affects one's decisions. The ethical decision making process is an excellent tool for generating discussion. Bring in an ethics vignettes (There are a number of good ones to choose from.) After the students read or watch the vignette, work through the decision steps with them. They may be annoyed at the process at first, but by the end of it they should understand both the value of the process and how it works.

DISCUSSION QUESTIONS

1.   The best approach is to do these all at approximately the same time. It is impossible to price a product without knowing the marketing costs charged to it. Similarly, the distribution method will have an impact on the type of promotion.

2.   The best way to ensure consistency is to ensure that the decision makers talk to each other. Delegating these tasks too much risks having the decisions made independently of each other, causing consistency problems.

3.   The advertising budget is important to ensure that the right amount of advertising is done at the right time using the right media.

4.   Clusters typically are better because the advertisements are more believable if they come from various sources at approximately the same time. In addition, once potential customers have been exposed to the advertisements repeatedly, they will remember them for a long period of time.

5.   The answer here is yes, but.... The amount of advertising needed may be a function of the price of a product, but there are many other factors. The nature of the product, itself, is a big factor. The amount that competitors advertise also affects the amount we must advertise. The seasonal and cyclical effects also must be considered.

6. Distributing silk plants within a two state region could be done initially by contract carrier and with additional orders by United Parcel Service (UPS). The initial shipments would likely be large enough to deliver in bulk, while the later orders would tend to be small enough to send by a package delivery service. Shipments within perhaps fifty miles could be handled by the company's van or small truck. Once the geographic territory had expanded to the entire east coast, then thought should be given to purchasing a larger, over-the-road truck.

7. Discount stores sell strictly on volume. They purchase such large amounts that producers are willing to give them volume discounts. Smaller stores seldom can match those prices because they cannot buy the volume. If the small firm is of the type that can join a cooperative buying service, they can come closer but still not match the discount price completely. Thus, the smaller stores must compete on a different front, most likely service.

8. Consistency is the meshing of all marketing related tactics. Advertising, pricing, service, in-store displays, and other aspects of the marketing function must send the same message. Even the firm's stationery, sacks and boxes, and product labels should have the same logo or message.

9. The process is essentially the same. The objectives of the finance function must, of course, be the objectives of the venture. The analysis will be more specific to the finance function, but the tasks of the analysis are similar.

10. A case could be made that all ratios are important. However, any ratios that deal with liquidity or cash flow are critically important for new and emerging firms. More established firms might be more interested in return on investment, but cash flow related ratios will still be important.

11. The high equity strategy has the advantage of limited debt service and the fact that equity is more patient than debt. A high debt strategy has the advantage of less owners to share the profits of the venture. Of course, the best strategy is to use a combination of debt and equity that will give a higher total capital and spread the risks better.

12. The need to look to the future regarding uses of cash is important because of the current and future sources of the cash. If we know that we will need a major infusion of cash in two years to build new plant and equipment, we must consider what sources of capital we will need then in order to balance it with our current sources and uses.

13. A policy guides day to day action. A strategy is a mode of action that aims us toward a particular objective. The two are related however, since the adoption of a strategy may affect policies. For example, a high growth venture strategy may dictate a human resource strategy of bringing in new workers and managers who can make a

contribution to the firm as quickly as possible. This may, in turn, dictate a policy of hiring only trained workers who have experience with other firms.

14. The speed with which they can make a true contribution is greater. On the other hand, you pay for what you get. Thus, initial salaries or wages will be higher, and this will affect short run profit.

15. Promote from within means filling any higher level vacancies with personnel already in the firm at a lower level. This is opposed to hiring new workers to fill those positions. In general, this is far superior due to the motivating influence of a promote from within strategy. The only time this would not be wise is if the firm is growing so fast that there are few experienced people inside the firm that are promotable.

16. Small firms have more flexibility with regard to ethics because they are not as constrained either by regulations or by public awareness. Thus, as long as a major ethical breach has not been made, they are somewhat more shielded from scrutiny.

17. The entrepreneur's ethical influence is so great because all of the entrepreneur's influence is great. Since the entrepreneur is simultaneously the owner, chief strategist, key manager, and prime source of the culture, all eyes look there for guidance.

18. The ethical strategy is important because it is visible and sets the overall tone for the rest of the venture's employees. The ethical decision making process is important because unique situations arise that are not covered by any strategy or code.

EXERCISE 9-1

A possible memo is the following:

To: Employees

From: Owner

Recent events in the industry suggest that some landscapers are prone to cut corners or do other things that could be considered unethical. I want to make it clear that our company will not engage in unethical behavior. I would rather lose money honestly than make money dishonestly. Even if our business must close, we will look back on it knowing that we did everything in the most ethical fashion possible. If you are ever tempted either by a customer's demands or by others in the industry, please see me immediately. I will always support you when your actions are ethical.

EXERCISE 9-2

Donald Burr's human resource strategy for People Express Airline made sense in the beginning. It was the epitome of an entrepreneurial venture. Employees working for a highly entrepreneurial venture are usually willing to work for long hours at lower than normal wages if they perceive a payoff in the future. Once the business grows, it must have more structure than an emerging venture does. Additional employees should have been added, and an additional management level would have been useful. On the other hand, many of People Express Airline's problems were either Burr's fault or caused by reaction from other airlines.

CONVENIESSE, INC.

This assignment continues that from Chapter 8. Here students should be encouraged to put meat on the skeleton plan developed in the previous chapter. In particular, they should be tasked with developing a marketing plan for Conveniesse, Inc. It should include the nature and amount of advertising, other promotional methods such as flyers in the office building, an open house, involvement in office building activities, and other innovative ways of attracting customers into the store. The financial plan should be worked out among the three owners to guide their acquisition of funding in the future. Their human resource strategy should delineate the number of employees, the amount of training offered, hours of work, and compensation.

CHAPTER TEN

FRANCHISING

TEACHING OBJECTIVES

Teaching objectives for this chapter are to have students understand:

1.   The significance of franchising in the economy.

2.   The advantages of franchising from the viewpoint of both the franchisor and the franchisee.

3.   The disadvantages of franchising from both the franchisor's and franchisee's perspective.

4.   The need to study a franchise carefully before purchasing one.

5.   The methods to use in studying a franchise.

6.   The need to study the franchisee agreement carefully.

7.   The nature of the franchise triad.

CHAPTER OUTLINE

I.   Franchising Defined

II.   Types of Franchising

III. Franchising Basics

IV.   Advantages and Disadvantages of Franchising

   A. Advantages to the Franchisee

      1. Established Product or Service
      2. Technical and Managerial Assistance
      3. Quality Control Standards
      4. Less Operating Capital
      5. Opportunities for Growth

   B. Advantages for the Franchisor

      1. Expansion
      2. Motivation
      3. Operation of a Non-Union Business
      4. Bulk Purchasing
      5. Shared Advertising

   C. Disadvantages for the Franchisee

      1. Failed Expectations
      2. Royalty Fees
      3. Over-dependence
      4. Restrictions on Freedom of Ownership
      5. Termination of Agreement
      6. Performance of Other Franchisees

   D. Disadvantages to the Franchisor

      1. Company-owned versus Franchised Units
      2. Franchisor-Franchisee Problems

V.   Investigating a Franchise

VI.   Financial Requirements

   A. Requirements for Franchisors

   B. Requirements for Franchisees

CONSIDER THIS!

* This is definitely true. It is tempting to consider McDonald's as the typical franchise. Nothing could be farther from the truth. Many franchises are virtually unheard of and may not be worth the fee.

* This is also true. They are small businesses because the franchisee is a small business person. On the other hand, the franchisor is typically a large business and has the strengths associated with large businesses.

* Franchising is not cheap. It should not be considered an inexpensive method of starting a business.

* A true entrepreneur will likely resist franchising since it does require playing by someone else's rules. Further, the inexperienced person or one who does not want to invest long hours each day would not make a good franchisee.

* Part of the decision process in investing in franchises is to determine whether the concept could be implemented just as well without a franchise.

CHAPTER SUMMARY

Tremendous preparation is needed before a franchisee opens a franchised outlet. There is a strong degree of personal involvement brought to the business activities by both franchisor and franchisee. To a franchisor, franchising means potential for growth at a rate that can far exceed the rate typical of growth through wholly owned outlets. To a franchisee, franchising means the opportunity for extensive training and preparation prior to opening an outlet, plus use of a recognizable name, trademark, or logo associated with the products or services to be offered.

Both franchisor and franchisee have advantages and disadvantages that stem from their involvement in a franchising relationship. The greatest advantage to the franchisee is the help available from the parent organization. Possibly the franchisee's greatest disadvantages are the restrictions on business practices and the inclination to over-depend on help from the franchisor. For the franchisor, perhaps the greatest single advantage is the chance to expand the business with limited capital risk and equity investment. Because of the investment by the franchisee, a franchisor doesn't have to inject large sums of money or incur major debt to expand the business into new locations. The greatest problem or challenge is maintaining control over an expanding franchise system while overseeing the general operations of each outlet.

The franchisee-franchisor business relationship is a common mission to ensure that both the franchisor and franchisee succeed. An individual franchisee is vulnerable if another franchisee does not maintain the same quality standards. Similarly, if the franchisor seeks to modify the product line, eliminate a service, or change an operating policy or other facet of the franchise system, it can be extremely difficult to achieve consensus among all franchisees regarding the proposed change.

Investing in a franchise, like any other business investment, involves risk. Seven steps for protection from the risks of franchising were presented. A potential franchisee will want to consider these steps before signing a franchising agreement.

The capital requirements of franchising are discussed from the perspective of both franchisor and franchisee. A franchisor will have capital requirements that must be addressed prior to development of a franchise system as well as on a continuing basis as the system is maintained or further developed. Typically, a franchisor's initial investment may range from $100,000 to over $1,000,000.

Like the franchisor, the prospective franchisee will also have financial requirements to consider. The capital requirements are divided into six categories: franchising fee, real estate or rental costs, personal living and travel costs, equipment costs, start-up expenses and inventory, and working capital requirements. Initial costs, as well as working capital requirements, can be substantial. Depending on the franchise an individual seeks, however, one can enter franchising for as little as $5,000. Entering a franchised business may be more costly than entering the same field of business as an independent entrepreneur. However, the added financial commitment can pay dividends for those seeking a safer way to enter business.

Typical elements included in a franchising agreement were listed to identify what a prospective franchisee should consider before buying a franchise. Finally, the existence of a triad or three part relationship was noted. This triad involves the legal agreement between the franchisor and franchisee, the business relationship between the two, and the recognition that each of the players is also an independent business.

TEACHING STRATEGY

This chapter is fairly straightforward. It lays out the advantages and disadvantages of franchising for both the franchisee and the franchisor. It then addresses items that should be considered in buying franchises in general and as well as a specific franchise.

An approach to take is to get the students to quit thinking of all franchises as a McDonald's. If you succeed at this, then the next step is to get them to think through whether they would really want to be a franchisee. Get them to think sequentially. That is, would they want to be any franchisee. Then what kind of franchise would they like. Then what specific franchise would they invest in.

Students should realize that franchisees really do depend on the franchisor to a large extent. The franchisee has some but not a lot of flexibility in decision making. Plus, franchising is not cheap. After adding the up front cost of franchise fees and other start-up costs, one must also add the royalty and advertising fees. These can be considerable.

The summary question is, "Can I do this by myself just as well as I can with a franchise?"

DISCUSSION QUESTIONS

1.   A person who was already a successful entrepreneur would probably not <u>need</u> the franchise as much as a new entrepreneur. On the other hand, an experienced entrepreneur would be able to grow the franchise quicker than the inexperienced person could. The inexperienced entrepreneur would benefit from the training provided by the franchisor.

2.   Talking with existing franchisees can give a level of objectivity that can not be gained from the franchisor. This is particularly true in regard to franchisor-franchisee relations.

3.   Talking to new, relatively new, and old franchisees is useful because it can yield information on how the franchisor relates to franchisees in those stages. It can also pick up information on the value of the training program.

4.   A franchise such as McDonald's is obviously well known, well accepted, and well run. It is also very expensive and has very strict rules. A lesser known franchise will typically be much less expensive, but it will also tend to be less valuable, and will offer less benefits.

5.   Typically it will not be possible to initially match a franchise with a free-standing business. This may or may not be important to the entrepreneur, depending upon the nature of the franchise and the experience of the franchisee.

6.   The advantage of franchising for the franchisor is that it provides quick expansion possibilities with less capital required.

7.   This is a good assignment. An even better assignment is for you to get some franchise packets in advance to hand out in class for students to analyze. These are easily obtainable from franchisors.

8.   The capital needs for a franchisee are significant. These include the franchise fee plus any required start-up costs such as building, equipment, leases, and the first few months' wages and other expenses. This may not, however, be significantly higher than a non-franchise start-up. The difference may be in the immediacy of the need for funds. A franchise may require over $100,000 of non-debt funds at the outset. A non-franchise start-up may have more flexibility than that.

9.   The three parts to the triad are the legal relationship, the business relationship, and the two businesses. The legal relationship establishes fixed responsibilities for each party. The business relationship is a dynamic interaction between the franchisee and the franchisor. The two separate business entities have separate goals and objectives. Hence, the three relationships within the triad form a complex interplay which must be carefully handled.

EXERCISE 10-1

I have used this as a test question by cutting out an advertisement and then having students analyze the information provided to determine what additional information would be needed to make a good decision.

EXERCISE 10-2

This is a fairly in-depth assignment, but it may be worth the time. It might also be good for a term paper assignment or an extra credit assignment. It could also be used as a group project in which several teams of students each interview pairs of franchisees and then report back to the class.

CONVENIESSE, INC.

Here, the three entrepreneurs are considering various methods of growth including the possibility of franchising. The assignment for the students is to analyze whether Conveniesse would be a good franchise candidate. Students will be tempted to say that they should since it appears to be similar to other convenience stores. Encourage them to think through the issues more carefully. Do these entrepreneurs seem like they could handle franchising on a major scale? Do they have the expertise? Is Conveniesse, Inc. just like any other convenience store? How many units per city are likely? Unless there is room for major growth via franchising, should they grow through company owned units instead?

The conclusion after analysis may still be that they should grow via franchising. As will be seen in the next chapter, they decided not to franchise, but that does not mean it was the correct decision. The issue is for the students to do the analysis to reach an objective conclusion.

CHAPTER ELEVEN

INTERNATIONAL ENTREPRENEURSHIP

TEACHING OBJECTIVES

The teaching objectives for this chapter are for the students to understand:

1. The nature of international business

2. The reasons why an entrepreneur will "go international"

3. The factors to consider in deciding how to export

4. How to decide what to export

5. The decision making regarding where to export

6. Sources of information on exporting

7. Other methods of selling in the international market

CHAPTER OUTLINE

I. The International Decision

    A. The need for planning

B. The need for commitment

C. The need for analysis

II. Deciding to Export

III. Deciding How to Export

    A. Indirect Exporting

        1. Commission Agents
        2. Export Management Companies
        3. Export Trading Companies
        4. Marketing Through Other Companies

    B. Direct Exporting

        1. Selling to Distributors
        2. Selling to Retailers
        3. Selling to End Users

IV. Deciding What to Export

V. Deciding Where to Export

    A. Conducting Market Research

    B. Sources of Market Information

VI. Implementing the International Strategy

    A. Establishing Relationships With Intermediaries

    B. Financing Considerations

    C. Controlling the Strategy

VII. Tapping the International Market

    A. Trade Shows

    B. Catalog Shows

CONSIDER THIS!

* Just as with businesses in general, exporters consist of a few large firms and a host of small firms.

* International decisions require careful thinking and planning. Large firms are not immune to mistakes.

* Although exporting is, by far, the most frequent method of international involvement, importing, joint ventures, licensing, and direct investment are all methods of international entrepreneurship.

* Small firms can easily spread themselves too thin by trying to capture all opportunities. Hence, they may fail through over-expansion.

* One of the areas in which the government does a very good job is in export assistance.

* Exporting must be considered a long-run strategy. It should not be considered a fill-in strategy during a downtime.

CHAPTER SUMMARY

The international arena is certainly an exciting possibility for entrepreneurial firms who desire additional growth. At the same time, it is not for everyone. Entering the international market for the first time can be a time consuming and frustrating adventure. If sufficient information and assistance can be obtained, the entrepreneur stands ready to achieve major growth compared to that possible in domestic markets.

The international decision should not be made independent of the firm's domestic strategy. In fact, the domestic strategy should be carefully analyzed to determine if an international thrust is advised. The strategic planning model introduced earlier in the text was adapted in this chapter for use in analyzing the international arena.

Decisions that are most important include: should the firm export, how should it export, what should it export, and to where should it export. Each of these decisions requires major amounts of study and research.

Firms may desire to export directly or indirectly. Direct exporting offers additional control of the process but is more costly and more difficult for first time exporters. Conversely, indirect exporting is much easier for the producing firm but has the disadvantage of loss of control over the product after it is sold to an intermediariy. Intermediaries who either purchase goods or provide assistance include export management companies (EMC's), export trading companies (ETC's), freight forwarders, or other companies which may purchase the firm's products to include with their own.

Significant advice and information are available regarding exporting. Most notable is the U.S. & Foreign Commercial Service of the U.S. Department of Commerce's International Trade Administration. A number of excellent books and periodicals are available that provide information on exporting.

Entrepreneurial firms may also be interested in other forms of international involvement. For ventures with products to sell outside the United States, either licensing or joint ventures are appealing to some. Other firms may be more interested in importing as part of their strategy.

TEACHING STRATEGY

Students are perhaps less familiar with the topics of this chapter than any other chapter in the text. Although business schools are beginning to teach international business, international entrepreneurship is a subset of the international business area. They will, in particular, be unaware of the technical aspects of exporting or importing. The goal of this chapter is to introduce the students to the topic. Those who are serious about the topic will want to increase their knowledge by contacting an international trade center near them.

The primary focus of this chapter is on exporting. Most entrepreneurs will choose this as their international strategy. Importing, joint ventures, and licensing are touched briefly at the end of the chapter.

An important point in the chapter is the need for planning and commitment. Planning is especially important when considering international ventures because of the added investment of time and money to begin the international strategy.

The major part of the chapter discusses the why, what, where, and how questions. That is, why should we export, what kinds of products are exportable, where are the markets for the product, and how should we export the product. The important aspect of the why question is the determination of the real motivation underlying the export decision. If, for example, the firm wishes to export to offset a temporary slump, the commitment may not remain after domestic sales return. The venture's products should be examined carefully to determine if it truly is an exportable product. Related to this is to ask where there is a demand for the product and what must be done to reach it. The last issue is to determine how to export. Many first time exporters will choose the indirect method of exporting because of the lower investment of time, money, and effort.

A good approach to covering this chapter is to invite a guest speaker either from a nearby international trade center or from a state or federal agency such as the Department of Commerce's International Trade Office. The advantage to this is that they can answer technical questions in addition to discussing the how-to of exporting. One such technical topic is the issue of getting paid when the products are purchased abroad in a currency other than U.S. Dollars.

DISCUSSION QUESTIONS

1. The advantage of exporting is simply that there are many markets beyond the borders of the United States. Thus, the opportunity for substantial increases in sales and profits exist. On the other hand, exporting is more difficult, at least initially, than selling domestically. Thus, a low growth entrepreneur might be well advised to grow domestically before expanding overseas.

2. The main concern is the firm's existing strategy. A complete analysis should be done of the venture's capabilities and opportunities to see if moving into the international arena is either warranted or possible. Only when this is done should secondary decisions regarding what, where, and how be addressed.

3.   The process is the same. The difference is that the international dimension is included here. In addition, the model focuses first on the firm's existing strategy and then looks at the international arena.

4.   The venture's overall strategy must be carefully analyzed first in order to determine if an international strategy is either warranted or possible. Further, analyzing the domestic strategy first may discover new markets that should be tapped before going international.

5.   No. All the international decisions are part of a package. In particular, the product decision influences where to export, how to export, and even if we should export.

6.   An export venture is more risky in the eyes of lenders and other investors who may not be familiar with exporting. Hence, getting funding for exporting will be more difficult unless a very convincing plan is presented.

7.   Included in the list would be items such as language, customs, currency related issues, tariffs, distribution channels, and government support. Ranking the importance of the items will be a function of the country and the entrepreneur's experience, but language and customs could heavily affect the success of the product.

8.   Consulting the National Trade Data Bank is a good start if that is in your university's library. If not, contact the Department of Commerce or your state's international trade division.

9.   An entrepreneur should NOT take advantage of all export opportunities for the same reason that NOT all domestic opportunities should be pursued. This will over-extend the venture's capabilities and possibly cause failure of the entire firm.

10.   The first control measure is to carefully analyze the project before beginning. A second control measure is to carefully pick any intermediaries that will be involved. A third measure is to visit the countries that will be importing the product.

11.   Eximbank provides funding to those desiring to export. Since many traditional banks will not provide export funding, the Eximbank was made available as an encouragement for international entrepreneurship.

12.   A joint venture consists of two companies working together to achieve goals that could not be achieved otherwise. The two companies often form a separate venture for a specific purpose. This differs from either direct or indirect exporting because there is no supplier/client transaction.

13. Licensing can be desirable. If the venture produces a product that is not easily exportable or if the entrepreneur does not want the level of involvement or risk necessary, licensing may be a desirable alternative. In this situation, the entrepreneur licenses the product to be manufactured and sold abroad by one or more firms. It then receives a royalty on the sale of the product.

14. The first information is the same as producing any other product. Information must be obtained that will aid in assessing the demand. In addition, information such as foreign sources of the product, exchange rates, shipping methods, and payment arrangements must be obtained. Some of the information can be obtained from the Department of Commerce. Other information can be gained from trade shows and other informal contacts with suppliers.

EXERCISE 11-1

This is a good assignment. It can either be done as an out-of-class assignment or an in-class discussion. If used outside of class, students should spend time in the library, perhaps with the National Trade Data Bank to gather information which would lead to a decision. If used as an in-class discussion, students should contemplate what there is about the product that would make it a good or bad product to export. For example, the mechanical sweeper is an industrial product probably made by only a few manufacturers. It would not be cheap to export, but could be done and would require a minimum of modification from country to country. Weed trimmers are low cost products and are likely made abroad now. Manufacturing them here for shipment abroad should be done only after careful consideration.

EXERCISE 11-2

This is a major outside assignment. This could even be a major consulting project for a team of students. This works best if it is for a real client rather than a hypothetical company. On the other hand, requiring the students to do a hypothetical export plan is a good assignment by itself.

CONVENIESSE, INC.

In this segment, the three entrepreneurs have an opportunity to expand into Canada. Students should be asked to consider just what, if any, differences there will be in Montreal and the rest of Canada. At the least, students should pick up on the language differences. They might also suggest different product mixes for Canadian stores. Does the name Conveniesse have any meaning in French? Will the beverage mix be the same as in the U.S.? Will any U.S. suppliers have difficulty? Will the laptop computers be programmed in French or English or both? Will currency exchange rates be significant?

CHAPTER TWELVE

STRUCTURING THE VENTURE

TEACHING OBJECTIVES

The teaching objectives for this chapter are for the students to understand:

1. The alternative ways to organize a venture's internal structure.

2. How to recognize when a given structure is not effective.

3. The unique features of a family-held venture as they relate to the venture's structure.

4. The reasons why a particular structure is appropriate.

5. The methods of assimilating new ventures into existing ventures.

6. Problems that can arise from inappropriate structure choice.

7. The value of a Board of Directors.

CHAPTER OUTLINE

I. Determining the Internal Structure of a Venture

    A. Basic Venture Structure

CONSIDER THIS!

*   In order to be efficient, the structure of the venture should be a reflection of its strategy. However, the firm's structure at a given time may also affect what strategy is selected. For example, a venture without a fully developed functional management structure could not be expected to immediately develop a high growth strategy.

* Many businesses that stagnate may do so because the entrepreneur was unwilling to add managerial staff and share power with them.

* Employees of both the acquired and acquiring firms will be anxious to see what the future brings. The structure of the combined firms will communicate significant messages to both. The entrepreneur considering what kind of merged structure to use must make that decision carefully and must communicate clearly to all employees.

* All of these factors can affect the decision.

* Culture is a significant and powerful force. Forcing two quite different cultures together is bound to create problems.

* A board of directors may be even more important for a smaller company than for a larger one. This is because the small firm may be more vulnerable as well as understaffed. An external board can provide information, contacts, and ideas, as well as a sounding board for the entrepreneur.

CHAPTER SUMMARY

Structuring a venture correctly can greatly affect the ability of the venture to compete over the long term. The discussion of venture structure includes both that of determining the organizational structure of a venture and the methods of meshing an acquired venture into an existing one.

The internal structure of a venture affects both the efficiency and effectiveness of the business. New and small ventures often utilize the basic structure which has only one person in a position of authority. This structure works well as long as the venture does not experience rapid growth and does not face a turbulent environment. If the venture does achieve growth, then the basic structure becomes very inefficient. A functional management structure will evolve to compensate for the entrepreneur's inability to manage the venture's growth. If even more growth is achieved or if acquisitions increase the size of the venture, then a divisional structure may evolve.

The structure of a venture is especially important if the business is a family firm. Although no particular structure is always best, the entrepreneur must consider the motivational impact of having family versus non-family members in authority positions.

In addition, management succession in the family venture must be considered as the structure is determined or adjusted.

New ventures that are purchased or developed must be assimilated into the existing structure. The structure used in assimilating the new venture can either add to or detract from the potential of both the new and old ventures. The choices of combined structures are to operate both as separate ventures connected only by a joint ownership, absorbing the new venture totally into the existing one, creating a subsidiary of the existing venture, and creating a new company that absorbs both the new and old ventures. The choice of structures depends of the relative cost of each structural type, the autonomy each allows, and the impact of the structural type on the motivation, power, and ego of the different players in the combined venture.

Boards of directors are not required in most new or small ventures. Yet they are a valuable part of any venture structure. Members of a board of directors that are carefully selected and well utilized can make a tremendous contribution to the survival of the venture.

TEACHING STRATEGY

Most students who take an entrepreneurship course have previously had a principles of management course. Thus, they should have been exposed to the basic, functional, and divisional forms of business. They key here is to examine how that fits new and growing ventures.

Students may not immediately catch on to the fact that the structure is a function of size more than time. Note to them that many ventures are small for twenty years and still function with primarily a basic structure. It is instructive to note examples in the community that students can recognize and discuss which structures they appear to have. Then lead them through a discussion of why a particular structure is good or bad for a specific business.

The family venture structure is particularly important both as the venture is launched and as it grows over a number of years. This is a good time to discuss bringing in non-family workers and non-family managers. It is always interesting to have students who have grown up in family ventures discuss the pros and cons of working with family and non-family workers. Some will report good relationships. Others will tell stories of their parents treating them worse than other employees so favoritism will not be suspected. Still others may tell stories of jealousies either among siblings or between family workers and non-family workers.

Students will typically not be familiar with the various methods of assimilating new ventures into existing ones. They almost certainly will not be aware of the advantages and disadvantages of each. List each of the methods on the board and have the students suggest advantages and disadvantages of each. Individual comments should be probed. The discussion of structure forms may say more about the individuals than it does the structure itself.

Chapter 3 briefly discussed advisory boards. This chapter covers it in more depth. This is really a second opportunity to hammer the importance of some sort of board of directors or an advisory board for the small firm. If you are personally on one or more boards, you may be able to share your own experiences.

DISCUSSION QUESTIONS

1. Structure is important because of both efficiency and effectiveness. An inappropriate structure can lead to inefficiency which in turn can result in lack of effectiveness. This is particularly true in new and growing businesses where the entrepreneur plays such a strong role.

2. The basic structure is often used in new and small ventures because it is not large enough to need the more advanced structure. As long as it is effective, it is more efficient. Only when the firm begins to grow does the basic structure become inefficient.

3. The bookkeeping/accounting function is often the first to be developed because it is a time consuming task that the entrepreneur often has little skill in that area. Sometimes a combination bookkeeper/office manager position is established to take care of the more mundane tasks. Later the bookkeeper position is changed to an accounting position.

4. The next position to develop will likely be a function of the entrepreneur's own skills. The additional person is hired (or promoted) to offset the entrepreneur's weaknesses. Thus, if the entrepreneur is a skilled technician, the first person hired may be a marketing person. If the entrepreneur is a strong sales person, the first person hired may be a purchasing person, an in-house marketing representative, or a technician/repair person.

5. The family and the family venture are most likely to experience conflict during the growth stage. In the beginning, the family typically supports the entrepreneur in the quest to launch the venture. Later, as the venture requires more and more of the entrepreneur's time, stress and conflict may arise. If the family and the venture survive the growth stage, the relationship between the two may stabilize again. During this period, family members may work in the venture, and some members may become involved in the management of the company. The remaining situation that may be

stressful will be when the venture is being harvested. This is why much planning should go into the harvest plan. This will be discussed in Chapter 16.

6.   Again, the growth stage is likely to cause conflict. If the venture experiences substantial growth, outside employees will increase in numbers. Managers may also be outsiders. Issues of power, compensation, benefits, and promotion will become significant. This, too, will be significant again when the harvest is imminent.

7.   A case can be made either way regarding the best structure for maximizing flexibility and the ability to react quickly to changes in the environment. For example, maintaining separate ventures is appealing because the separate ventures means that the managers are close to the customers and are therefore most able to read changes in buying patterns or customer profiles. On the other hand, if the entrepreneur must be present to make every decision, this structure will slow the decision process. The key to flexibility may not be tied to the actual structure as much as it is to the entrepreneur's management style.

8.   Entrepreneurs tend to have a high need for autonomy. This is a key reason why they start a venture in the first place. Some will also have a higher than average ego. Putting these two together suggests that an entrepreneur will not be happy working for someone else after having been totally in charge. Submitting the acquired venture to either a subsidiary status or totally absorbing it into the existing venture will certainly bruise the ego of the acquired firm's owner. If the deal includes bringing that owner in, the acquiring entrepreneur should not be surprised if the arrangement does not last long.

9.   There are not too many direct disadvantages. One is the duplication of management staff. Related to this is that the entrepreneur must spend considerable time traveling between the two ventures if tight control is desired. If the acquired firm is well managed, there are more advantages than disadvantages to keeping the firms separate.

10. They are seldom used for two reasons. First, the entrepreneur is busy and does not want to take the time from the venture to do the planning required to set up the board. Second, the entrepreneur may not want to share power with outsiders even though they were hand-picked.

11. Boards of directors are almost certain to be more prevalent in the growth oriented venture. In some cases they will be required by investors. Regardless, it is important for the growth venture to have the expertise of a competent board. A small business venture that does not intend to grow could still benefit from a board, but it is not as critical to the firm's success if the environment is benign.

EXERCISE 12-1

Various answers could be given to each of the situations listed. If these are used as graded exercises, the grading should be based on the justification rather than the specific answer.

1.   Joe Machias is typical of the small business owner. He is the top mechanic but spends part of his time dealing with customers. This is understandable since we assume that he has built a solid and loyal customer base. If the business is at or near capacity (as constrained by facilities) there may not be too much that can be done. Joe may want to consider taking himself out of the mechanic tasks and spend most of his time in administration or dealing with customers who demand special attention. This could reduce his stress without hurting the business. It might require adding a mechanic.

2.   The best suggestion here might be to leave the two businesses separate, at least for the short run. If the new business does not provide enough revenue to support the administrative manager, she might then want to consider merging the two locations. Since the businesses are service businesses, keeping the identity and location the same will be better for customer continuity. As for the structure of the original venture, the business may have room for expansion, but Adams may be reaching her limit of management before long. She could add one more accountant, but a better suggestion would be to hold off until she sees whether the acquired firm can be self-supporting. If not, she can use the excess space to house the remaining staff of the acquired firm.

3.   A firm cannot continue to grow at that rate for long without becoming inefficient and perhaps ineffective. Adding a layer of management would allow for even more growth. Given the technical knowledge required in the business, a wise idea might be to add a manager to the technical side and a marketing person to help generate more revenues.

4.   If the transmission shop has a good reputation (Many do not.), Machias could leave it as it is and either convince the owner to stay for a while as manager or promote someone from that shop or his own transmission specialist to be the manager of the acquired shop. If the reputation was not good, he could eliminate any mechanics or customer service representatives that hurt the reputation. He could also change the name to match his own shop to give the obvious tie to his operation. He could either assign his transmission specialist to run the new shop or he could hire additional help in his own shop so that he could spend time there.

5.   Since the car wash is moderately successful, it must be operating at least at an acceptable level. There is no rush to change it drastically, and none of the apparel store managers would likely want to move to the car wash. Thomason could leave it alone for now until she gets the struggling store stabilized. An additional manager could be added as a trouble-shooter who initially concentrates on the struggling store. If the store

manager appeared to be the problem, either training or termination might be called for. If location or other external problem was the cause, then the trouble-shooter could address it.

6.   Manufacturing a line of computer equipment is far different from other office equipment even though the markets are similar. One must question whether that is a wise move given the competitive nature of the market. If he does add it, Montgomery should consider starting a completely separate division for the computer equipment. The marketing function might use the existing sales force if they are adequately trained.

A better choice is to expand the office equipment sales into the eastern U.S. This would not require additional production facilities immediately, and any additional facilities could be added incrementally. The marketing function would need to expand to accommodate the additional markets.

EXERCISE 12-2

Avery probably acted hastily in combining the two staffs. Unless there were compelling reasons to absorb one into the other, the two ventures could be kept separate. Even if Ekstra physically moved into Avery facilities, it still could be kept as a separate entity at least for the short run. Later, the two staffs could be slowly combined. This would prevent the Ekstra people from being considered as less important.

EXERCISE 12-3

Obviously, the president needs to add at least one managerial position. The question is what the position should be. Either a vice president for human resources or a vice president for finance should be added. Since the market is growing, the president can only encounter still more stress unless someone is added. Since there is no indication that the firm is in financial trouble, a human resource V.P. seems to be the best choice. This would allow the president to focus more on planning and obtaining future financing if necessary. A part-time accountant or a CPA firm could help out in the accounting area. Alternatively, a controller could be hired. This person would take over the accounting function, do more analysis of the firm's condition, and help manage the overall operation.

CONVENIESSE, INC.

The chain of Conveniesse stores has now grown to ten with some in Canada and some in the U.S. Sarah has moved back to Montreal and manages the Canadian division. Jason was in charge of the U.S. based stores, and Yolanda was now the president as well as in charge of all marketing. Plans exist for increasing the number of stores substantially both in the U.S. and in Canada.

The student assignment is to analyze the chain's organization structure and to recommend a better one. The major strength of the current structure is that the two divisions each have a V.P. in charge. This is a geographical structure although the major difference is only that one division is in Canada and the other is in the United States. The weakness of the structure is that, except for marketing, none of the functional areas have a manager. Thus, Jason and Sarah are both generalists running their particular division almost solo. Yolanda handles marketing aspects for the entire chain and this makes sense given her expertise. The three meet frequently to handle management issues.

If the firm continues to grow, structural changes will have to be made. Vice presidents for finance and marketing should be added soon. Another person in charge of store expansion would also be useful. Have the class discuss what would be an optimal strategy now, with a few more stores, and with perhaps twenty more stores. Have someone do an organizational chart on the board. Ask the following questions: If the new vice presidents are added, then what role will Jason and Sarah play? What happens if the U.S. division grows rapidly and the Canadian division stabilizes at slightly higher than it is now? How large can Conveniesse, Inc. grow without a major change in structure?

CHAPTER THIRTEEN

MANAGING GROWTH

TEACHING OBJECTIVES

The teaching objectives for this chapter are for the student to understand:

1. The need to keep the venture's resources in line with the natural growth of the market.

2. The need to continue growth once the market tapers off.

3. The problems of maintaining and encouraging growth while controlling it.

4. The causes, effects, and solutions to stress in a growth oriented venture.

CHAPTER OUTLINE

I. Enabling Growth

   A. Human Resources

   B. Physical Resources

   C. Supplier Availability

   D. Distribution

E.   Financial Resources

II.   Growth Extending Actions

A.   Geographic Expansion

B.   Expansion Through Acquisition

III.   Rejuvenating Growth

IV.   Controlling Growth

A.   Identifying Control Problems

B.   Controlling Through Budgets

C.   Implementing Control

V.   Managing Stress in Growth Ventures

A.   Sources of Entrepreneurial Stress

B.   Managing Entrepreneurial Stress

VI.   Summary

CONSIDER THIS!

*   Keeping growth alive may indeed be more difficult than starting it. Because of the additional human, financial, and physical resources required, it is difficult to react timely to the demands of growth.

*   Maximizing growth may lead to uncontrolled growth which, in turn, may lead to wildly expanding costs. These can then lead to bankruptcy if not controlled.

*   The amount of growth will be the lesser of (a) the amount of natural growth in the market and (b) the firm's ability to keep up with the growth.

*   Growth can be maintained beyond that of the market as a whole by either moving into new markets, by purchasing competitors, or by bringing out related products.

*   Substantial research suggests that entrepreneurs may thrive on stress to an extent and therefore do not exhibit the indicators of stress to the extent that other individuals do. In addition, even though many stressors exist in entrepreneurial ventures, the entrepreneurs can often control the stressors better because of the flexibility they have in running their own venture.

CHAPTER SUMMARY

This chapter deals with managing a growth oriented venture. Launching a venture is difficult. It may pale, however, in comparison to the challenge of maintaining and controlling growth once the venture is launched. The two tasks of maintaining and controlling growth can, to an extent, work against each other. Yet, actions can be taken to let the venture grow at its natural rate, and other actions can be taken to extend the growth beyond its natural peak. Still other actions are required to rejuvenate growth after the product enters the maturity phase. Controlling growth without eliminating it is particularly difficult in entrepreneurial firms because the freedom and autonomy may be a major reason why the growth is achieved in the first place. Restricting growth may have adverse side effects.

A key to managing growth ventures is to be able to evaluate performance. Performance evaluation can be best done via budgets and ratio analysis. Several ratios were suggested that are particularly appropriate for entrepreneurial ventures.

Many entrepreneurs thrive on the excitement and pressure of entrepreneurship, and research tends to support this contention. At the same time, entrepreneurs must be able to identify stress both within themselves and among their subordinates. Failure to manage stress appropriately can cause lost productivity because of turnover or absenteeism of workers and because of physical or emotional wear and tear on the entrepreneur.

TEACHING STRATEGY

Two types of students may be uncomfortable with this chapter. The first is the student who thinks that too much attention is given to growth ventures since the vast majority of ventures are in the low growth category. The second type of student may feel that the chapter unnecessarily attempts to constrain growth. They feel that the role of the entrepreneur is to get as much growth as possible in the shortest time as possible without regard to control. They feel that discussing ways to control or constrain growth is the antithesis of entrepreneurship. Neither conclusion is totally correct, nor are they reasons to denigrate the value of the chapter.

The first part of the chapter addresses the problem of keeping up with the growth or growth enabling actions. Try to impress on the students the difficulty of the decisions related to enabling growth. Unfortunately, adding staff, facilities, or even financing can not be done in a nice smooth method. The decision to add facilities, for example, is a major one since increasing the amount of equipment or warehousing can only be done in blocks of capacity. Students should be made aware of the difficulty of making decisions when the entrepreneur has the choice of limiting growth versus making significant investments in the venture in hopes that growth continues.

The second part of the chapter deals with extending growth beyond the normally expected amount. Some of these factors fall in the area of competition for market share. Others require geographical expansion or the development of new products. In any of the cases, substantial investment of time and energy is required. A major difference between extending growth and enabling growth is that enabling growth focuses inward while extending growth focuses outward. Rejuvenating growth is similar to extending growth, except that the actions taken are more dramatic.

The last section of the chapter deals with managing entrepreneurial stress. Students may not identify with this unless they were raised around a growth oriented family business. This is a good opportunity to address the sometimes parallel and sometimes opposite demands of the family and the family business. It is also an opportunity to discuss the energizing power of entrepreneurship. A number of studies have shown that entrepreneurs put in long hours with much uncertainty. Yet, other studies have also shown that entrepreneurs do not necessarily react badly to these stressors. Some entrepreneurs are energized by the venture and thrive on the action. Still, actions should be taken to reduce the amount of stress to the extent that it is deleterious for the entrepreneur or the venture.

DISCUSSION QUESTIONS

1. The "natural growth rate" for a venture is that rate that the venture would realize if it just kept up with its competitors as the market grew. For new ventures, the entrepreneur must at least keep up with the natural growth of the market, or the venture will fall behind the competition.

2. Although the enabling and extending actions could be done at the same time, they usually are not. The reason is that when the entrepreneur is struggling to keep up with the growth, little attention is given to extending growth. In addition, resources will be quite limited because of the growth, and this leaves few, if any, resources to use for growth extending actions.

3.   It is not uncommon for ventures to fail because of too much growth. When a firm's owners are struggling to keep up with growth, they lose control of the venture's operation. Defects creep in, costs go up rapidly, short term financing causes debt service to grow, and employees must be added too rapidly to train properly.

4.   Controlling growth is a dilemma because too much growth can cause problems while too many controls can stifle creativity. It is certainly risky to allow growth to continue unchecked. Conversely, restraining entrepreneurial employees too much can reduce their motivation.

5.   There is no single answer to this problem. Involving employees in the development of budgets helps them see potential problems. Delegating control to workers within some parameters makes use of their talents while constraining their range of movement.

6.   An interesting assignment. This is good for either extra credit or take home exam.

7.   In high growth ventures, performance will almost always be over budget. Regardless of how optimistic the planning is, both revenues and costs exceed estimates. Still, the venture benefits from budgets. The reason is that the entrepreneur can see how much each item exceeds the budget and get an idea of the relative changes in each.

8.   Monitoring the venture's financial performance does not automatically mean close monitoring of individual performance by employees. Hence, sometimes we may want to give an employee substantial freedom of movement because that freedom may support the venture's growth.

9.   Entrepreneurs have a strong need for autonomy, an internal locus of control, and a high need for achievement. They rise to a challenge and feel that they can surpass it. Thus, stressors may be seen as challenges. Beyond that, entrepreneurs can often structure their activities such that stressors do not have the negative impact that they do for others.

10. The entrepreneur can begin to isolate venture caused stress from others by being alert to employee behavior and willing to discuss problems on a one-to-one basis. Seldom can anyone be totally successful in removing stress from employees, but the entrepreneur should monitor employee actions to see if problems are developing.

EXERCISE 13-1

This is a good exercise to use fisCAL. If an entrepreneur is willing to share financial information, fisCAL can do a ratio analysis as well as cash flow projections and a valuation.

EXERCISE 13-2

This exercise is one of a company whose growth is beginning to get out of control. Knowing only what is presented in the exercise, the answer appears to be one of insufficient staff. If the backlog of claims processing is consistent and increasing, the company's owners must take actions to speed up the processing, and this can be done best in the short run by increasing personnel. Since growth is projected to increase for a while, the entrepreneurs may want to look at their processing system. Perhaps there are ways to reduce the processing time per claim.

CONVENIESSE, INC.

In this vignette, the three entrepreneurs begin to exhibit some stress associated with the growing chain. As a result, Sarah decides to pull out and focus strictly on the Canadian side. This leaves Jason and Yolanda to manage and grow the U.S. based stores. After a year or so of stabilizing, they begin to refocus on growth.

The assignment for the chapter asks a number of questions that Jason and Yolanda should consider. These should stimulate class discussion.

CHAPTER FOURTEEN

INTRAPRENEURSHIP

TEACHING OBJECTIVES

The teaching objectives for this chapter are for the student to understand:

1. The nature of intrapreneurship
2. Barriers to intrapreneurship
3. How to encourage entrepreneurship in large corporations
4. How to evaluate intrapreneurial proposals
5. Different ways to structure companies to accommodate intrapreneurial activities
6. The unique challenges of entrepreneurship in not-for-profit organizations

CHAPTER OUTLINE

I. The Nature of Intrapreneurship

II. Barriers to Corporate Entrepreneurship

    A. The Inherent Nature of Large Organizations

    B. Need for Short Run Profits

    C. Lack of Entrepreneurial Talent

    D. Inappropriate Compensation Methods

III. Planning for Corporate Entrepreneurship

   A. Committing the Organization

   B. Determining the Corporate Entrepreneurship Model

   C. Developing an Intrapreneurial Culture

   D. Identifying Intrapreneurial Talent

      1. Identifying Individual Intrapreneurs
      2. Identifying Team Members

   E. Rewarding Intrapreneurs

IV. Evaluating Intrapreneurial Projects

V. Administering Intrapreneurial Projects

VI. Entrepreneurship in Not-For-Profit Organizations

VII. Summary

CONSIDER THIS!

* Large corporations do retard entrepreneurship. Their rules, bureaucracy, structure, levels of management, and traditions all work against entrepreneurship.

* True entrepreneurs are seldom comfortable in large corporations. Yet many people have some entrepreneurial tendencies who may work well in larger firms.

* Many new products are created or developed by individual entrepreneurs. Corporate entrepreneurship is also responsible for many new products.

* New products developed by corporate entrepreneurs are produced and sold by the parent company. Others may be assigned to new product divisions. Still others may be developed by separate ventures spun off by the parent company.

* Government has all the problems of large corporations plus a unique culture only evident in government agencies. Not-for-profit organizations such as charitable organizations have problems because of an intense focus on programs rather than overall management of the organization.

CHAPTER SUMMARY

Corporate entrepreneurship, or intrapreneurship, has many similarities with new venture entrepreneurship. It requires innovation, risk taking, commitment, an objective analysis of opportunities, and sufficient funding. Entrepreneurship in the corporate setting, however, faces a number of obstacles. The large size of a corporation stifles entrepreneurship because of the number of layers in the hierarchy and the necessary controls in place to direct such a large organization. Large corporations do not attract true entrepreneurs because of the limited autonomy within a bureaucratic system. Further, if entrepreneurs do find their way into a large corporation, they typically do not stay. The need for fixed time frames and budgets in large corporations makes investing in entrepreneurial ventures difficult. Finally, compensating intrapreneurs is complex within the framework of a traditional corporation.

Five steps must be taken to develop intrapreneurship in large corporations. First, the corporate management must be fully committed to entrepreneurship. Second, a model or structure for corporate entrepreneurship must be determined. Third, an intrapreneurial culture must be developed throughout the organization. Fourth, intrapreneurs must be identified and encouraged. And fifth, a reward system for intrapreneurs must be developed. Once corporate entrepreneurship is endorsed and implemented, then proposals must be evaluated, and successful proposals must be housed somewhere in the overall corporate structure.

Entrepreneurial proposals within a corporation must be evaluated much as any new venture proposal might be evaluated by venture capitalists. Strategic fit and the corporate culture are the two most important issues in determining whether a proposal will be funded. Other criteria include the amount of funding needed, the competition, and the probability of high rates of return.

Entrepreneurship in the not-for-profit organization exists in a broad sense even though the concepts of personal capital investment, the profit motive, and new venture creation are not present. Encouraging entrepreneurship in the not-for-profit organization may be even more difficult than in the corporation because of the nature of the organizations, their managers, and the culture of the organization. Not-for-profit organizations, however, can benefit from entrepreneurial actions that make them more competitive or more cost effective.

TEACHING STRATEGY

Teaching this chapter is not difficult once we accept the premise that entrepreneurship is possible in large corporations. After spending much of the semester suggesting that entrepreneurship is better than life in the corporate world, we must now turn the tables to say that entrepreneurship can exist in the large corporations -- if the culture and organizational structure can be changed.

Most students in an entrepreneurship class can readily identify with the barriers to corporate entrepreneurship. The more difficult task will be the discussion of ways to instill intrapreneurship in mature organizations. Focus on the need for a CEO who is willing to change the corporate culture. Focus on the need to identify intrapreneurs. Lastly, note that there are a number of different organizational structures which can be used to implement intrapreneurship. It is not absolutely necessary for the entire corporate culture to be changed, although it certainly is useful. Even creating a corporate venture capital unit is helpful. Adding a new products division or subsidiary is better.

Spend some time comparing the evaluation of intrapreneurial projects to entrepreneurial projects. Note that some of the criteria may be different, but the evaluation process will be similar.

Finally, encourage the reading of the Appendix to Chapter 14, the story of Art Fry and the Post-It Note. Many of us academics have heard that story many times and may be tired of it. Yet, students are usually somewhat awed by the process at 3M and how the Post-It Note was really developed.

DISCUSSION QUESTIONS

1. The similarities are that both require some amount of risk taking, both focus on opportunities, and both require an amount of capital that may or may not be returned. The difference is that intrapreneurship occurs in established corporations while new venture creation is done by an individual entrepreneur. New venture entrepreneurship is developmental; intrapreneurship tends to be restorative.

2. It is technically possible, but not likely to happen. This does not mean that we do not want to try. Most companies will never succeed in driving out all their competition, but they still act as if they want to.

3. Barriers to intrapreneurship include the size of the firm, the short run focus, the culture, and the inability to attract and adequately compensate entrepreneurial people. Some of these are surmountable, but they require commitment of the CEO and the entire management of the company. Even so, it will be difficult.

4.   The scenario must have, as its first or an early step, the total commitment of the CEO. The second step must be the total convincing of the next level of top managers of the value of intrapreneurship, and communicating the CEO's personal commitment to the concept. They must accept the idea as a long range change in the organization's mode of operations. Next, these managers must work with sequentially lower layers throughout the organization to both change the culture and begin to identify intrapreneurs and intrapreneurial projects. Throughout the entire process, top management must constantly reinforce the change.

5.   Not likely. Middle managers, accustomed to working in the midst of the bureaucracy will react with disbelief that it will ever work. They may see intrapreneurship as the latest fad (as some are seeing total quality management), and will be resistant to giving up old ways of operation. If top management endorses the concept, they will attempt to permeate the organization with the new idea. They may, however, be unaware of the strength of old traditions.

6.   A compensation plan for intrapreneurs must somehow include rewarding the intrapreneur for success while not penalizing failure. Further, it must reward both intrapreneurial and traditional workers who may be working side by side. This is a difficult task to do well over time particularly if the intrapreneur is successful. Factors to be considered include the differences in the motivation of intrapreneurs, the longer term commitment to the intrapreneur before success occurs, and the different goals of each.

7.   Yes. Although it is not optimal, some segments of the company can be designated as intrapreneurial units while others remain in a traditional framework. It requires substantial planning and may even require moving people around within and among buildings.

8.   The process is similar, especially with regard to the external or market aspects of the proposal. The differences will occur within the organizations. The large corporation may include a higher hurdle rate than does the smaller firm. The larger firm may have a number of different proposals at the same time competing for funds. And the larger firm may have to consider its overall mission and how the new proposal fits that mission.

9.   Politics are significant in organizations moving toward intrapreneurial cultures because the normal hierarchical relationships are being challenged and changed. Intrapreneurial teams cut across departments and levels within the organization. Pay structures differ from the traditional. Non-salary reward systems change. All of this disrupts the status quo and will be resisted by some managers throughout the organization.

10. From the outside, the only difference in an entrepreneurial not-for-profit organization and a non-entrepreneurial one would be the response time and willingness to adapt to

different situations. Inside, the culture will differ. The organization will not be seen as a bureaucratic maze or regulations and patronage. Instead, it may focus on how to improve service, how to be more creative, and how to encourage its workers to be innovative in their approach to traditional problems.

11. First, the personnel in not-for-profit organizations have little business backgrounds. Intrapreneurship includes both innovation and the ability to manage a project. Second, not-for-profit organizations often have a very narrow focus. Hence, the workers may not be sufficiently trained in a broader focus to capture innovation.   Third, not-for-profit organizations are often so strapped for funds, that they do not have the flexibility required for intrapreneurial projects that may fail.

12. This is anybody's guess. Intrapreneurship has some similarities to total quality management which was first seen as a great concept and has now been criticized by many. The reason intrapreneurship is uncertain is the same as why TQM is being criticized. It takes total commitment from the top to make either of them work.

EXERCISE 14-1

This would be an interesting exam question. Remarks should include such things as the need for innovation, the challenges to be overcome, the need for willingness to change, the recognition that normal hierarchical relationships will be disrupted from time to time, the acceptance of failure as part of innovation, and the top management's full commitment to the process.

EXERCISE 14-2

This exercise would be fairly time consuming, but could create good discussion in class. It could be used for a short project grade or for a special assignment.

CONVENIESSE, INC.

In this vignette, Jason and Yolanda have been meeting with their managers. Some concern and tension abounds because there is disagreement regarding the need for new life in the organization. The consensus at the end of the meetings is that Conveniesse, Inc. has become somewhat sluggish and has lost its vitality. Some of the units are in danger of being eliminated from their location, and most have not seen much gain in sales in recent years.

The assignment is to recommend solutions to the problem. Discuss whether new paint and motif are sufficient. What, if anything, can be done to rejuvenate the stores? Maybe nothing can be done. If so, then what?

CHAPTER FIFTEEN

VALUING THE VENTURE

TEACHING OBJECTIVES

The teaching objectives for this chapter are for the student to be able to:

1. Differentiate between "price" and "value."

2. Understand when a venture should be valued.

3. Identify factors to consider in reaching a value.

4. Differentiate between the perspectives of buyers, sellers, and financiers.

5. Understand various evaluation methods.

6. Realize the role of risk in valuation.

7. Understand the effect of the "deal" on final price.

CHAPTER OUTLINE

I.   Price Versus Value

II.   Occasions to Value a Venture

VI.   Computing the Venture's Value (Micro-Print)

    A.   Asset Based Approach

    B.   Market Comparables Approaches

    C.   Net Present Value Approach

        1.   Estimating Future Profits
        2.   Calculating Estimated Future Cash Flows
        3.   Applying the Discount Rate

    D.   Comparing the Results

VII.   The Effect of the "Deal" on Price

VIII. Summary

CONSIDER THIS!

*   Valuing a venture utilizes one or more formulas to calculate the value. Yet these values are estimates only, and each method produces a different answer. Hence, it is part objective and part subjective.

*   The "correct price" is whatever a buyer and seller agree upon. There may not be one correct value since a number of factors go into the valuation in addition to the valuation methods.

*   So many factors enter the valuation process as well as the negotiation process that the price range may be quite wide.

*   Some methods are more appropriate than others for a given situation, but there are also reasons why any method is appropriate in different situations.

*   Because of the different perspectives of the value analysts, the data presented will yield different answers as the analysts make different assumptions.

*   An experienced analyst knows that the valuation methods do not give precise, unequivocal answers. Hence, the analyst will combine past experience, the current situation facing the firm, and the valuation methods to reach a defendable value.

CHAPTER SUMMARY

This chapter discusses one of the most difficult aspects of entrepreneurship, that of valuing a venture. It is easy to see after reading the section on factors influencing value and, especially, the section on methods of calculating value why many entrepreneurs do a poor job in this area.

It is important to differentiate between value and price. The most appropriate value is estimated by one of the methods discussed in this chapter. The most correct price is ultimately the price on which all interested parties agree, and this may be adjusted by factors included in the deal.

There are many occasions in which a venture may need to be valued. These include the purchase or sale of a venture, obtaining financing for the venture, bringing in or buying out partners, taking the venture public, harvesting the venture, settling estates, and others.

A myriad of factors exist that will affect the value of the firm. These include, among others, the nature of the assets, the industry, the intended use of the purchased venture, and the perspective of the individual doing the valuation.

There are four basic approaches to valuing a firm. The first is the comparable firm approach. It is simple to use providing that a similar firm is available and can be accurately compared with the firm under consideration. The lack of availability of adequately comparable firms causes this approach to have limited usefulness. The asset based approaches value the actual assets of the venture. Four asset based methods were discussed. These include book value, market value, replacement value, and liquidation value. The market comparables approach assumes the similarity of publicly traded firms in the same industry as the one being valued. Publicly available ratios from the industry or similar firms are combined with the target firm's data to determine a value. The net present value approach is the most accurate of the approaches but requires a knowledge of statistics and finance to do the valuation well. Whatever method, the final value determined must be discounted by a factor to account for uncertainties associated with a new or small firm. The actual price agreed upon will usually be affected by the "deal" between the buyer and seller.

TEACHING STRATEGY

The key to teaching this chapter is to get the students to realize that valuing a venture is both objective and subjective. The chapter presents a number of valuation methods. As is seen in the Micro-Print Venture Perspective, however, the methods can yield quite different values. The task is to utilize as many methods as possible to determine values, and then to either pick the one or ones that seem most logical or to combine them in some way to get a weighted average.

The subjectivity of this is illustrated well by the Martin Enterprise case. I recommend strongly that this case be assigned at the same time as the chapter. The case is long and somewhat complex, but it docs a good job of illustrating both the objective and subjective nature of the valuation process. I also recommend that fisCAL be discussed here in terms of valuation. It presents four valuation methods and then combines them with weights chosen by the user. Again, the methods are objective, but the weights are subjective. Note also that for Micro-Print, fisCAL develops a final value that is different than that calculated in this chapter. I am including a letter to me from The Halcyon Group defending their choice in comparison to that presented in the chapter. The reason I have included this is to show that their assumptions differ somewhat than the chapter's assumptions, and the choice of assumptions affects the resulting valuation.

It is tempting to conclude from this that valuation is witchcraft and, as a result, is a waste of student's time. However, the chapter is very important, and the methods do give estimates of a venture's value. The analyst's job is to utilize the methods to arrive at a conclusion and then adjust those results based on experience.

A teaching strategy that I have used successfully in the past is to invite a local business broker or valuation expert in to talk to the class. Without any prompting from me, the broker I use supports the notion of the chapter of the importance of the valuation process and the view that valuation is both and art and a science. To make the discussion even more relevant, I suggest providing the valuation expert with a copy of the Micro-Print information prior to the visit. Have the person do a valuation based on the methods the firm uses, and then compare it with that done either by the chapter or by fisCAL. The odds are that the result will be similar but different than either the text or fisCAL.

Other points to make in this chapter is to clearly differentiate between the value and the price. The value is some figure arrived at by an objective formula or method. The price should be based on the value, but it will likely also be based on a number of additional factors including some which do not appear rational to the outside observer. These include whether the owner plans to retire or not, how long the business has been in business, the owner's need for capital, the owner's ego, what the buyer intends to do with the venture, the reason for the sale, the reason for the purchase, and a host of other ideas. Consider the Campground For Sale! -- Sold! case. The potential buyers were convinced that they wanted to buy the campground, and they were convinced that the price was reasonable. No amount of cajoling by the consultants would convince them otherwise. Thus, the price offered was in no way based on value.

In summary, this is an interesting chapter to teach, and it is a challenge to get the students to come away from the discussion with a knowledge of valuation methods while not being discouraged by the subjectivity inherent in the process.

DISCUSSION QUESTIONS

1. Price and value are related, but not necessarily closely related. The price should be a function of a carefully determined value, but either the buyer or seller may have reasons to offer or ask a price that is substantially different from the calculated value.

2. It is important to value a business prior to bringing in a new partner in order to estimate the capital infusion required for the new partner. Whether the firm is a partnership or corporation is of no importance.

3. A case could be made that a number of different factors are important for any of the ventures. The following are ones that seem particularly important.

    Small manufacturing venture - age of equipment, amount of inventory, number and type of customers, long term contracts, growth rate over past few years.

    Growing, but unprofitable software firm - cash flow, breadth and depth of product usage, trends in industry, competitor products.

    Dentist office - stability or growth of cash flows, value of customer list, equipment value, profitability.

    Service business - cash flows, trends in industry, owner investment.

4. Asset based methods are typically inaccurate because the assets are seldom worth precisely what their book value suggests. Further, market value for the individual assets is often difficult to assess. Still further, the market value for the individual assets does not imply the value of those assets in a going concern.

5. The present value approach, if used totally correctly, is quite complicated. For example, rather than simply selecting a discount rate, correct application of the method calculates the discount rate based on the variance of the cash flows over time. Some will use a modified net present value approach which short-cuts some of the difficult calculations, but this reduces the accuracy.

6. This is a good discussion or test question. Certainly errors could be made in the data collection, both in the accuracy of the data and in the choice of variables. Errors could be made in choosing profits versus cash flow. A common error is to use the inappropriate valuation method. Another error is to fail to use more than one method or to weight a combination of methods wrong. Finally, qualitative judgments can affect the result.

7.   Possibly. Rapid growth firms often have high losses as well as negative cash flows. Yet, if we can project future cash flows with some accuracy, the net present value method will still be useful. Most other methods would be less useful for the growth firm but might by acceptable for low growth ventures.

8.   The better question is which methods would not be appropriate. The answer to this is that any asset based approach would be inappropriate since there are relatively few assets. (I use a variation on this question frequently as an essay question. It does a good job of separating out the astute thinkers from the others.)

9.   The difference in using five year averages versus the last year is that one presents a historical average while the other accounts for the significance of the most recent data. This could be especially significant for a firm that is just taking off after a period of stability.

10. The most significant problem is that comparables aren't always comparable. They utilize either industry averages or figures for publicly traded firms. These may both be quite different from the firm being valued. If these are used, attempt both to get industry figures and data on traded firms and compare the results.

11. Increases or decreases in these variables represent inflows or outflows of cash and must be taken into account in order to get an accurate calculation of actual cash flow for the firm.

12. Some analysts feel that the venture is worth something at the end of ten years and that value must be accounted for in determining the overall value of the firm. Others feel that ten years hence is so uncertain that no value should be given beyond that period. This may be especially true in the case of small businesses.

13. Smaller firms are inherently more risky than larger firms. Thus, the calculated value should be discounted to account for the additional risk. On the other hand, the premium for a one-person control is because the owner has total control over the venture as well as receiving the total benefits of the venture's operations. This is better than sharing the benefits of a publicly held firm.

EXERCISE 15-1

This is the essay question mentioned above that I frequently use on exams. It does a good job of assessing what students really know about valuation concepts. Note that the venture is a service firm, and book value methods are useless. Consulting firms are not often sold, so the Comparable Firms approach is also likely to be of limited value. The net present value method is the method of choice. The answers to the second part of the question offer opportunities to assess the students' reasoning ability even though the answer is most likely that the valuation methods should be the same regardless of the reasoning. An exception to this might be that if a 50-50 merger is desired, an accurate value of the venture may not be as important as a general view of the relative value of the two firms.

EXERCISE 15-2

These are good for class discussion. Answers will vary by team. The object is not to arrive at the "most correct" answer as to work through the process of reaching a figure. The exercise gets students thinking about the subjectivity in the valuation process.

CONVENIESSE, INC.

In this segment Yolanda instructs a subordinate to arrive at a value of the firm using a number of different methods. There is not enough information given for students to complete a valuation. But they can give thought here to how to value a firm that is made up of convenience stores spread around a large geographical region.

CHAPTER SIXTEEN

HARVESTING THE VENTURE

TEACHING OBJECTIVES

The teaching objectives for this chapter are for the students to understand:

1. The nature of harvesting a venture.

2. Reasons for harvesting a venture.

3. That both healthy and ill businesses may be harvested.

4. Various methods of harvesting a venture.

5. Why some methods of harvesting are better than others for specific situations.

6. The types of harvesting that are most appropriate for different levels of ventures.

7. The types of bankruptcy and their significance.

8. The need to plan a harvest strategy.

CHAPTER OUTLINE

I.   The Need for a Harvest Strategy

II.   Reasons for Harvesting a Venture

    A.   Harvesting Because of Changes in Personal Situations

        1.   Retirement
        2.   Relocation
        3.   Change in Life Cycle Stage
        4.   Stress

    B.   Harvesting Because of Unmet Expectations

    C.   Harvesting in Order to Pursue Other Interests

    D.   Harvesting for Personal Wealth

    E.   Passing on the Family Venture

    F.   Harvesting and Estate Planning

    G.   Facilitating Growth

III. Methods of Harvesting a Venture

    A.   Direct Sale

    B.   Employee Stock Option Plan

    C.   Management Buyout

    D.   Leveraged Buyout

    E.   Merger

    F.   Going Public

    G.   Liquidation

    H.   Bankruptcy

    I.   Passing the Venture to Family

IV.   Matching Harvest Methods with Reasons for the Harvest

V.   Developing the Harvest Plan

VI.   Summary

CONSIDER THIS!

*   I would speculate that more businesses close because of personal reasons than because of failure. This would include the retirement or death of an owner, relocation, changes in life stages, and a host of other reasons.

*   Harvesting actually ends the business only in liquidation. In other forms of harvest the business continues, although it may be in a different form.

*   There are many different ways to harvest a venture. Some are profitable and some are not.

*   The employee stock option plan is an excellent way to harvest the venture since it leaves the venture in the hands of the employees. This has powerful motivational effects in addition to creating wealth for the original entrepreneur.

*   A quite small percentage of businesses ever go public -- probably less than one percent.

*   LBOs offer a way to purchase or harvest a business when it might not otherwise be possible. It has some serious disadvantages, however, for new or small firms because of the amount of debt on the balance sheet.

*   Firms filing Chapter 11 bankruptcy continue to operate after filing.

*   If a business is small, the entrepreneur has few heirs, and those heirs are already in the business, the task will be simple. On the other hand, if the business is growing, the family is large, or there are multiple businesses, and only a portion of the heirs will be involved in the venture, the task will be much more complex.

*   It would be a travesty for an entrepreneur to lose much of the value a firm has developed over a number of years simply because of insufficient planning of the harvest strategy.

CHAPTER SUMMARY

Harvesting the venture is the natural ending of the entrepreneurship cycle. Like the rest of entrepreneurship, the harvest must be well planned in order to succeed. Careful thought and thorough analysis will aid in successfully preparing for and executing the harvest.

Numerous reasons exist for harvesting a venture. Perhaps the most frequent is simply changes in the entrepreneur's personal situation. This may be retirement, relocation, a change in the health of the entrepreneur, or a change in the life cycle stage of the entrepreneur. The venture may be harvested because it no longer meets the expectations of the entrepreneur. This does not mean that it is a failure, but rather that the venture did not meet goals envisioned by the entrepreneur. If, indeed, the venture was doing extremely poorly, harvesting the venture may be the only way to protect any part of the entrepreneur's original investment. The desire for personal wealth is a stereotypical goal of entrepreneurs, and harvesting a highly profitable venture is the epitome of entrepreneurship. Some harvests provide the entrepreneur with substantial capital to use either for future investments or for underwriting a comfortable lifestyle. Passing the venture onto family members or caring for one's estate planning are also reasons to harvest a venture even though some may not feel that passing the venture on is truly harvesting it. Finally, in some cases, harvesting the venture is the only way to allow for the venture to grow.

Just as there are a plethora of reasons to harvest a venture, there are many methods of harvesting it. A direct sale to an unrelated person is perhaps the most common and easiest to do. Once a buyer is found, the process is only to value the company and agree on a price and terms. Establishing an employee stock option plan has many advantages. It provides a ready buyer for the venture, rewards loyal employees, and can be a powerful motivating tool. It is somewhat time consuming to develop the plan which can take a number of different forms. Selling the company to key managers is another frequent harvest method. This may done with or without a leveraged buyout. The leveraged buyout, often in conjunction with the management buyout, provides a means to purchase the venture when cash is not available. But it leaves the venture highly leveraged and may prevent future expansion. The merger is desirable when the entrepreneur desires to stay with the firm at least temporarily but wants to reap the benefits of possible synergies with the acquiring firm. Taking the company public via an initial public offering is a complex, expensive process. If successful, however, it can make the entrepreneur quite wealthy while providing funds for significant expansion. Not all harvest methods are of a positive nature. Liquidation may be appropriate when the firm is not doing well or when the entrepreneur simply decides to close the business. Sometimes the liquidation involves the bankruptcy of the venture, although some do not. Conversely, the Chapter 11 bankruptcy does not require the closing of the venture.

It is important that the entrepreneur develop a harvest plan. The plan should include the type of harvest selected, cultivating outsiders that may be involved in the process, acquiring the expertise needed to process the harvest, valuing the company, and making strategic changes necessary to position the venture for harvest. The plans for the harvest should be communicated to employees in the venture, but the timing of the communication must be carefully considered. In order to harvest the venture at a desired date, reverse planning should be done in order that all the necessary actions gel at the appropriate time.

TEACHING STRATEGY

The strategy for this chapter is to work with students to underscore the value of planning a harvest. Use examples that you are aware of or develop hypothetical situations that illustrate the perils of not planning at the time of harvest. In particular, try to illustrate how an unplanned harvest can result in a rushed valuation or perhaps a sale without a valuation. Examples could also illustrate how the death or illness of an owner leaves the business without a plan.

Note to the students the number of reasons for harvesting a venture. In particular, note that many of the reasons fall under the category of personal reasons. This is especially true among low growth ventures. It is also important to note that only one of the harvest methods -- liquidation -- requires the business to be shut down. In all other cases, the business continues, but in a different form.

Key on the matrix showing the appropriate methods of harvesting for each reason for harvest. Not that there are a variety of methods to harvest a venture for most of the reasons. For example, harvesting for personal reasons might result in a sale, a management buyout, a liquidation, passing the venture on to family members, and others.

Finally, the steps in a harvest plan should be discussed. Discuss the concept of the reverse time-table. Students may not initially consider the importance of counting backward from a harvest date to begin the actual planning. They may also not have previously considered the need to make changes in the venture and its strategies in advance in order to be ready to harvest at the desired time. Get students to debate this statement, "A harvest plan should always be current even if no harvest is contemplated." A case could be made that always focusing on the harvest could cause short-sighted actions rather than a longer term focus. The flip side is that not focusing on the harvest can result in the loss of many of the gains the entrepreneur has worked for over many years. There certainly are pros and cons of each view.

DISCUSSION QUESTIONS

1.   The importance of developing a harvest plan, like the importance of developing a venture strategy is in the process itself. In addition to yielding a document that can be consulted when needed, the process generates knowledge for the entrepreneur to use in making logical operational decisions. It also means that the entrepreneur is prepared when a harvest opportunity arises. Without the harvest plan, unfortunate surprises may occur.

2.   Most low growth entrepreneurs do not plan a harvest for the same reason that they do not plan a venture strategy. That is that they are too busy running the venture and dealing with short term problems to plan for the future. In addition, many entrepreneurs do not ever expect to retire or sell the business. Hence, they see no reason to plan for that eventuality.

3.   Both the reasons and the methods could change with changes in the environment.

    a.   If a high inflation rate is accompanied by a high interest rate, a direct sale might be enticing providing a cash buyer could be found. High inflation might create problems in making a profit, compared to what could be made with investments.

    b.   New competitors are likely to take some market share away. If the firm were marginally profitable before, breaking even might be difficult now. Thus, either a sale, a merger, or perhaps a liquidation might be appropriate.

    c.   A recession certainly can hurt any business. If profits are squeezed too much, a merger with a competitor might be appropriate or perhaps a direct sale or liquidation.

    d.   A sudden debilitating illness can develop a critical need to exit the venture rather quickly. Here, a management buyout could be desirable as could a direct sale. A liquidation would not be appropriate here because of both the time and stress associated with it.

4.   For low growth ventures, the sale, liquidation, passing the venture to family members, and merger are appropriate. Growth ventures could use the merger, the public offering, or the direct sale. Both could use the ESOP.

5.   The management buyout could also be a leveraged buyout. Most others are mutually exclusive.

6.   It is likely that some matches other than those indicated could be appropriate for specific situations. The matrix is designed to account for the most common occurrences.

7.   The reverse time-table is important because it gives the entrepreneur an idea of how long it will take to put the venture into a harvestable condition. In so doing, it will also help identify kinds of actions that should be taken in order to be on schedule.

8.   For an ESOP, all key managers -- and especially the controller -- should be involved from the outset. Once the general concept has been researched, then other workers should be informed of the potential for the ESOP. Then the managers should work out details which will again be communicated to those lower in the organization. A liquidation may require the help of outside specialists. Key managers would normally also be involved. In the family transfer situation, key managers and key family members should be included early.

9.   If the company is to be taken public, key managers must be informed as early as possible. This is so they will be aware of the reasons for the investment bankers' frequent visits and the CEO's preoccupation with the project. Otherwise, they could be misled into thinking the business was going to be sold. In addition, if the entrepreneur is taking the venture public, other managers must be delegated day to day responsibility for operations. If the harvest is via merger, the entrepreneur may want to wait until the merger is reasonably firm before communicating to any but the closest confidants. Once the plans are in place, then the word must be quickly spread in order that all understand the nature of the merger.

10. Determining when to communicate the harvest plan is certainly an ethical issue. Waiting until the owner shuts the doors to tell workers that the firm is being liquidated is unconscionable. On the other hand, communicating it too soon can cause real morale and turnover problems. Thus, the ethical issue is "How much lead time should workers be given before a liquidation?" The same issue holds for other harvest methods, but the magnitude of the result will not be as great. Still employees must be informed sufficiently early so they can make plans.

EXERCISE 16-1

Since Micro-Print, Inc. was growing and was generally profitable, there would be no reason to liquidate or declare bankruptcy. Conversely, it was not in such good shape that taking it public would be logical. Hence, the methods available would be to sell it, to merge with another firm, to sell it to managers, or to pass it on to family members if applicable. An ESOP would also be appropriate. We would want additional information about possible family members' wishes, the nature of competition, who possible buyers might be, and key managers' interest in continuing with the firm either as part owners or working for someone else.

EXERCISE 16-2

This is an excellent project, but it must be assigned early in the term in order to give sufficient time. It will provide a great service to the SBDC since most do not have good information on harvesting ventures.

CONVENIESSE, INC.

In this final segment of Conveniesse, Inc., the two entrepreneurs have tired of operating the chain and are looking at the possibility of selling out or merging with someone else. This would be a good time to review the entire entrepreneurial process with the students. The original three entrepreneurs did some planning, launched the venture, financed it with some debt and some equity, grew it, considered franchising it, took it international, addressed the issue of stagnation, and finally began the harvest process which included valuation of the corporation. The remaining task is to decide if they want to harvest it and how they should do it. Students should discuss whether harvesting it now is a good idea and which of the possible companies identified would be a good match.

VIDEOS

Adopters using **Entrepreneurship: A Planning Approach** receive copies of the Blue Chip Enterprise Initiative's video tapes featuring fifty business situations illustrating entrepreneurial management. The videos were produced in cooperation with Connecticut Mutual Life Insurance Company, Nation's Business, and the U.S. Chamber of Commerce.

The videos come on four cassettes and focus on ventures which have overcome some adversity in order to be successful. Due to copyright provisions, the tapes are not in order based on issues discussed. The following pages note the companies included along with a very brief description of the company. Instructors may choose to show entire video tapes, single segments or a group of selected segments that illustrates particular points. In addition, those companies marked with a * have more lengthy writeups included at the end of this section. They may be copied for handouts prior to showing the tape if desired.

WALLACE CO., INC.

Wallace Co., Inc., of Houston, Texas, is a distributor of pipes, valves and fittings for the engineering and construction industries. Family-owned and founded in 1942, Wallace Co.'s nine regional offices employ a staff of 280 and generated sales of $90 million in 1990.

KL SPRING AND STAMPING CORPORATION

A renewed initiative helped KL Spring & Stamping Corporation become recognized as a leader in its industry. This Chicago-based manufacturer began facing numerous problems in the early 1980's, as did many other companies supplying the price-sensitive automotive industry.

* STOCKPOT SOUPS

Founded in 1981, Stockpot Soups is a manufacturer of fresh soup concentrates, with 100 employees.   Like many small start-up companies in its early years, Stockpot faced the daunting challenge of convincing distributors to carry its products. The firm also needed to increase its recognition among customers, and to control labor and facility costs.

KIAMICHI RAILROAD COMPANY, INC.

Persistence, enlightened human resource management, customer-driven service innovations and a community focus enabled national designer Kiamichi Railroad Company, Inc. to maintain a profit from the first month of operations. Traffic volumes forecasted for the seventh year were reached in just 17 months - in the very market where two successive national rail lines failed to keep operations going.

SUMMIT AVIATION, INC.

In 1987, Summit Aviation was beset by the same adverse forces buffeting general aviation nationwide. Operating capital was tight, as was lending. At the same time, the company faced a crisis caused by the death of its founder, Richard C. duPont, Jr., whose intense commitment had seen Summit through hard times in earlier years.

CONTINENTAL TRAFFIC SERVICE, INC.

Through aggressive marketing and effective employee relations, Continental Traffic Service, Inc. dramatically increased its sales and customer base. Continental Traffic Service, Inc., is a freight-bill payment company based in Memphis, Tennessee. Founded in 1952, the company now employs a staff of 85 in three locations, and grossed $400 million in sales in 1990.

THE TLC GROUP

The Total Logistic Control Group (TLC) of Zeeland, Michigan, provides third-party logistical services to customers on a national scale. TLC was established in 1904 as a wholesale produce company and had become a small, regional refrigerated warehousing and distribution company by the early 1950's. In the late 1970's, TLC added dry warehousing to its service offerings. The past five years have brought a six-fold expansion of the warehouse business and creation of a full-service trucking company.

TRANSAMERICA ENERGY ASSOCIATES, INC.

Founded in Atlanta in 1982, TEA is a sophisticated temporary-help agency that provides engineers and skilled negotiators to electric transmission, telecommunication and pipeline companies, as well as government agencies, for the purpose of right-of-way and land acquisition. TEA also performs route engineering and design services for telecommunications companies as well as construction and inspection services for cellular telephone operating companies.

AMERICAN CALCULATOR AND COMPUTER COMPANY, INC.

American Calculator and Computer Company (AC3) was established in 1980 by Fred Nunnelly in the back room of a Birmingham Phillips 66 service station. To purchase his start-up inventory, Nunnelly used the remaining $300 limit on his credit card for a cash advance. From this modest beginning, Nunnelly build AC3 into a company with 250 employees and annual sales of $100 million, a 500 percent sales growth in the last three years.

FOX MANUFACTURING COMPANY, INC.

Founded in 1974, Fox Manufacturing/Autumn Wood is a family owned manufacturer and retailer of contemporary and southwest-style furniture. A devastating fire at the company sparked a company-wide commitment of unprecedented levels. Not only was Fox intent on resuming operations - its goal was to do so in only eight weeks, and emerge as a rejuvenated, improved facility offering enhanced services.

R.W. SUMMERS RAILROAD CONTRACTOR, INC.

Resilience and drive have made the history of R.W. Summers Railroad Contractor, Inc. a poignant success story. Based in Bartow, this railroad contracting firm - the largest in the state - was beset by tragedy and misfortune, yet it persisted and succeeded.

MINARIK ELECTRIC COMPANY

Established in 1953, Minarik Electric Company employs 96 workers in manufacturing and 150 workers in distributing industrial motor controls and programmable controllers. By updating its technology and making effective use of its managerial staff, Minarik was able to overcome fierce competition and regain lost market share.

THE OLYMPIAD

The Olympiad is a Burlington, Vermont, health club offering squash, racquetball, aerobic, and cardiovascular exercise. Founded in 1982, the firm has 63 employees. By introducing a number of new personal services, the Olympiad was able to fend off its competition and increase customer sales.

TRAILCO LEASING

Trailco Leasing, specializing in equipment leasing and sales, is a $7.5 million company based in Greensboro, North Carolina. Founded in 1983, the company now has 41 employees in four locations. By borrowing assets to build its fleet, Trailco Leasing financed its own business expansion.

* VCW, INC.

VCW, Inc., showed how with persistence and creativity a small insurance agency could overcome many obstacles and evolve into a $20 million business over the course of a decade.

* SUPPORTIVE HOMECARE

Supportive HomeCare is a state licensed home health agency serving the Fox River Valley providing skilled nursing care, personal hygiene care, and homemaker/companion services to people of all ages in their home. Founded in Oshkosh in 1983, the agency currently employs a staff of 162. By implementing an innovative marketing program and cost effective hiring plan, Supportive HomeCare increased sales in spite of many changes in the marketplace.

* KELLY TRUCK LINE, INC.

Kelly Truck Line, Inc., located in Pittsburgh, Kansas has 185 employees. Founded in 1957, the trucking company has annual sales of $14 million through its operations in the U.S., with bases in Kansas, Missouri, Texas, Ohio, Arkansas. In October of 1984, it entered into a leveraged buyout of the existing business. During the span of five years, Kelly Truck Line retired its leveraged buyout and replaced an aging fleet with new top of the line equipment. It has grown from a $5 million a year company to $14 million and has been able to attract major corporations throughout the country as it expanded its growing client base.

CYCLE SPORTS OF SALEM, INC.

Founded in 1981, Cycle Sports is a family-owned retailer of motorcycles, jet skis, snowmobiles and related parts and service. The company has 13 employees and annual sales of $3.6 million. Cycle Sports was being pulled in many different directions by family ownership. Competing loyalties, and feeling they had little stake in the company, made employees ambivalent about their performances. Their frustration prevented much needed sales from developing, thus further damaging morale. An astute family member saw that an infusion of new blood was the only solution to forging a new and focused vision.

BALLARD & SONS OF CHARLESTON, INC.

Ballard & Sons is a family-owned contracting firm specializing in asbestos abatement, insulation, lead abatement, and indoor air quality. When the company started in 1984, it had a minimal amount of capital, and cash flow problems were a constant threat, but those are not unusual situations for a new company. The family entered the business knowing they would have competition from larger companies that were already entrenched, but they were ready to compete. By taking care of business and concentrating on quality, Ballard & Sons has realized 150 percent sales growth in the last three years.

EAGLE BRONZE, INC.

Eagle Bronze is a $600,000 casting company. The company manufactures bronze and ferrous alloy castings for artists and industrial customers. Founded in 1986, the company now employs a staff of 28. By providing customer service and a highly motivating training program, Eagle Bronze, Inc. increased sales 500 percent in three years.

NORTON MANUFACTURING COMPANY, INC.

Norton Manufacturing Company is a manufacturer of precision-machined crankshafts. Founded in 1950 as a small three-man tool and die shop, the firm now employs a staff of 96. By modifying its product to meet the needs of a new industry, Norton Manufacturing Company created a new market for its work. The growth is a result of product diversification.

HEIDI'S FAMILY RESTAURANT

Through hard work, perseverance and an innovative business strategy, Heidi's Family Restaurant turned several bankrupt or closed businesses into highly successful enterprises. Heidi's Family Restaurant operates three restaurants and a bread store. In 1986, the company opened its first Heidi's Family Restaurant in Carson City, followed by restaurants in Minden (1988) and Reno (1990). Heidi's The Bread Store, opened in 1990.

STONYFIELD FARM, INC.

Founded in 1982, the Londonderry yogurt manufacturer had achieved $2.3 million in revenues by 1987 but still did not have an efficient manufacturing plant of its own. In October of that year, the company which manufactured under contract for Stonyfield declared bankruptcy, leaving Stonyfield with no ability to continue production.

The company created a permanent manufacturing facility, which opened in 1989, and along with it a management structure to prevent the crisis from recurring. As a result of its recovery program, sales grew from $2.3 million to $6.6 million. With an annual growth rate of over 60 percent in several of the region's largest chains, Stonyfield Farm is among the fastest growing brands on the shelves. The company has opened several major national markets and launched three new product lines. In 1990 it was one of only three companies to be awarded for Ethics in Business by *Business Ethics Magazine*.

MICROTEST, INC.

Microtest develops and markets products which increase the reliability and productivity of Local Area Networks (LANs). The company has pioneered several "firsts" in the industry with diagnostic and connectivity products which provide innovative and cost-effective solutions to businesses with LANs.

SEITZ CORPORATION

The Seitz Corporation manufactures thermoplastic mechanical drives, such as gears and pulleys, and perforated forms pin feed tractors for printers. Family-owed and founded in 1949, Seitz's two plants employ 200 workers. The Seitz Corporation of Torrington created and implemented the "World-Class Excellence Through Total Quality" program to turn around a drastic decline in sales due to foreign competition. By promoting and encouraging employee involvement in the success of the company, this program helped sales reach $19 million in 1990.

* NEW PIG CORPORATION

New Pig Corporation is a global manufacturer and retailer of industrial absorbents. Founded in 1985, the firm employs 175 at its three plants in Tipton, Pennsylvania, and warehouses in Tipton and Reno, Nevada. In 1990, the company reaped sales of $18,400,000. Through highly-resourceful marketing tactics, New Pig Corporation overcame a lack of production and distribution capabilities to become one of the fastest growing companies in the nation.

FM CORPORATION

Established in 1980, the FM Corporation manufactures custom molded structural plastics, employs a work force of 160 and reports a 49 percent increase in annual sales over the last three years. By effectively managing its human and financial resources, the FM Corporation was able to overcome a near fatal loss of $3 million and emerge a strong company that now enjoys $10 million in annual sales.

AUSTAD'S

Austad's is a family-owned business and was the first company to supply golf equipment through the mail. Founded in 1963, the firm today has 270 employees, and a robust $56 million in annual sales. An innovative strategic plan broadening its market focus enabled Austad's to overcome competition and reap high profits.

LIFELINE SYSTEMS, INC.

Established in 1974, Lifeline manufactures and provides personal response services and equipment. The personal response industry services individuals who require emergency assistance due to health problems or security needs. Effective use of management resources enabled Lifeline Systems, Inc. to overcome inefficiency and position the company to take advantage of tremendous growth opportunities.

COMPHEALTH, INC.

CompHealth is the leading temporary medical staffing agency in the U.S., serving hospitals and health care facilities nationwide. Founded in 1978, the firm maintains three regional offices and 190 employees, and enjoyed $54.5 million in annual sales in 1990. By employing solid strategic marketing, CompHealth's "new owners" transformed an $800,000 debt into record-setting earnings.

NORTON'S SHIPYARD & MARINA, INC.

Norton's Shipyard offers and performs a variety of services for recreational boaters. Founded in 1945, the firm has annual sales of $1.3 million, employs a staff of 12, and has grown to provide space for 160 slips and 160 moorings. By effectively marshalling all their available resources, the staff and management of Norton's Shipyard & Marina Inc. banded together to rebuild the company after a devastating fire.

SCIENTECH, INC.

Based in Idaho Falls, SCIENTECH, INC. is an employee-owned company providing assistance to clients in the energy, environment, information management, and defense fields through offices in nine cities. The company has been profitable for six consecutive years, but it has had growing pains. Rapid growth, changing and shrinking markets, intense competition, technological advances, and cash flows challenges all pecked at the company, but SCIENTECH emerged victorious.

MARESCO INTERNATIONAL CORPORATION

Through a name recognition strategy, a shared risk agreement, and creative positioning, Maresco International brought a U.S. manufacturer of low-tech, high-cost fork lift trucks into a highly competitive international marketplace, and earned the manufacturer immediate and sustained profitability. Founded in 1983, the small, Bridgewater-based export management company faced this challenge at a time when the U.S. dollar was at an all-time high against all other foreign currencies.

MILA ADMINISTRATIVE SERVICES, INC.

MILA provides temporary and permanent employee placement to businesses and operates computerized office technology training. Established in 1981, MILA currently employs over 110 workers. In 1990 it reported annual sales of over $2.6 million, a 225 percent increase in three years.

FARR MANUFACTURING & ENGINEERING COMPANY

Farr Manufacturing and Engineering Co. builds custom-designed industrial equipment such as ovens, furnaces, and pollution control equipment, as well as heat treating equipment for synthetic fibers. Founded in 1985, the firm employs a staff of 68 and last year reaped sales of $3,778,000. With clever marketing and entrepreneurial determination, Farr Manufacturing and Engineering grew from a tiny, two-person operation into a thriving, multi-million dollar success story.

RICHTMAN'S PRINTING AND PACKAGING

When Richtman's Printing and Packaging, now in its 50th year, was purchased in 1982 by then pre-press employee Wm. J. Engelhardt, it was on the verge of bankruptcy. Through aggressive sales and a reputation built on providing the highest quality products on time with very competitive prices, the company recovered and has grown to include three locations and sales growth of 50 percent over the last three years.

TRANSAMERICA TELEMARKETING, INC.

This year, TransAmerica Telemarketing Inc., expects to earn more than $4 million by providing telemarketing and direct mail services. In the last three years, the company has grown 12 percent, but only after overcoming the obstacles that were caused by its being operated and managed in two separate offices - one in Washington, D.C., and another in Harrisonburg, Virginia.

SENIOR MARKET SALES, INC.

Effective management of its legal and regulatory environment and a strategic growth strategy have helped Senior Market Sales, Inc. (SMS, Inc.) to enjoy substantial success over the past three years. Despite strong competition in seniors health and life insurance marketing, the five-year-old company grew 341 percent in sales to $51,000,000.

CULLIGAN WATER CONDITIONING OF HAVRE

Culligan Water Conditioning, a water conditioning equipment dealer and bottled water business, is based in Havre, a small community in the heart of an agricultural region. Established in 1946, the family-run business was purchased by its current owner, Thomas Bravard, in 1974. Its main challenge was to maintain cash flow and grow the business in an economically depressed region.

DELTA WIRE CORPORATION

Founded in 1978, Delta Wire corporation is a manufacturer of high carbon specialty steel wire for global markets. The firm employs a staff of 91 and has had increasing sales each year. By training its work force to implement the highest quality control standards, Delta Wire Corporation sustained a leadership position in the highly competitive steel wire industry.

HOMARUS, INC.

With the help of an L.L. Bean Smoker, Karen Ransom and Peter Heineman started Homarus, Inc., a manufacturer and supplier of smoked fish with annual sales of $5.8 million, in his mother's backyard in 1976. Homarus counts among its customers some of the world's most prestigious hotels an shops, as well as international airlines, export and mail order companies. Over the past three years, the company has achieved 35 percent and 25 percent growth in sales and employees, respectively.

MOODY-PRICE, INCORPORATED

Moody-Price, Incorporated has been in business since 1955 and employs 130. It is a distributor of industrial instrumentation and accessories with sales offices and stocking locations throughout the South. Moody-Price, Incorporated (MPI) realigned its product mix so as to be less dependent on the oil and gas industry in order to survive in its market while competitors went out of business or abandoned their customer base.

PEVCO SYSTEMS INTERNATIONAL, INC.

Pevco Systems International, Inc. headquartered in Baltimore, Maryland, was established in 1978. Currently employing 19 people, the $3 million company specializes in manufacturing pneumatic tube systems for health care, industrial and commercial applications. From 1978 to 1983, Pevco evolved from a one-man sales organization to a full-service company specializing in the sale, installation, engineering and service of pneumatic tube systems. Sales increased from $1.3 million in 1985 to $3.2 million in 1989, while total general and administrative expenses were reduced by 37 percent. Concentration on core products has built a solid customer base offering the latest state-of-the-art computer-controlled pneumatic tube systems.

MIDAMERICA SAVINGS BANK

Headquartered in Waterloo, Iowa, MidAmerica is a full-service financial institution with eight branch locations. But in the late 1980's the bank faced a number of serious challenges. The effects of Iowa's agricultural recession included a loss of 10,000 jobs and 10 percent of the population in Waterloo alone. By expanding its involvement in the community and maximizing existing resources, MidAmerica Savings Bank was able to rebound and rebuild a successful business.

CREATIVE APPAREL, INC.

Creative Apparel has 80 employees and has its plant and retail outlet headquartered in Belmont, Maine. An additional plant is located at the Passamamquoddy Tribe's Indian Township Reservation in Princeton, Maine. The company manufactures outerware and other forms of clothing, and projects 1991 sales at $3.5 million. Creative Apparel, Inc. used human resources, training, and technological updates to gain a year-round flow of work and international distribution. As a result, sales have grown in excess of 400 percent over the last three years.

BTG INC.

BTG Inc. is a software developer that provides system integration and systems engineering services. Founded in 1982, the firm has four locations, 285 employees, and earned $27.5 million in its last fiscal year. By integrating a progressive "prototyping" process, BTG Inc. became one of the nation's fastest-growing small businesses.

GBC, INC.

GBC was established in Honolulu in 1972 as a wholesale distributor of tourist souvenir and curio items. After many successful years in business, the owner opted to concentrate efforts on the packaging products end of the business, and sold the souvenir business. Diversification and innovation pulled GBC, Inc., dba GBC Boxes and Packaging, through when hard times hit.

OIL TECHNOLOGY, INCORPORATED

It takes true grit to start a new company to address the needs of a new market. Oil Technology, Inc., founded in 1982, took the leap into a particularly tough market, and has passed the test of time. In fact, company sales have grown 400 percent in the last three years, making Oil Technology the leader in on-site oil recycling for the steel industry.

STEAM WAY INTERNATIONAL, INCORPORATED

Steam Way International, Inc. made a dynamic comeback when Ralph Bloss purchased the company and effectively merged a sound business plan with a genuine concern for the environment.

Since 1982, annual sales have increased almost 600 percent and the company has grown from 8 workers to 38. Founded in 1966 as one of the original manufacturers of the "steam" carpet cleaner, Steam Way quickly became a leader in the professional carpet and upholstery cleaning industry. By 1981, however, the founder had focused his attention on other enterprises and talked of liquidating Steam Way. Then vice-president, Ralph Bloss purchased both the equipment and chemical divisions of the company and chose to try to restore its much depleted market share and regain Steam Way's name recognition.

MILTON SEIFERT & ASSOCIATES

When Dr. Milton Seifert started his own practice in 1972, his goal was to satisfy patients with cost-effective, quality care. It was his belief that he would have a good business if he practiced good medicine. Having grown more than 25 percent in the last three years, Milton Seifert & Associates owes its success to an uncompromising commitment to quality and an alliance with its patients.

AIR RELIEF, INC.

Located in Mayfield, Kentucky, Air Relief, Inc. is a supplier of air compressor parts and service. The $7 million company, headed by Paul Hayes and D. Fleming, was formed in 1985 and employs 80 people. An innovative co-op manufacturing program helped Air Relief, Inc. meet the demands of rapid growth.

VIDEO CASES

Selected videos among the fifty presented here are supplemented with additional information and discussion questions. It is suggested that the cases be provided for students to analyze and discuss in class. Once discussion ends, the video segment can then be shown to illustrate the solutions chosen by the entrepreneurs.

STOCKPOT SOUPS

Kevin Fortun began his career in the restaurant business as a dishwasher. He later worked his way up to steakhouse manager while attending Oregon State University. After graduation, he returned as a buyer. During this time, however, he came to realize that a restaurant's homemade soups varied greatly in quality even though cooks supposedly followed identical recipes. Fortun concluded that, if his own restaurants were having trouble with consistency of soup quality, certainly other restaurants were too. In addition, using instant or concentrated soups produced inferior soups, but making soups from scratch was extremely labor intensive. This could easily take two hours of a cook's time which was already a big problem in restaurants.

Fortun was convinced that centralized production of soups, using precise recipes and cooking cycles would eliminate the inconsistency. Working at night for two years, he developed soup concentrates which could be packaged in cryovac bags and stored for up to 90 days without freezing. The soups could then be reconstituted with water or milk.

Fortun opened Stockpot Soups as a producer of soup concentrates which would then be sold through distributors to restaurants and other institutional meal providers such as universities, hospitals, and corporate cafeterias. Unfortunately, distributors were not interested in carrying his products which caused cash flow problems. He also had problems of product recognition.

DISCUSSION QUESTIONS

1.   How do you get reluctant distributors to carry your product?

2.   How can you increase your cash flow while waiting for industry sales to pick up?

3.   How do you sell a food product made in the state of Washington nationwide?

ENTREPRENEURIAL RESPONSE

1.   In order to get reluctant distributors to carry his product, Keven Fortun went directly to some large customers such as chain restaurants or grocery chains that also included a restaurant or deli. Once he convinced them to use his products, the customers put pressure on the distributors to carry the product. The distributors then sold the soup products to others on their customer list. Stockpot Soups are now sold in forty-two states plus Canada, Europe, Japan, Australia, and other countries.

2.   Fortun intended to sell the soup wholesale through distributors. But since he needed some additional cash flow, he opened a small deli-type store in a mall. This brought in a positive cash flow until the industry sales caught on. Incidentally, in spite of their profitability, Fortun decided not to pursue the restaurant business directly since he felt they were in the soup making business and not the restaurant business. Possible licensing of the restaurants is a possibility though.

3.   Kevin Fortun originally envisioned selling Stockpot Soups throughout the west coast. Thus, his original idea included packaging that would allow shipment. To gain the rapid growth, he brought in his brothers, Mike and Steve. Mike's task was to develop a nationwide distribution of the product. Currently their sales are in forty-two states plus several international companies.

SUPPORTIVE HOMECARE

At the age of 28, Terri Hansen quit her full-time job because she saw a gap in home care services, and she was sure she could provide what was needed. She began Supportive HomeCare in the upstairs of her home in 1983 with her partner and three part-time employees. She targeted clients who needed long hour care service any time of day or night including weekends. Services provided included skilled nursing services, lab work, counseling, home aide service such as bathing, exercising, dressing, and homemaker/companion services, grocery shopping, and meal preparation.

Hansen's agency grew rapidly for four years both in terms of sales and employees. Then at least two things happened. Competition from a number of sources began to cut into her market. In addition, significant funding cuts from third party providers decreased the demand for Supportive HomeCare services. Further, additional regulations coupled with a tight labor market made hiring and training additional workers difficult.

QUESTIONS FOR DISCUSSION

1. Given the adverse environment that is developing, what should Supportive HomeCare do? Should they close?

2. If a decision is made not to close, what should be done to increase revenue or decrease cost in order to survive?

ENTREPRENEURIAL RESPONSE

1. Supportive HomeCare did not close. Instead, Terri Hansen decided to diversify. First, she expanded geographically by offering the services in neighboring cities. Second, she began two new divisions of Supportive HomeCare. Personnel Resource Network offers specialized home management services to well people who do not require any medical services. It also works as an employment agency for medical staffing with customers including nursing homes, hospitals, medical clinics, and day care centers. Lifestyle Connections provides health promotion, wellness, and consultation through screenings, programs, and classes for individuals, elderly housing complexes and businesses. Third, she created a totally new company called Creative Management and Marketing Resources, Inc. to provide consulting to businesses regarding general management problems.

2.   Supportive HomeCare cut expenses by eliminating some employees and thereby increasing the efficiency. As shown in question 1, they also diversified greatly out of the direct home care services. They did not close the business, but did realize that it would not survive without expanding the customer base within the home care business and expanding business outside of that sub-industry.

NEW PIG CORPORATION

How do you develop and sell a mundane industrial product to handle dirty jobs? How can you convince customers to buy products from you that do nothing but help clean up drips and spills on factory floors? That is the problem that faced Ben Stapelfield and Don Beaver in the central Pennsylvania town of Tipton.

Stapelton and Beaver ran a cleaning company that targeted industrial customers. They grew tired of continually cleaning up spills or removing oil soaked clay around leaky machinery. They began experimenting with ways to absorb liquids. They tried rags, athletic tube socks filled with clay, and panty hose filled with sawdust. They finally hit upon the idea of a fabric tube 42 inches long and filled with ground up corncobs.

Customers liked the idea of the corncob-filled socks because of their absorbent ability. But banks refused to lend them money because of the perceived riskiness of the venture. The product was too mundane and there was not a marketing plan to get the product out to a wide variety of customers scattered over the entire country. Stapelton and Beaver pooled their life savings, took out second mortgages on their homes, and convinced a few investors to invest in their idea. But the problem was still one of how to market the product.

QUESTIONS FOR DISCUSSION

1.   How would you market the absorbent tubes? Who would be your customers and how would you reach them?

2.   What kind of innovative promotion campaign would attract industrial customers to purchase the products?

3.   What rate of growth would you expect from this kind of product?

ENTREPRENEURIAL RESPONSE

1.   Stapelton and Beaver selected an unlikely name for their company, the New Pig Corporation, and an unlikely method of marketing the product -- direct mail. They felt that mail order catalogs (called Pigalogs) could explain and show the benefit of the products more effectively and efficiently than other methods. This would also allow them to specifically target their customers who were manufacturers and other customers with likely industrial spills.

2.   The innovative marketing was based on the belief that only with catchy and cleverly presented messages would these mundane products get and keep the attention of industrial customers. Hence, the company's name was New Pig Corporation. Catalogs were called Pigalogs. The toll-free number was 1-800-HOT-HOGS. Pictures and cartoons of pigs accompanied descriptions of products. A folder containing brochures and pigalogs was bright blue with a bright pink "Oink" on the front and pigtails inside. Even a survey of customers was entitled the Repork Card, and a newsletter was called the New Pork Times.

3.   With a product as mundane as corncob-filled socks, growth would be expected to be small and slow. However, due to their effective marketing, New Pig Corporation has grown from three employees to 225 and now projects 1992 sales of $35 million. Their product line now includes hundreds of cleaning products aimed at the industrial market.

VCW, INC.

V. Cheryl Womack left a career as a teacher and joined an insurance company. Within 18 months, she was promoted to senior rater. She was later hired away by a second firm that specialized in trucking insurance and particularly focused on owner-operators. She worked there for five years before asking to be allowed to go out and sell on the road. Her boss told her that women don't go out on the road. So she left the company and formed her own insurance agency.

Womack formed an insurance agency catering to independent truckers called VCW, Inc., and also started the National Association of Independent Truckers. The NAIT provided an opportunity for her to provide group insurance to independent operators. At the time she began VCW, she worked out of her house with one employee. Nine years later her agency had sixty employees, sold to 8000 independent truckers, and had revenues of more than $21,000,000. In spite of this growth, VCW was faced with a number of challenges. Among them were that Womack's insurance provider dropped the workers' compensation insurance, VCW's mainstay insurance line. Later, the state of California required truckers to carry workers' compensation insurance on their employees.

DISCUSSION QUESTIONS

1.   How does a woman succeed in two male-dominated industries -- insurance and trucking?

2.   How do you market to independent truckers?

3.   How do you find an insurance provider when your existing provider quits carrying the primary policies you sell?

ENTREPRENEURIAL RESPONSE

1.   To answer the question simply, a woman succeeds in male-dominated industries by very hard work, aggressiveness, and a refusal to give up. In addition, innovation in new areas that have not been tried before create one's own opportunities. The National Association of Independent Truckers is an example of Womack's innovativeness. She decided that if she could develop the concept of an association for independent truckers, that she could provide them services that large trucking organizations have as well as having a ready source of customers for her insurance sales.

2.   Developing the NAIT was primarily by word of mouth. Once it was launched successfully, it became a natural method of reaching independent truckers for the sale of insurance.

3.   Again, hard work and perseverance were the key. In the case of the required workers' compensation insurance, she literally travelled the entire country and made hundreds of phone calls before she found a carrier.

KELLY TRUCK LINE, INC.

This case is the story of a company which overcame a number of challenges in order to survive in a competitive environment. It also is a good example of the perils of leveraged buyouts. Michael Kelly bought Kelly Truck Line in 1984 via a leveraged buyout. Although it was the best method to acquire the truck line at the time, the ensuing difficulties caused by the leveraged buyout nearly ruined the company.

Because of the poor financial condition after the LBO, the company's insurer refused to renew their policy because the company was too high risk. Their new carrier increased their rates 300% and then went into receivership, locking up $143,000 of KTL's deposit with them. Further, KTL's equipment was old and inefficient, but it could not be replaced because of the poor financial condition. This, in turn, caused drivers to quit and work for other companies that had newer equipment.

Kelly Truck Line was a diversified trucking company. That is, it owned a several types of trailers -- grain, hopper, pneumatic, van, flatbed, and lowboys. Some of this equipment had only seasonal usage. Further, drivers were not well trained in the variety of trailers. To make matters worse, half of their truck tractors were recalled because of a manufacturer's defect and were out of service for six weeks.

QUESTIONS FOR DISCUSSION

1.   Is Kelly Truck Line's situation similar to other companies who went through a leveraged buyout?

2.   Can anything be done to save KTL? Can they survive given their current situation?

3.   Develop a strategy for Kelly Truck Line.

ENTREPRENEURIAL RESPONSE

1.   Every company's situation is unique. However, their situation is not atypical of the problems caused by leveraged buyouts. The often massive amount of debt required to purchase the company leaves the business in such poor financial condition that outsiders dealing with them react negatively. Further, it is nearly impossible to launch an agressive strategy to overcome the situation. If demand falls for any reason, servicing the debt becomes virtually impossible.

2.   Michael Kelly determined that he <u>had to get rid of the debt.</u> Thus, he decided to get rid of all the trailers except the flatbeds. The capital raised by the sale of the other trailers allowed him to reduce the debt and replace some of the older equipment. It also allowed drivers to know only one kind of trailer rather than several. Unfortunately, this reduced sales to only those that use flatbed trailers. To overcome that, he hired some outside sales persons to generate sales within a more narrow geographic region in order to focus their efforts on a more restricted area.

3.   Kelly Truck Line's new strategy was what Porter would call a focus strategy or a niche strategy. By focusing on only the flatbed hauling market, they could specialize with limited equipment.

CASES

The case teaching notes that follow were all provided by the case authors. Their efforts are appreciated. The notes have been edited only slightly to conform to the style of this manual. Typographical errors are mine.

CASE A

THE ARTISAN'S HAVEN

<u>CASE SUMMARY</u>

John Owen was 55 years old when he was laid off by the large chemical firm for which he had worked for 33 years. At first John was upset and frustrated, because he did not know what to do. He did not want to retire at age 55, but he did not want to take a job working for anyone else, either. Retirement would have meant a very modest lifestyle for him and his wife, Katie, and he did not like that idea.

Katie suggested that John open a business to sell arts and crafts, because his hobby for many years had been making gold jewelry. In fact, John had become an accomplished goldsmith. Katie was an amateur interior designer, and she thought that she could go into business with John and that they could spend more time together. They opened a store in Trenton, New Jersey in 1974, and by 1980 they owned six stores in New Jersey and Pennsylvania. In 1980 at age 61, John decided to sell his stores and retire. His net worth was in excess of $1,000,000, and he and Katie wanted to move to Athens, Georgia.

163

It took John less than a year to realize that retirement was not what he wanted, so he opened a store in Athens to sell arts and crafts. The name of the store was The Artisan's Haven. The Artisan's Haven became quite popular, and John and Katie became involved in prominent social and professional circles in Athens. In addition, John and Katie took $50,000 in salary from the business in 1981. It was turning into a real success story.

In July, 1987, John had a massive heart attack, so Katie insisted that he sell the business. John agreed, but they did not have any idea how much it was worth. For all practical purposes, John and Katie were the business. It was a success because of their hard work, their knowledge, and because they had gotten to know their customers and their suppliers personally. The value of the business, therefore, would not be easy to determine.

CASE OBJECTIVES

1. To expose students to critical intangible issues that underlie important finance/accounting decisions in businesses.

2. To explore the non-financial issues that come into play in valuation decisions.

3. To focus students' attention on the critical issues that determine business success or failure.

CASE ANALYSIS

1. External Environment

   a. No direct competitors in Athens, Georgia.
   b. The nearest direct competitors are in Atlanta, Georgia about 65 miles away.
   c. Their is a national trend among consumers toward quality goods and services.
   d. Their is a trend in Athens toward higher quality goods and services, too.
   e. Their is a national trend and a trend in Athens toward high quality arts and crafts as well.

2. Organizational and Internal Issues

   a. John and Katie are heavily involved in the business. Except for part-time employees, they are the business.
   b. John and Katie are the management team.
   c. Their customers are loyal to them because of their knowledge, expertise, and friendliness.

d. Their part-time employees are loyal to them because they are personal friends and because they appreciate John and Katie giving them jobs that are not burdensome and that allow them to do something constructive.

e. Their suppliers are loyal to them because they are friends and because John has given them help by organizing their guild.

3. Scenarios for Valuation of the Business

Presently, the success of the Artisan's Haven relies primarily on the leadership of John and Katie Owen. Consequently, the future success of the business will depend on the ability of the purchaser to run the business in a manner that is consistent with the Owens' style and qualities. Simply stated, the value of the firm cannot be determined by interpreting the past financial data. Instead, the value of the firm was, and will continue to be, created by the owners themselves.

It is obvious from both the income statement and the comments in the case that advertising is not correlated with sales volume. Instead, it is tied almost exclusively to the personal effort of the Owens. Therefore, the Owens' ability to find an interested buyer who possesses the same basic characteristics they possess will determine to a large extent the price they can get for their business.

A study of the income statement reveals the following:

1. Sales: in all probability, sales will fall or at best remain constant with the addition of new management and owners. As stated above the sales are directly correlated with the effort of the Owens themselves.

2. Cost of Goods Sold: will increase. The Owens ability to make and buy quality merchandise enabled them to keep their costs down. Now that they are disassociated from the business, prices will most likely rise.

3. Wages to Officers: will have to be decreased. More money will have to be left in the business to increase retained earnings and decrease the debt to equity ratio. This will be required in order for them to gain outside financing. Obviously, this is dependent on whether the new owners need outside financing.

4. Other Wages: will increase. Presently, the Owens have two elder workers who appear to work for them because they enjoy their company. They work for $5.00 per hour and it is doubtful that new owners will be able to find quality workers for this price.

5. Advertising: would probably increase slightly. There seems to be no connection between sales and advertising in this business. It is likely that new owners will

increase the advertising budget to let the community know about the new store. However, it is also possible that they might not want to publicize the change in ownership.

6.   Interest: will increase. As explained above, interest payments should increase as bank debt is incurred. This assumes that outside financing is necessary.

7.   Taxes: will increase slightly, because more money will be left in the business.

A study of the Balance Sheet reveals the following:

1.   Inventory: one must question how quickly the new owners will be able to sell the merchandise on hand. Inventory is directly related to sales which depends on the success of the new owner.

2.   Retained Earnings: as explained previously, this must be increased in order to bring the debt to equity ratio to an acceptable level.

In conclusion, the outlook for the sale of this business is not good. The only good alternative the Owens' have is to find a buyer(s) who is (are) very similar to themselves (i.e., people who will run the business in a similar way). Additionally, it is very likely that John Owen will not be willing to continue working for the business after he sells it because of his heart attack.

The following are three scenarios that students could develop using the data in the case. Of course, they all assume that John and Katie will no longer be involved with the business. The following tables first present historical data and then project that data based on the three scenarios.

INCOME STATEMENT

	1981	1982	1983	1984	1985	Actual 1986
Sales	16,610	55,673	78,736	105,928	123,683	153,186
Cost of Sales	8,305	27,837	35,968	43,441	60,201	75,806
Gross Profit	8,305	27,836	42,768	62,487	63,482	77,380
Expenses:						
Rent	3,900	7,800	7,800	7,800	7,800	7,800
Wages to officers	10,000	11,000	15,500	20,000	25,000	50,000
Other wages	0	0	0	4,526	9,688	10,803
Utilities	434	612	712	862	1,002	1,165
Advertising	35,000	2,000	2,000	2,000	2,000	2,000
Travel	391	774	933	1,171	1,394	1,654
Supplies	649	835	971	1,175	1,366	1,589
Insurance	145	560	560	560	560	560
Depreciation	168	535	535	535	535	535
Interest	0	278	278	278	409	409
Total Expenses	50,687	24,394	29,289	38,907	49,754	76,515
Profit after tax	(42,382)	3,442	13,479	23,580	13,728	865
Tax	0	0	0	0	5,805	423
Net Income	(42,382)	3,442	13,479	23,580	7,923	442
Officers pay & N.I.	(32,382)	14,442	28,979	43,580	32,923	50,442

Balance Sheet

Assets	1981	1982	1983	1984	1985	1986
Cash	0	68	5,823	16,532	22,018	20,996
Inventory	18,000	26,262	30,651	35,398	40,782	62,168
Prepaid Expenses	2,089	1,973	1,862	2,239	2,355	2,451
Total Current Assets	20,089	28,303	38,336	54,169	65,155	85,615
Long Term Assets:						
Equipment	4,675	4,675	4,675	5,752	5,752	7,860
Furniture	3,897	3,897	3,897	3,897	3,897	4,623
Less: Acc. Dep.	168	703	1,238	1,773	2,308	2,843
Total P,P & E	8,404	7,869	7,334	7,876	7,341	9,640
Total Assets	28,493	36,172	45,670	62,045	72,496	95,255
Liabilities & Stockholders Equity						
Current Maturities	278	278	278	278	278	597
Accounts Payable	2,122	7,899	10,211	14,447	17,901	21,870
Accrued Expenses	1,093	1,240	1,829	1,942	2,068	2,189
Total Current Liab.	3,493	9,417	12,318	16,667	20,247	24,656
Long Term Debt	47,382	45,695	38,813	27,259	26,207	34,115
Total Liabilities	50,875	55,112	51,131	43,926	46,454	58,771
Stockholder's Equity						
Common Stock	20,000	20,000	20,000	20,000	20,000	30,000
Retained Earnings	(42,382)	(38,940)	(25,461)	(1,881)	6,042	6,484
Total Equity	(22,382)	(18,940)	(5,461)	18,119	26,042	36,484
Total Liab. & Equity	28,493	36,172	45,670	62,045	72,496	95,255
ROE(N.I. based)	189.36%	-18.17%	-246.82%	130.24%	30.42%	1.21%
ROE(N.I. & officer based)	144.68%	-76.25%	-530.65%	240.52%	126.42%	138.26%
Debt to equity	-2.12	-2.41	-7.11	1.50	1.01	0.94

Income Statement
Year to Year % Change

	1982	1983	1984	1985	1986
Sales	70.17%	29.29%	25.67%	14.36%	19.26%
Cost of Sales	70.17%	22.61%	17.20%	27.84%	20.59%
Gross Profit	70.16%	34.91%	31.56%	1.57%	17.96%
Expenses:					
Rent	50.00%	0.00%	0.00%	0.00%	0.00%
Wages to officers	9.09%	29.03%	22.50%	20.00%	50.00%
Other wages			100.00%	53.28%	10.32%
Utilities	29.08%	14.04%	17.40%	13.97%	13.99%
Advertising	-1650.00%	0.00%	0.00%	0.00%	0.00%
Travel	49.48%	17.04%	20.32%	16.00%	15.72%
Supplies	22.28%	14.01%	17.36%	13.98%	14.03%
Insurance	74.11%	0.00%	0.00%	0.00%	0.00%
Depreciation	68.60%	0.00%	0.00%	0.00%	0.00%
Interest	100.00%	0.00%	0.00%	32.03%	0.00%
Total Expenses	-107.78%	16.71%	24.72%	21.80%	34.97%
Profit after tax	1331.32%	74.46%	42.84%	-71.77%	-1487.05%
Tax				100.00%	-1272.34%
Net Income	1331.32%	74.46%	42.84%	-197.61%	-1692.53%
Officers pay & N.I.	342.22%	50.16%	33.50%	-32.37%	34.73%

Year to Year % Change
Balance Sheet

Assets	1982	1983	1984	1995	1986
Cash	100.00%	98.83%	64.78%	24.92%	-4.87%
Inventory	31.46%	14.32%	13.41%	13.20%	34.40%
Prepaid Expenses	-5.88%	-5.96%	16.84%	4.93%	3.92%
Total Current Assets	29.02%	26.17%	29.23%	16.86%	23.90%
Long Term Assets:					
Equipment	0.00%	0.00%	18.72%	0.00%	26.82%
Furniture	0.00%	0.00%	0.00%	0.00%	15.70%
Less: Acc. Dep.	76.10%	43.21%	30.17%	23.18%	18.82%
Total P,P & E	-6.80%	-7.29%	6.88%	-7.29%	23.85%
Total Assets	21.23%	20.80%	26.38%	14.42%	23.89%
Liabilities & Stocks					
Current Maturities	0.00%	0.00%	0.00%	0.00%	53.43%
Accounts Payable	73.14%	22.64%	29.32%	19.30%	18.15%
Accrued Expenses	11.85%	32.20%	5.82%	6.09%	5.53%
Total Current Liabilities	62.91%	23.55%	26.09%	17.68%	17.88%
Long Term Debt	-3.69%	-17.73%	42.39%	-4.01%	23.18%
Total Liabilities	7.69%	-7.79%	-16.40%	5.44%	20.96%
Stockholder's Equity					
Common Stock	0.00%	0.00%	0.00%	0.00%	33.33%
Retained Earnings	-8.84%	-52.94%	-1253.59%	131.13%	6.82%
Total Equity	-18.17%	-246.82%	130.14%	30.42%	28.62%
Total Liab. & Equity	21.23%	20.80%	26.39%	14.42%	23.89%
ROE(N.I. based)	1121.96%	92.46%	289.66%	-327.75%	-2411.28%
ROE(N.I. & officer based)	289.74%	85.63%	320.63%	-90.25%	8.56%
Debt to Equity	12.25%	66.05%	572.42%	-49.50%	-7.62

Percentage of Sales

	1981	1982	1983	1984	1985	1986	ERR
Sales	100.00%	100.00%	100.00%	100.00%	100.00%	100.00%	100.00%
Cost of Sales	50.00%	50.00%	45.68%	41.01%	48.67%	49.49%	50.00%
Gross Profit	50.00%	50.00%	54.32%	58.99%	51.33%	50.51%	50.00%
Expenses:							
Rent	23.48%	14.01%	9.91%	7.36%	6.31%	5.09%	4.86%
Wages to officers	60.20%	19.76%	19.69%	18.88%	20.21%	32.64%	32.64%
Other wages	0.00%	0.00%	0.00%	4.27%	7.83%	7.05%	7.05%
Utilities	2.61%	1.10%	0.90%	0.81%	0.81%	0.76%	0.79%
Advertising	210.72%	3.59%	2.54%	1.89%	1.62%	1.31%	2.97%
Travel	2.35%	1.39%	1.18%	1.11%	1.13%	1.08%	1.08%
Supplies	3.91%	1.50%	1.23%	1.11%	1.10%	1.04%	1.04%
Insurance	0.87%	1.01%	0.71%	0.53%	0.45%	0.37%	0.35%
Depreciation	1.01%	0.96%	0.68%	0.51%	0.43%	0.35%	0.32%
Interest	0.00%	0.50%	0.35%	0.26%	0.33%	0.27%	2.02%
Total Expenses	305.16%	43.82%	37.20%	36.73%	40.23%	49.95%	53.11%
Profit after tax	-255.16%	6.18%	17.12%	22.26%	11.10%	0.56%	-3.11%
Tax	0.00%	0.00%	0.00%	0.00%	4.69%	0.28%	0.00%
Net Income	-255.16%	6.18%	17.12%	22.26%	6.41%	0.29%	-3.11%
	-194.95%	25.94%	36.81%	41.14%	26.62%	32.93%	29.53%

BEST CASE SCENARIO -- Sales Increase at 10%

ASSUMPTIONS

COGS	50.00%	Annual Increase *	10.00%
Sales Growth Rate	10.00%	Inflation adjustment	5.00%
Interest on LTD	10.00%	Tax Rate	30.00%
Hourly wage paid*	$5.40		

* These figures relate to labor costs for in store help.

NOTE: COGS will increase as the new owner has to purchase more of the merchandise. Interest payments will increase as new owner will not be able to obtain funds at the current interest rates.

Pro Forma Income Statement

	1987	1988	1989	1990	1991	Underlying Assumptions
Sales	168,505	185,355	203,891	224,280	246,708	Tied to variable
Cost of Sales	84,252	92,678	101,945	112,140	123,354	Sales tied to variable
Gross Profit	84,252	92,678	101,945	112,140	123,354	
Expenses:						
Rent	8,190	8,600	9,029	9,481	9,955	Increased 5% annually
Wages to officers	55,000	60,500	66,550	73,205	80,526	Percent of sales
Other wages	11,880	13,068	14,375	15,812	17,394	Tied to variables @20/hr
Utilities	1,328	1,514	1,726	1,967	2,242	Increase at historical rate
Advertising	5,000	5,000	4,000	2,500	2,000	
Travel	1,819	2,001	2,201	2,422	2,664	Percent of sales
Supplies	1,748	1,923	2,115	2,326	2,559	Percent of sales
Insurance	588	617	648	681	715	Increased 5% annually
Depreciation	535	535	535	535	535	Straight line
Interest	3,412	4,580	5,822	7,072	8,278	Tied to LTD & variable
Total Expenses	89,500	98,338	107,001	116,001	127,867	
Profit after tax	(5,248)	(5,660)	(5,056)	(3,861)	(3,513)	
Tax	0	0	0	0	0	Carry forward ignored
Net income	(5,248)	(5,660)	(5,056)	(3,861)	(3,513)	
Officers pay & N.I.	49,753	54,840	61,494	69,344	77,012	

NOTE: Those lines that are "Tied to variable" are based on the percent stated on the assumptions sheet.

Balance Sheet

Assets	1987	1988	1989	1990	1991	Underlying Assumptions
Case	23,096	25,405	27,946	30,740	33,814	Percentage of sales
Inventory	68,385	75,223	82,746	91,020	100,122	Percentage of sales
Prepaid Expenses	2,574	2,702	2,837	2,979	3,128	Inflation adjusted
Total Current Assets	94,054	103,331	113,529	124,740	137,056	
Long Term Assets:						
Equipment	8253	8665.65	9098.932	9553.879	10031.57	Increase of 5%
Furniture	4854.15	5096.857	5351.700	5619.285	5900.249	Increase of 5%
Less: Acc. Dep.	3,378	3,913	4,448	4,983	5,518	Straight line
Total P,P & E	9,729	9,850	10,003	10,190	10,414	
Total Assets	103,783	113,180	123,531	134,930	147,478	
Liabilities & Stockhold:						
Current Maturities	627	658	691	726	762	Inflation adjusted
Accounts Payable	23590.64	25949.70	28554.67	31399.14	34539.06	Percent of sales
Accrued Expenses	2527.569	2780.325	3058.358	3364.194	3700.613	Percent of sales
Total Current Liabilities	26,745	29,388	32,294	35,489	39,002	
Long Term Debt	45,802	58,216	70,717	82,781	95,331	Plug
Total Liabilities	72,547	87,604	103,011	118,270	134,332	
Stockholder's Equity:						
Common Stock	30,000	30,000	30,000	30,000	30,000	
Retained Earnings	1236.5	-4423,85	-9479.74	-13340.6	-16853.8	Function of income
Total Equity	31,237	25,576	20,520	16,659	13,146	
Total Liability & Equity	103,783	113,180	123,531	134,930	147,478	
ROE(N.I. based)	-16.80%	-22.13%	-24.64%	-23.18%	-26.72%	
ROE(N.I. and officer based)	159.28%	214.42%	299.68%	416.25%	585.82%	
Debt to equity	1.47	2.28	3.45	4.97	7.25	

MOST LIKELY SCENARIO -- Current Customer Base Allows Sales to Hold Steady

ASSUMPTIONS

COGS	50.00%	Annual increase	10.00%
Sales growth rate	0.00%	Inflation adjustment	5.00%
Interest on LTD	10.00%	Tax Rate	30.00%
Hourly wage paid*	$5.40		

* These figures relate to labor costs for in store help.

NOTE: COGS will increase as the new owner has to purchase more of the merchandise.
Interest payments will increase as new owner will not be able to obtain funds at the current interest rates.

Pro Forma Income Statement

	1987	1988	1989	1990	1991	Underlying Assumptions
Sales	153,186	153,186	153,186	153,186	153,186	Tied to variable
Cost of sales	76,593	76,593	76,593	76,593	76,593	Sales tied to variable
Gross Profit	76,593	76,593	76,593	76,593	76,593	
Expenses:						
Rent	8,190	8,600	9,029	9,481	9,955	Increased 5% annually
Wages to officers	50,000	50,000	50,000	50,000	50,000	Percent of sales
Other wages	11880.00	13,068	14,375	15,812	17,394	Tied to variables @20/hr
Utilities	1,328	1,514	1,726	1,967	2,242	Increase at historical rate
Advertising	5,000	5,000	4,000	2,500	2,000	
Travel	1,654	1,654	1,654	1,654	1,654	Percent of sales
Supplies	1,589	1,589	1,589	1,589	1,589	Percent of sales
Insurance	588	617	648	681	715	Increased 5% annually
Depreciation	535	535	535	535	535	Straight line
Interest	3,412	4,219	5,262	6,510	7,953	Tied to LTD and variables
Total Expenses	84,176	86,796	88,818	90,728	94,036	
Profit after tax	(7,583)	(10,203)	(12,225)	(14,135)	(17,443)	
Tax	0	0	0	0	0	Carry forward ignored
Net Income	(7,583)	(10,203)	(12,225)	(14,135)	(17,443)	
Officers pay & N.I.	42,418	39,797	37,775	35,865	32,557	

NOTE: Those lines that are "Tied to variable" are based on the percent stated on the assumptions sheet.

Balance Sheet

Assets	1987	1988	1989	1990	1991	Underlying Assumptions
Cash	20,996	20,996	20,996	20,996	20,996	Percentage of sales
Inventory	62,168	62,168	62,168	62,168	62,168	Percentage of sales
Prepaid Expenses	2,574	2,702	2,837	2,979	3,128	Inflation adjusted
Total Current Assets	85,738	85,866	86,001	86,143	86,292	
Long Term Assets:						
Equipment	8253	8665.65	9098.932	9553.879	10031.57	Increase of 5%
Furniture	4854.15	5096.857	5351.700	5619.285	5900.249	Increase of 5%
Less Acc.Dep.	3,378	3,913	4,448	4,983	5,518	Straight line
TOTAL P,P & E	9,729	9,850	10,003	10,190	10,414	
Total Assets	95,467	95,716	96,004	96,333	96,706	
Liabilities & Stockhold:						
Current Maturities	627	658	691	726	762	Inflation adjusted
Accounts Payable	21446.04	21446.04	21446.04	21446.04	21446.04	Percent of sales
Accrued Expenses	2297.79	2297.79	2297.79	2297.29	2297.79	Percent of sales
Total Current Liabilities	24,371	24,402	24,435	24,469	24,506	
Long Term Debt	42,195	52,615	65,095	79,526	97,305	Plug
Total Liabilities	66,565	77,017	89,530	103,995	121,811	
Stockholder's Equity:						
Common Stock	30,000	30,000	30,000	30,000	30,000	
Retained Earnings	-1098.5	-11301.6	-23526.3	-37661.8	-55104.9	Function of income
Total Equity	28,902	18,698	6,474	(7,662)	(25,105)	
Total Liability & Equity	95,467	95,716	96,004	96,333	96,706	
ROE(N.I. based)	-26.24%	-54.57%	-188.84%	184.49%	69.48%	
ROE(N.I. and officer based)	146.77%	212.84%	583.52%	-468.09%	-129.68%	
Debt to Equity	1.46	2.81	10.06	-10.38	-3.88	

WORST SCENARIO -- Sales Slide at a 10% Annual Rate

ASSUMPTIONS

COGS	50.00%	Annual Increase*	10.00%
Sales Growth Rate	-10.00%	Inflation Adjustment	5.00%
Interest on LTD	10.00%	Tax Rate	30.00%
Hourly wage paid*	$5.40		

* These figures relate to labor costs for in store help.

NOTE: COGS will increase as the new owner has to purchase more of the merchandise.

Interest payments will increase as new owner will not be able to obtain funds at the current interest rates.

Pro Forma Income Statement

	1987	1988	1989	1990	1991	Underlying Assumptions
Sales	137,867	124,081	111,673	100,505	90,455	Tied to variable
Cost of Sales	68,934	62.040	55,836	50,253	45,227	Sales tied to variable
Gross Profit	68,934	62,040	55,836	50,253	45,227	
Expenses:						
Rent	8,190	8,600	9,029	9,481	9,955	Increased 5% annually
Wages to officers	45,000	40,500	36,450	32,805	29,524	Percent of sales
Other wages	11880.00	13,068	14,375	15,812	17,394	Tied to variables @20/hr
Utilities	1,328	1,514	1,726	1,967	2,242	Increase at historical rate
Advertising	5,000	5,000	4,000	2,500	2,000	
Travel	1,489	1,340	1,206	1,085	977	Percent of sales
Supplies	1,430	1,287	1,158	1,043	938	Percent of sales
Insurance	588	617	648	681	715	Increased 5% annually
Depreciation	535	535	535	535	535	Straight line
Interest	3,412	3,859	4,774	6,124	7,899	Tied to LTD and variable
Total Expenses	78,851	76,319	73,901	72,033	72,179	
Profit after tax	(9,918)	(14,279)	(18,065)	(21,780)	(26,951)	
Tax	0	0	0	0	0	Carry forward ignored
Net Income	(9,918)	(14,279)	(18,065)	(21,780)	(26,951)	
Officers Pay & N.I.	35,082	26,221	18,385	11,025	2,573	

NOTE: Those lines that are "Tied to variable" are based on the percent stated on the assumptions sheet.

Balance Sheet

Assets	1987	1988	1989	1990	1991	Underlying Assumptions
Cash	18,896	17,007	15,306	13,775	12,398	Percentage of sales
Inventory	55,951	50,356	45,320	40,788	36,710	Percentage of sales
Prepaid Expenses	2,574	2,702	2,837	2,979	3,128	Inflation adjusted
Total Current Assets	77,421	70,065	63,464	57,543	52,236	
Long Term Assets:						
Equipment	8253	8665.65	9098.932	9553.879	10031.57	Increase of 5%
Furniture	4854.15	5096.857	5351.700	5619.285	5900.249	Increase of 5%
Less: Acc.Dep.	3,378	3,913	4,448	4,983	5,518	Straight line
Total P,P & E	9,729	9,850	10,003	10,190	10,414	
Total Assets	87,150	79,915	73,467	67,733	62,649	
Liabilities & Stockhold:						
Current Maturities	627	658	691	726	762	Inflation adjusted
Accounts Payable	19301.43	17371.29	15634.16	14070.74	12663.67	Percent of sales
Accrued Expenses	2068.011	1861.209	1675.088	1507.580	1356.822	Percent of sales
Total Current Liabilities	21,996	19,891	18,000	16,304	14,782	
Long Term Debt	38,588	47,736	61,243	78,987	102,376	Plug
Total Liabilities	60,584	67,627	79,244	95,291	117,158	
Stockholder's Equity:						
Common Stock	30,000	30,000	30,000	30,000	30,000	
Retained Earnings	-3433.5	-17712.4	-35777.0	-57557.4	-84508.6	Function of income
Total Equity	26,567	12,288	(5,777)	(27,557)	(54,509)	
Total Liability & Equity	87,150	79,915	73,467	67,733	62,649	
ROE(N.I. based)	-37.33%	-116.21%	312.69%	79.04%	49.44%	
ROE(N.I. and officer based)	132.06%	213.40%	-318.25%	-40.01%	-4.72%	
Debt to Equity	1.45	3.88	-10.60	-2.87	-1.88	

CASE B

INTERNATIONAL LEARNING CORPORATION

CASE SUMMARY

International Learning Corporation grew out of the graduate work undertaken by Robert Owen in a leading university department dedicated to learning theory. Owen determined to bring his ideas and the expertise of the department to commercialization. Initially he funded the product development through case flow generated from consulting and advances from family members. Owen recognized early that the firm would need more funds than he could generate personally or, initially, from operations. The case provides opportunity to evaluate the industry segment in which Owen has chosen to compete. He developed a business plan and searched for various alternative venture capital sources. After two years Owen found himself out of cash but with offers from three venture capital firms. The case poses the dilemma of which of the three to choose.

CASE OBJECTIVES

This case provides the student with the opportunity to make decisions at various points over two years of a company's history. The case focuses on three alternative venture capital proposals which Owen must choose between.

Suggested Assignment Questions: International Learning Corporation

1. Evaluate Robert Owen's business activities to date.

2. Which venture capital opportunity should Robert Owen take? Why?

3. What strategic and operational suggestions do you have for him, i.e., what can he do to maximize the possibility that his firm will succeed?

Analysis

1. Evaluate Robert Owen's business activities to date.

Owen apparently has a good deal of talent with regard to software development, business jargon, and his potential market. In addition, he is able to engender a great deal of loyalty to his vision. As the case concludes, he has convinced at least three other well-trained individuals to invest a considerable amount of their professional lives into the company. Madelaine, at least, has worked for two years at $500/month -- hardly a living wage. Owen has put $100K in the budget for back wages for himself and these individuals. Even if only half that amount is owed, each individual has essentially worked as much as a year gratis for the company!

Technical Capability. It is difficult to assess Owen's technical capability. Certainly he demonstrated in a basic university math course the applicability of his concepts. Are they transferable into the corporate world? He has several hurdles. One is his ability to craft appropriate products and the second to overcome the switching costs, i.e., to convince corporate America to invest in his product and in the development of expertise among their own staff in using his products.

Knowledge of the Market. Owen has likely developed a good deal of knowledge about his potential clients/market through his consulting activities. His initial direct mail piece (Exhibit I) commands attention and connotes a professional orientation toward the market place. Students will no doubt note that there was about a 14% response to this mailing piece. Moreover, Owen visited twenty firms. Assuming that he asked appropriate questions, this activity in itself would give him a reasonable base of information for initiating his activities. Note, however, that within a year Owen felt that his activities, i.e., the application of his ideas to non-computer based training would not succeed. There was resistance in the market to his theory and methodology. One might validly ask the question whether the corporate training market would be more easily persuaded to use the concepts in computer-based training. Further, there was no interest in ILC by the larger consulting (presumably training) companies. We might ask if the experts in the field did not want to buy into Owen's ideas, would the customer?

Owen appears to have developed basic knowledge of his market (see Exhibit III) and his competitors (see Exhibit IV). It is clear that there is opportunity. The micro-computer based training market is expected to nearly double each year over the five year span exhibited. Further, at $5B expected in 1988, it is not a small market. Certainly a number of small firms can find opportunity in such an industry. Moreover, Owen wants a firm with $200M in sales in 1990. If the 1990 market is $8B, Owen wants only 2% of the market -- a modest goal assuming that he can get appropriate financing and that his product will achieve the results he promises.

Development of the Business Plan. Owen's business plan is, like his mailing piece, professionally done. Obviously, he has done a good deal of thinking about how to approach his market. Further, his summary especially indicates that he is able to crystallize his ideas in a format that is easy to understand. The results are significant -- here is an unknown entrepreneur without any track record in running a company who interested ten venture capital firms in his company and has three offers in hand.

2. Which venture capital opportunity should Robert Owen take? Why?

Essentially, Owen has to make the traditional tradeoff between how much control/equity he gives up and how much money he currently gets in order to develop his product. He would be in a stronger position, of course, if he had a prototype completed and one or two customers in line. Then he would be seeking venture capital only for the marketing effort. At the present time he is seeking capital for completion of the prototype and the marketing effort. Moreover, his marketing efforts at $75,000 may be woefully inadequate given the size of some of the current competition (see Exhibit IV).

3. What strategic and operational suggestions do you have for him, i.e., what can he do to maximize the possibility that his firm will succeed?

Owen has to do three things: (1) finish the prototype, (2) begin marketing activities, and (3) maintain relationships with the venture capital firm. The latter issue is highly dependent on the first two. It is difficult for a student to determine how reasonable Owen's estimates of the required time to prototype completion. The prototype, however, has to be completed before he can aggressively approach the market. In addition, ILC -- either in the form of the venture capital firm or in the person of Owen -- has to make decision about his role. Heretofore, he has been the marketing arm (e.g., getting out of the direct mail piece, marketing himself as a consultant, putting together the business plan, selling the company to the venture capitalists) of the firm in addition to being the central "Dr. Land" of ILC. Can he play both roles? It is unlikely and he will thus have to choose between the two activities. It is likely that the venture capital firm would prefer that he remain in house and complete the prototype. ILC could more likely hire a "marketing type" with experience in the training industry than a genius product designer.

What kind of marketing person should be sought? This question is difficult to answer until ILC has worked out how they are going to approach the market. For example, if ILC decides to sell or license the Learn! system to the market, their selling job at $20K is considerably different than as if they attempt to sell off-the-shelf courses at $30-700/course. Moreover the market for customized courses is different than the off-the-shelf courses. We have no idea from the case nor the business plan, whether Owen understands the different distribution systems that will be necessary for these different kinds of products.

CASE C

DOORSTEP VIDEO, INC.

CASE SUMMARY

Doorstep Video, Inc. is a case in entrepreneurship and the process of gathering the information needed to make a decision on whether or not to start-up a company based on a novel idea -- the home delivery of rental video-tapes and VCR equipment. The case provides a concept that is easy to understand and one that students can relate to. The setting is one that is familiar to almost all college students.

Two college age students, one of whom is still in college and one who is just about to graduate and who has a firm job offer, are considering setting up a small warehouse from which they will deliver rental video tapes. They believe that a profitable business can be built around the home delivery of rental tapes just like a profitable business has been built around the home delivery of pizza. They plan to start with a small capital base, and with a minimum of overhead expenses, build up inventory with the cash flows generated from the business.

OBJECTIVE OF THE CASE

This case presents the information available to two college age entrepreneurs who are trying to decide if they should start a business for the home delivery of rental video tapes and VCR equipment in a small North Carolina town of approximately 28,000 people.

QUESTIONS

1. Is home delivery a potentially profitable niche in the rental video tape industry?

Home delivery of rental video tapes probably is not a profitable niche. A break even analysis (see attached) shows that the firm would need 546 rentals per day to break even. This is about all one would expect in a small town with plenty of other rental outlets. The lack of marketing research shows up here for there is no known number of people, or percentage of potential customers, who would prefer to call in an order rather than go browse through a store's video library. As renters of video tapes, ask the class if they would frequently call for delivery, or would they rather go to the store and browse through the selection? My guess is that most would rather browse through the selection and at a later date may have one delivered that they remembered that they would like to see. Although home delivery sounds like a good idea, videos are not like pizzas which are limited in the number of types that one may wish. New videos are constantly reaching the market, and more importantly, viewers' moods change and the type of movie they wish to see corresponds with these mood changes.

2. What potential problems do you foresee in the home delivery of rental video tapes?

The biggest problem is generating the amount of business that will make the venture profitable. This will require some very creative advertising and excellent service on delivery for all new customers. Not only must this business generate new business, but they must take some business from existing competitors.

3. What would you do to make this startup have a better chance of being successful?

Starting small and building a base of loyal customers through excellent delivery time, delivery of a list of videos for rent with each actual rental, and expansion to walk-in traffic seem to be some ways of making this venture successful. Maybe even a pick-up service would help. Their job is to establish a record of service that will build a large enough group of customers for this type of service that will ensure profitability.

4. What are the strengths and weaknesses of Doorstep Video?

(See next section.)

5. What are the opportunities and threats facing Doorstep Video?

(See next section.)

6. What is the future of the rental video tape industry? How will it evolve?

This question should open the class up as most students should have some idea of where they think this industry is heading. The point of this question is two-fold. First have the students state where they think the industry is going in the future, and then how a firm can position itself to be ready for this future.

7. Would you give up a good paying job with managerial potential to start a small business in a relatively small town?

Students should be asked this question, and then answer why or why not. Certainly the entrepreneurial type will usually answer in the affirmative, while the more traditional student would not. Reasons will vary from the chance to be your own boss and the ability to control one's own future, to lack of security and lack of potential business.

8. Would you proceed with the startup of Doorstep Video? Why or why not?

Certainly, this is the question that will be the most interesting from a teaching standpoint. Make the students defined why they would or would not proceed with the startup. After this discussion, you may wish to tell them what actually happened. Realize that at the time the case was written, the success of this business was anything but certain. Many new video rental stores do not make it through the first two years. (See Epilogue)

CASE ANALYSIS

After a general discussion of the rental video tape industry, a SWOT analysis of Doorstep Video is a necessary step before making a determination of the potential of starting a business that delivers rental video tapes.

Strengths

1. Youthful enthusiasm -- acceptance of little or no pay.
2. Low overhead.
3. Willingness to work hard to establish the business.
4. New idea that will attract some business.

Weaknesses
1. Garret's limited business experience.
2. Limited market.
3. Low capitalization.
4. A very competitive industry.

Opportunities

1. Expand to delivery and walk-in business.
2. Sales of video tapes, accessories, electronic equipment.
3. Delivery of snack foods with video tapes.
4. Expansion of the home delivery concept.
5. Open additional stores in the same area.

Threats

1. Competition from chain stores.
2. Ease of entry into the business -- increased local competition.
3. Potential liability problem with drivers.

In addition to the SWOT analysis, students should calculate a break even analysis and a pro forma income statement for the first three months of operation. (See attached break even analysis and pro forma statement.) NOTE: The pro forma income statement indicates that Clay and Garret have underestimated the cost of the delivery of cassettes. See Exhibit 4 from the case for comparison. The payroll of $1,100 leaves only $400 for delivery expenses per month after Garret's $700 is subtracted. Based on the estimate of 513 rentals per week and delivery cost of $0.71 per tape, the total monthly delivery payroll would be 513(.71)(13 wks.)/3 months = $1,578.

Students should be prepared to present their analysis to the class and be able to defend their projections. The case discussion should focus on the potential profitability of the business venture, the ability of the two entrepreneurs, and the competitiveness of the industry.

EPILOGUE

The final decision to open a rental video tape delivery company was made by the two entrepreneurs in early May. The final decision was triggered by their desire to own their own successful business and the acceptance of the idea by both parents. Doorstep Video opened on June 12th and has been profitable every month since then except for the first month. As planned all profits during the first year were used to expand the firm's inventory of tapes. At the end of the first year, Doorstep Video had almost 1,000 tapes as compared to their opening inventory of less than 550 titles.

After only six months, Doorstep Video expanded to a storefront business and walk-in traffic now accounts for 60 percent of the total rental business. In addition, Doorstep Video sells electronic equipment, primarily Hitachi VCRs, televisions, and stereos. Doorstep Video has no investment in the electronic equipment and only carries display models in the store. However, if a customer wanted to purchase a piece of equipment,

Doorstep Video can make the delivery within a matter of hours as the distributor is located in a nearby city. With the expansion to a storefront operation, Doorstep Video purchased a computer and software that was designed to give video rental stores accurate inventory management. The computer system has proved to be both accurate and efficient, allowing for the expansion of the rental base without requiring additional store personnel.

Pro Forma Income Statement
Doorstep Video, Inc.
For Three-Month Period

Revenues:

Video rentals (513/wk.)($2.63)(13 wks.)	$17,539	
VCR rentals (7/wk. @ $5/rental)	455	
Total revenues		$17,994

Expenses:

Video purchases		$ 4,500
Payroll: Garrett ($700)(3 months)	2,100	
Delivery: (513)(.71)(13)		4,735
Advertising		900
Taxes	1,100	
Telephone		345
Rent & Utilities		300
Misc. expenses		360
Insurance		90
Total expenses		$14,430

Net Income $ 3,564

NOTE: Depreciation expenses are not shown above but should be included in the student's pro forma statement. An argument could be made for depreciating the tapes over a two year period. If so the depreciation expenses would be $2,019. Conversely a good argument could be made to expense the costs, which would eliminate the positive net income.

Variable Costs

The variable cost for delivery of video tapes is based on an estimate that drivers can average delivering seven tapes per hour. This average seems reasonable in that most customers order more than one tape. In fact Clay assumed 4 deliveries (7 tapes) per hour.

$$VC = \$3.35/7 + .40(4)/7 = \$0.71 \text{ per tape}$$

Fixed Costs - Month

Videos	$1,500
Payroll - Garrett	700
Advertising	300
Taxes	370
Telephone	115
Rent & Utilities	100
Misc. Expenses	120
Insurance	30
Total	$3,235

Break Even Point

$$BP = \text{fixed cost/contribution margin} = 3{,}235/(2.63-.71)$$
$$= 1{,}685 \text{ rentals per month.}$$

This is 393 rentals per week or 56 rentals per day.

CASE D

WISCONSIN SEALCOATING

CASE SUMMARY

The student is placed in the role of a small business consultant who has just been hired to replace a consultant who will be leaving. The senior consultant has a client who needs his business plan updated, so she decides to train her replacement in business plan preparation. The student is provided information on the client, Mr. Peter Radtke and his company, Wisconsin Sealcoating of Appleton, Wisconsin.

The case presents the history of Wisconsin Sealcoating, discusses the current personnel, including the owner and his wife, and the current services provided. The company's material resources and financial condition are described. Operating statement information for the past three years is provided. Environmental factors, in terms of competition, technology, and market conditions, are then discussed. The case ends with a discussion of the company's current marketing efforts and Mr. Radtke's managerial philosophy and short-term goals.

TEACHING OBJECTIVES

1. To provide students with the opportunity to develop a business plan, pulling together all that they've learned in their marketing, management, finance, and other classes.

2. To focus the student's attention on the problems a small business can have with understanding the needs of their customers and learning how to segment the marketplace in order to meet the different needs.

QUESTIONS

1. What additional information should the student collect?

2. In Appendix A, the authors have included certain sections of the February 1988 Strategic Plan for Wisconsin Sealcoating. If the instructor so chooses, s/he may pass out copies of this Appendix and have the students evaluate the information as prepared by the owner.

3. After the students have prepared their versions of a business plan for the company, the instructor can share with them the material found in Appendix A. The students can then discuss how their plans differ from and are similar to the plans prepared by the owner.

DISCUSSION

This is an actual company that is located in Appleton, Wisconsin. Mr. Radtke has sought the services of the Small Business Development Center at the University of Wisconsin Oshkosh, where Dr. Cornwall has consulted with him over the past three years. Mr. Radtke has graciously given us permission to develop this case. The only fictitious information in the case are the names of the staff, including those of the owner and his wife, the names of the competitors, and the masking of the years for the financial statements. A model for formulating a strategic business plan that the SBDC uses is provided in Appendix B of this Note.

The student should do some library and outside research on the sealcoating industry, in order to get a better understanding of the business situation that is presented here. Information should be available at any area technical school.

The instructor should caution the students about the financial data that are presented in Appendix 1 of the case. These data were taken directly from the business plan. There were no explanations of some of the categories used, such as Gross Wages and Miscellaneous. There were several errors in the year-to-year change percentages, so these were not included. The students can calculate those percentages themselves. The Balance Sheet looks questionable, especially in the first column (2nd Prior year). The financial ratio calculations should be double-checked, then compared to industry ratios for the mid-1980s.

There are some problems with the SWOT Analysis that the owner has prepared (see Appendix A). As one reviewer of this case has noted, some of the factors are questionable. "How is the company's marketing plan an opportunity? This is an internal factor and if indeed it is a strength then the company can use this strength to take advantage of opportunities in the external environment. Some factors listed under Opportunities are extremely questionable - Company acceptance by customers, Knowledgeable, etc." The owner does not address how he plans to handle the health and safety problems related to the sealers.

OBSERVATIONS & UPDATE

Even with the current business plan, the client is still having problems with marketing. He fails to see what the different segments of the market want and need. He really does not understand segmentation. The segmentation process was explained to the client this past summer. Hopefully, he now has a better understanding of his market, and this understanding will be reflected in future business plans and marketing strategies.

In a meeting with the owner during the summer, several updates and comments were provided by him. Regarding the current work force, Todd has left the company and two new workers have been hired. Jack has been a real asset to the company and will be going to college. The owner hopes to create a full-time position for him.

With regard to their financial condition, they have expanded their line of credit to $40,000 for the summer months. This lets them take advantage of cash discounts provided by suppliers. Mr. Radtke said that he has enough work this summer. It's been near perfect for his business, since the state has been withering under a drought during May, June and July.

One competitor, Vende Hey, has moved into a new type of work. They now provide asphalt repair work in the form of on-the-spot patching. They've purchased a mobile truck that carries special equipment that actually heats the pavement before the repair material is applied. There are big upfront costs associated with this work.

Wisconsin Sealcoating has entered into the small crackfilling market. Peter bought a small piece of equipment to take care of small, on-the-job projects, as a convenience to the client. He makes this service available, but is not heavily marketing it. They have also added some pavement sealing work to their tennis court resurfacing work in Door County. Peter is looking at the potential market in asphalt sealing there, and may pursue the market more aggressively in the future.

As of December, 1988, the owner has made the following observations about his current situation. With regards to their sealcoating operation, they now have the necessary equipment and staff to do almost any size job. They have not utilized or expanded their sealing operation as they should have. Increases in sales for this year is largely due to subcontracting (to a friendly competitor) of hot crackfilling work -- a service Wisconsin had not been able to offer before. The important competition from formidable outside companies has been in the area of larger accounts. The area sealing competition has remained active but not so vigorously that he feels they could not become more dominant.

With regards to their tennis operations, they have very strong public work competition and have never been able to consistently be priced competitively. There have been several attempts to "unseat" them with their Kossel account. They have remained strong in this area. Privately contracted work has been their strong area because of their personalized and quality service.

With regards to staffing, Peter considers his foreman to be technically superior to any in the area; however, they are limited to only one effective crew because of their dependence on him. Mike and John will be returning next year. Bill will be returning on probation, due to poor performance this year. The worker who was hired to replace Todd will return, possibly as a sealing crew leader. Jack has been a good worker, doing well in school, and will return next year. Hopefully he will be able to help Peter with sales as well.

Finally, with regards to cash flow, Wisconsin has encountered a problem with one accounts receivable. It is now tied up in Chapter 11 bankruptcy. There is hope that eventually they will be paid by the problem customer. Cash flow over the winter will be a problem. Peter is hoping to find some type of work which may help out. This situation has and will temper their spending decisions for 1989.

APPENDIX A

SWOT ANALYSIS

External Environment:

Opportunities

Limited good competition
Large, growing market
Company acceptance by customers
Established in the marketplace
Knowledgeable
Satisfied customers
Customer interest in new products
  (crackfilling, consulting)
Complete service available
Rejuvenator Sealer - new product
Contractor Relationships - growth area
Asphalt Repairing - larger work
  open market
Marketing plan
Most competitive sales efforts
  are the "shotgun" approach
No large company name recognition

Threats

Increasing number of competitors
Pricing drops
Equipment needs = expense
VSC has a small sales force
Previously tarnished industry image
Customers often buy on price
Consulting is time consuming
Contracts are "one-shot" deals with
  very little repeat business
Long term: Health or safety constraints
on types of sealers used and methods
of application and disposal (?)

Internal:

Strengths

Returning work force of four
Have sales/office help
Knowledgeable foreman (1)
Concerned management
Experienced owner/salesman
Operationally good equipment
Hire summer help
TJTC and job training available
Modest long term debt

Weaknesses

Seasonal work

Difficulty of getting and keeping good
  people seasonally
Financial cycle - seasonal
One man management
- maintenance
- sales
- communications
- training
- some equipment limitations
Limited earning power of the short season

ALTERNATIVE STRATEGIES

I.   BROADENING OUR MISSION

(Related Diversification)

A. Products:
    - Rejuvenator Sealer
    - Paving brick installation
    - Thermoplastic striping
    - Sealing building foundations
    - Sell Silica Sand (bulk)
    - Grinding of pavements (milling)
    - Trucking, hauling of waste, septic?
    - Mudjacking
    - Manufacture sealing equipment/tools
    - Exterior cleaning services (sidewalks, exteriors)
    - Provide contract sweeping services
    - HiPressure water jetting

B. Market:
    - Specialize in areas: churches, property management,
                  HUD facilities, factory, chains
    - Expand into regions: Oshkosh, Sheboygan, Rural

C. Technical:
    - Handicap access work
    - Floorings, protective coatings

(Vertical Integration)

    - Broker the sale of sealer and crackfiller
    - Manufacture of tools and equipment

(Horizontal Integration)

    - Start a sweeping service

(Joint Venture)

A. Shared Experience
    - Quote contractors on a fixed-rate schedule as subcontractors

(ie: we'll seal their driveways)
- Follow-up previous years customers of paving customers
B. Competitors:
- Contract their work, in exchange for (?) our doing theirs

WITHIN OUR PRESENT MISSION

(Vacant Niche)

- Offer complete, annual maintenance services for large pavement
  owners and managers

(Specialist)

- Consulting Services: parking maintain, and tennis court

(TLC)

(Distinctive Image)

(Grow and Build)

- Expand capability to install sealer. Our sealcoating equipment
  is not being fully utilized.
- Build organization, invest in people. Develop the role of Adm.
  Assistant. Purpose to have an operational manager to allow me to
  pursue other things.
- Expand crackfilling services
- Small asphalt paving, larger repairs.

(Long-run Focus)

- Provide the personnel incentive for company to grow.
- Look toward a full service organization.

POSSIBILITIES BETWEEN I. AND II.

(Market and Product Development)

- Parking lot maintenance service

STRATEGIC DECISION

I. **VIABLE ALTERNATIVES**

- Develop Marketing Plan (Item B)	Related Diversification
- Emphasis on Property Managers	Related Diversification
- Expand Crackfilling Services	Related Diversification
- Rejuvenator Sealer	Related Diversification
- Subcontracting Expanded (Item A)	Joint Venture
- Expand Asphalt Repair Capacity	Grow & Build
- Consulting: Pavement, Tennis	Specialist
- Pavement Maintenance	Vacant Niche

II. **SWOT ANALYSIS**
Aggressive philosophy. Diversification on existing strength

GRAND STRATEGY SELECTION MATRIX
Market, product development, innovation, or joint venture

MODEL OF GRAND STRATEGY CLUSTERS
Market and product development

III. **COMPARE TO PREMISES (Can Do & Can't Do)**

Condensed List From I.

Marketing Plan Development:
    property managers
    Oshkosh area contractors

Expanded Services:
    rejuvenator sealer
    crackfilling (hot)
    asphalt repairs (larger)
    subcontracting (fabric, grinding, concrete work)

Vacant Niche:
    Pavement maintenance service

Specialist:
Consulting on pavement and tennis

(Analysis)

Marketing Plan

In the past we have not had a formal marketing strategy. Basically, we solicited work through yellow pages, contractors, and public bidding. I believe there is more work available. The common trap is to spend too much time selling small rather low dollar profit jobs. I think it's time to utilize the availability of our past customer files, computer, and office assistant to expand our sales. The payoff is more growth in sales and better types of contracts.

The primary obstacles I see is the limitation on my time. It is apparent that my time is best spent soliciting large accounts. One possible solution is to develop the administrative assistant's role (full time?). Hopefully, this position can pay for itself by yielding greater efficiency, communications, and improved sales. Other possible ways to relieve the sales bottleneck are to use office temporary help for clerical work to relieve and speed up the office work during peak times. This will allow us to turn-around quotations faster and make personal presentations and follow-ups on our bids.

Utilizing the computer, we can expand our mailing list in the off-season to keep in touch with our market and to locate prospects. Contractors in this field have often used this technique although our attempts have been sporadic and unprofessional - yet sometimes effective.

This should not be an overly costly process and actually should more than earn the money spent.

Services

1. **Rejuvenator Sealer:**
    This is an old product which the market place has not seen. It has a higher cost to the customer but offers the additional benefit of rejuvenation over conventional sealers. We already own the basic equipment to apply this product so there is no large start-up costs to incur.

2. **Crackfilling:**
    This is the "hot" topic in our industry. The hard question is whether to get into the hot pour market, which requires an investment of approximately $5-10,000. Used equipment will likely become available in time.

    In the private sector, hot pour crackfilling is still expensive and new. Most customers are paying extra for the hot pour crackfilling but not buying the complete installation that costs even more but makes the whole process worthwhile. These "half-way" type purchases may disappoint those customers who later closely examine the work.

Presently, we are using high-grader cold pour crackfillers and this product will hold acceptance due to reduced costs to the customer plus ease and safety for the contractor.

We are the only one, of the larger contractors, not installing their own hot-pour crackfiller. This has cost us some jobs.

3. **Asphalt Repairs (larger):**
   In 1987 we purchased an old dump truck which now makes hauling a ton of asphalt much easier. There is good profit in asphalt patching, however we are often not equipped to handle larger repairs without subcontracting or renting. Watch for used equipment to handle this need?

4. **Subcontracting:**
   This proved to be a very profitable segment of our business in past years. Our out-of-pocket expense was low and by dealing with good subcontractors, our risks were low. I believe we should aggressively provide any work that our subcontractor base can realistically provide. It also puts us in a better working relationship with some of the contractors.

   The one negative aspect of this program is that the selling effort does not generate any work for our employees. This hasn't been a problem so far.

5. **Additional equipment considerations are:**
   Box truck for the tennis court crew. This would permit them to haul more product and keep the equipment permanently on the truck. It would save some labor costs by reducing loading and would be convenient to the crew. I'm inclined to wait on this item and work on our profitability and cash flow situation.

VACANT NICHE

Pavement Maintenance Service:
This should be an effective idea for past customers and large owners of asphalt. What I'd like to do is contract to maintain their surfaces. To my knowledge this is not being done in Wisconsin.

The idea is to provide all or most of the services a pavement owner is looking for. They are:
- Sweeping
- Crackfilling
- Sealcoating
- Striping
- Repairs

- Snow removal

I can envision this to be attractive to property managers since it should ease their work. Further, properly done, I'm sure this regular care could save our large customers money. Since it is a new idea, it will require selling and I have no idea if it will be as well received as I think.

The advantage I foresee is the development of a large customer base utilizing all of our services on a regular basis. With good relations, I believe contracts will be renewable and competition will be squeezed out. Further, we will have some reliable, steady work to plan on. In general, this idea should work well with our company culture. It may also work in very well with my efforts in consulting (see Specialist).

With a few years of promotion I think this could catch on.

One risk I see is the possible drain on sales time during such a promotional period. This program may require help, so the company's regular sales don't drop. It's possible that many of our regular sales customers will actually accept this proposal at the same time.

Another problem I see is our current lack of ability to provide sweeping and snow plowing services. It is possible that these could be dropped from the list of services or have it subcontracted.

The income from this work will likely be less than we're accustomed to, however the prospect of steadier work may make this worthwhile.

<u>Specialist</u>

For the past two years, I have done consulting work for the Marcus Corporation. I think this has been beneficial to everyone. I believe I should continue this work and strive to expand it.

It would also be a good idea to develop a good idea for monitoring the projects I've done in the past to keep myself active on their care and in some cases it may also find maintenance work for the company.

SUMMARY

1. Develop a Marketing Plan
   A. Key is efficiency
   B. Utilize your assistant

2. Experiment with Rejuvenator Sealer and test market it

3. Crackfilling and Asphalt Repairs

A. Watch for equipment availability
B. Be prepared to purchase when the conditions are right
C. Continue selling using your past installation methods

4. Consulting and Preventative Maintenance

Concerns:
Presently no alternatives for expanding our work season have developed. Perhaps preventative maintenance programs can open doors into property management? Consulting could be more year long also.

IMPLEMENTATION

We will work to aggressively market our current services and expand within our existing framework developing the personnel and equipment resources we already have available.

I. POLICIES AND PROCEDURES

A. Marketing Plan
- Key is efficiency
- Utilize assistant
- Utilize computer, files, contractors
- Increase sealcoating sales

B. Test Market Rejuvenator Sealer
- Offer test samples
- Sell as an option to get pilot jobs

C. Crackfilling and Repairs
- Determine type and dollars willing to spend on equipment
- Continue selling these services as in the past
- Be prepared to buy when conditions are right

D. Consulting
- Be active with Marcus Corp. divisions
- Develop monitoring schedule of past jobs
- Develop references and prospects

E. Preventative Maintenance
   - Test market
   - Develop a pricing framework and try to line up some pilot contracts

F. Profitability
   - Monitor finances
   - Utilize tax and job training programs
   - Monitor labor costs
   - Quick startup in Spring
   - Expand sales
   - Hire early and carefully

DECISION PREMISES

Current Strategy

Assess Environment

Internal Resources

Values, Aspirations,
& Ethics of Management

ALTERNATIVE STRATEGIES

Broadening Our Mission
* Related Diversification
* Vertical Integration
* Horizontal Integration
* Joint Venture

Within Our Present Mission
* Vacant Niche
* Specialist
* TLC
* Distinctive Image

* Grow & Build
* Long-run Focus

STRATEGIC DECISION

Examine viable
Alternatives

Compare to
Premises

FORGE AHEAD!

IMPLEMENTATION

Change Structure?

MOTIVATION!!

Policies &
Procedures

Monitor &
Control

Adapt & Change

CASE E

SOUTHERN CABINET COMPANY

CASE SUMMARY

Southern Cabinet Company (SCC) is a successful, growing, small business ($2.5 million in sales) that seems to have found a niche as a manufacturer and supplier of kitchen and bathroom wooden cabinets for new residential construction. SCC is located in a rapidly growing Sunbelt city. It was founded in 1954 by Bill Martin, who is the current president and chairman. In 1984, there were 32 employees in the shop and 6 in the office. The company's current level of operations seems to be straining the administrative skills of the management team. Bill is faced with a series of major strategic decisions about SCC's future - (1) possible offer to buy the business, (2) sales expansion and the accompanying problems of growth, (3) build his own plant on land recently acquired or other land, (4) organizational changes required to keep the company viable, and (5) how to convince Mike to join SCC. Key personnel are somewhat old and trained successors have not been developed. Bill has a son-in-law, Mike Norris, who has a recent MBA and has been offered a position with the company. The company's financial performance has been extremely sound over the past five years. Many of SCC's competitors were seriously hurt during these years because of high interest rates and high inflation.

CASE OBJECTIVES

1. To provide a vehicle for the examination of the "entrepreneurial spirit."

2. To analyze the operation of a successful, profitable small business.

3. To analyze the financial operations of this small business to determine a fair selling price.

4. To examine the propriety of a conservative growth strategy versus an aggressive expansion strategy.

5. To examine the prospects for a young, well educated, experienced MBA graduate who is considering joining a small business founded and operated by a family member.

6. To evaluate the pros and cons of market niche concentration strategy for a small business.

SUGGESTED CLASSROOM APPROACHES TO THE CASE

1. This is an excellent case to use at the beginning of the course to deal with a maturing Stage I corporation, or as a discussion case anywhere in the course.

2. It is an excellent entrepreneurship case in a basic business (home construction).

3. It allows for a discussion of how this company survived during a period of high inflation and interest, with a solid financial performance.

4. This case allows for a discussion of the strategic objectives of the company and the personal objectives of the owner. He is 64 and has a possible offer to buy his business.

5. It also allows for a discussion of the role his son-in-law, Mike Norris, recent MBA, should play if he accepts an offer to join the company. Also, what issues should be resolved in the offer (gaining interest in company, buy-out plan, training, etc.) to Mike.

QUESTIONS

1. Why has SCC been a profitable small business?

2. What characteristics, behaviors, and traits of Bill Martin correspond with what is known about entrepreneurs?

3. What are the positive and negative factors which Mike Norris should consider before making a decision on Bill Martin's offer to join the business?

4. Is it possible for SCC to slow its growth and consolidate its gains during the next two years?

5. Using the current facilities, how can SCC handle increases in profitable sales?

6. If Bill Martin decided to sell SCC, what would be a fair selling price?

7. What level of sales would be required for profitable operations if Bill Martin decided to build the new facility?

8. If you were in Mike Norris' position and you accepted Bill's offer to be Executive Vice President, what would ;you expect in the way of responsibilities, authority, compensation and career future?

9. What would happen to SCC if Bill Martin became ill or died?

10. What are the major problems facing SCC in the next 5 years?

11. If you were a bank loan officer and Bill approached you for a loan to finance the new facility, what factors would you consider in making your loan decision? What covenants would you place on a loan for $600,000?

12. What are the key ingredients to continued survival and success of SCC?

This case is about a successful, growing, small business that seems to have found a niche as a manufacturer and supplier of cabinets for the residential construction industry. Southern Cabinet Company (SCC) is located in a rapidly growing urban area in the Sunbelt. SCC in the past few years has experienced growth in profit and sales that are even greater than the growth in residential construction in that geographical area. The two key people in the case are Bill Martin, 64, the founder and principle owner and his son-in-law, Mike Norris, 34, a recent MBA graduate who has discussed with and advised Bill about the business, and, at the time of the case is considering joining the management at SCC.

The products of SCC are semi custom-made high quality kitchen and bathroom cabinets. Orders and specifications for cabinets are made by residential contractors through the VP of Sales, Harry Wood. The materials for the cabinets are cut, assembled, finished and stored in an assembly line process. Since manufacturing is done only after orders have been placed, until recently there has been little need for finished inventory storage space. Because of the large increases in sales what was a small storage problem has become a large one and additional nearby storage space has been leased.

The key production management people are Jim Mayo, 70, and Oscar Syatt, 58. The operative level employees (about 25) are hired as unskilled labor, but on-the-job training enables them to have flexibility in performing most of the production jobs. The average pay for these non-union employees is $6.50/hour. During high production periods there is considerable opportunity for overtime, and when units of cabinets (called pieces) exceed 500/week bonuses are paid. Mike has noted that the labor cost of these bonuses increases disproportionately when the production level reaches 800-900 pieces per week.

SCC has used a micro then a minicomputer to handle its accounting and inventory operations. But the current computer and software system may not be able to handle a large expansion in business.

The current managerial and administrative staff seems to be very effective, loyal, and committed to SCC, and hourly employees are hard-working and loyal with a minimum of turnover.

Even though the early 80s recession caused some decrease in the rate of residential construction, SCC has shown a steady increase in sales and profit. Based upon sales figures for the early months of 1984, record sales of $2.5 million are expected. With this increasing level of business SCC is faced with the following:

1. Even though finished pieces are held only a few weeks, additional storage space is needed.
2. The lease on the current building which houses manufacturing and administration offices has increased to $5600/month and the current lease expires in late 1984.
3. SCC recently purchased 3 acres of land for $90,000 and had architectural and engineering plans developed for a new $800,000 facility.
4. Since purchasing the land, its value has increased to $250,000.
5. The new facility, if properly operated, will more than double SCC's capacity, and when operated near capacity will reduce variable and average cost/unit considerably.
6. Bill believes that some stock pieces would smooth production cycles. But there are obvious advantages and disadvantages to this option.

Recently Bill has been approached by a business broker who has discussed with Bill the possibility of selling the business. Bill does not seem particularly interested in selling because he seems to enjoy the stimulation of the business.

FINANCIAL RATIO ANALYSIS
Southern Cabinet Company
*1984 data ends April 30, 1984

YEARS

	1979	1980	1981	1982	1983	1984
RATIOS						
Liquidity Ratios						
Current	2.47	2.44	3.35	4.97	4.86	12.67
Quick	1.74	1.81	2.42	3.59	3.56	9.21
Inventory to Net Working Capital	.50	.44	.39	.35	.34	.30
Cash Ratio	.32	.82	1.22	2.11	1.76	4.98
Profitability Ratios						
Net Profit Margin	5.8	10.5	12.8	7.9	9.1	15.9
Gross Profit Margin	22.4	29.4	31.8	26.1	29.2	30.1
ROI	20.2	25.2	33.4	20.0	20.0	23.1
ROE	26.7	28.0	29.2	16.6	15.9	24.6
EPS	N/A	N/A	N/A	N/A	N/A	N/A
Productivity of Assets	1.2	1.0	1.0	.7	.7	N/A
Activity Ratios						
Inventory Turnover	12.7	12.1	10.6	10.6	10.1	7.1
Days of Inventory	37	42	50	46	51	74
Net Working Capital Turnover	6.3	5.3	4.2	3.7	3.4	2.1
Asset Turnover	3.5	2.4	2.6	2.5	2.2	1.5
Fixed Asset Turnover	51.6	16.9	25.4	22.6	12.1	7.1
Average Collection Period	53	41	41	34	46	58
A/R Turnover	7.0	8.8	9.0	10.9	7.9	6.3
Accounts Payable Period						
Cash Turnover	12.6	39.3	45.1	52.9	49.0	74.3
Leverage Ratios						
Debt Ratio	37.7	36.2	28.4	17.6	16.8	5.9
Debt to Equity	.6	.6	.4	.2	.2	.1
L.T. Debt to Total Capital	.002	.07	.03	.004	0	0
Times Interest Earned	N/A	N/A	N/A	N/A	N/A	N/A
Coverage of Fixed Charges	N/A	N/A	N/A	N/A	N/A	N/A
Current Liabilities to Equity	60.3	49.2	36.8	21.0	20.2	6.3
Other Ratios						
Price Earnings	N/A	N/A	N/A	N/A	N/A	N/A
Dividend Payout	N/A	N/A	N/A	N/A	N/A	N/A
Dividend Yield	N/A	N/A	N/A	N/A	N/A	N/A
Cash Flow/Share	N/A	N/A	N/A	N/A	N/A	N/A

Net Working Capital
1979: 243484; 1980: 267254; 1981: 456230
1982: 521787; 1983: 579767; 1984: 723470

CASE F

GAL-TECH AND MELANIN

CASE SUMMARY

Gal-Tech Corporation is a Texas Corporation chartered in December, 1987. Gal-Tech's principal product is a melanin concentrate. This concentrate is then incorporated into glass and plastic products, specifically sunglasses.

Melanin is a natural product found in the skin and the human eye. It is nature's way of protecting the human eye from light radiation, as it absorbs the harmful light rays in proportion to their damaging effects. Competitors' methods of blocking the harmful effects of the sun are not only less effective, but sacrifice color vision.

Gal-Tech is now actively pursuing product manufacturers to incorporate the melanin concentrate into their products. In order to expand its marketing and production facilities, Gal-Tech is seeking capitalization of $250,000.00 This capitalization will provide plant and equipment, and management, marketing, and production personnel. Firms in the sunglass industry have already shown an interest in melanin. This industry had sales in 1987 of $1.3 billion. Gal-Tech projects that in three years it will conservatively have gross annual sales and license fees of $1,710,000. Based on this project, Return on Equity will be approximately 35 percent. After three years in operation, income is expected to grow rapidly as the public becomes more aware of the product and more uses are discovered for it.

James Gallas, Ph.D. is the inventor and developer of the melanin concentrate. He is the Chairman of the Board of Gal-Tech Corporation. It is through his insight and guidance that melanin will become the consumer's choice in radiation protection. Dr. Gallas has chosen Dr. Melvin Eisner, Ph.D., who has been working with him since 1982 in the development of the melanin concentrate, to be President of the corporation. Other officers and management personnel will be included on the basis of the overall needs of the corporation, including production, administration and finance, and marketing.

Students read the material in the first part of the case and then analyze the opportunity and the business plan that is written by the case author.

OBJECTIVES OF THE CASE

This case will give students an opportunity to analyze a business plan designed to bring a new invention, melanin concentrate, to market. The case is suitable for graduate or undergraduate courses in policy, entrepreneurship, or technology transfer. The case could be introduced to the students as an example of technology transfer. The situation this case describes is an example of one of America's strengths: technological innovation and ingenuity in creating new products and services. The focus of the case is on bridging the gap between the scientific aspects of technology and the reality of operating a business through the vehicle of a business plan. It is intended that the students examine the case, analyze the information and the business plan that presents a strategy that will hopefully make this venture a business success.

TEACHING STRATEGY

Begin an open class discussion about the importance of technology and innovation, mention their role in the industrial revolution of the eighteenth and nineteenth centuries and highlight the relevance of technology in maintaining industrial competitiveness in the twentieth century and perhaps speculate into what is coming in the twenty-first. Then, indicate that an example of an opportunity for such business evolution is Gal-Tech. The students' role is to carry it out. The invention process tends to arouse the students' interest, but they should be led to conduct a thorough examination of the facts. Instructors should ask specific questions of the students to avoid off-the-wall general comments which have little depth.

Ask the students to act as business consultants and utilize all their skills to guarantee that this scientific discovery can be considered a commercial success.

1. **Analyze the business plan. Does it appear to be in an appropriate format? Does it make a convincing case for investment?**

The plan uses a format which is acceptable. It might be somewhat weak in the analysis of the market, but it covers other areas sufficiently well. Making a "compelling" case is difficult with a totally new product. It does, however, explain the nature of the product to the extent that risk-prone investors should at least be interested in additional investigation.

2. **How can Gallas extent the protection of his patent beyond the 17 year protection?**

   A. He can develop a trade name such as "galenite" which would remain proprietary after the patent has run out.

   B. He could continue to invent and patent new uses and methods of incorporating melanin into other products. Each new patent would have a 17 year life.

3. **Can a world-wide global perspective be attempted? How can Gallas participate in this globalization of markets?**

   A. Licensing.

   B. Patent in specific foreign countries.

4. **What can Gallas do if someone infringes on his patent?**

   A. Use the legal power of his lawyers.

5. **Develop a SWOT analysis of Gal-Tech.**

   Strengths:
   - new unique and natural idea, performs better than existing products
   - patent ownership
   - contact with not only manufacturers, but with the distributors as well
   - Gallas manufactures the product himself
   - low production costs and short production period

   Weaknesses:
   - financial backing (lack of capital)
   - too eager to offer a percentage of the company as a form of pay
   - lack of business experience - no demonstrated success in developing a successful business product

   Opportunities:
   - growing health consciousness about eye protection among consumers
   - rapid expansion of the sunglass industry (sales increasing)

- interest of well established sunglass companies
- new markets (windows, contact lenses)

Threats:
- there are already companies established that produce an eye protection block
- public may not like the "look" of the new glasses
- FDA approval for contact lenses

CASE G

MOVIES R US: A CASE STUDY

CASE SUMMARY

This is an actual case. The names and locations have been changed to disguise the identity of the people involved, but the details are accurate. The dialogue has been dramatized, but is a close representation of the actual interview.

The case requires the student to extract from the interviews and exhibits relevant information for a diagnosis of the firm's problems. The case displays an excellent example of failure to manage. The owner/manager in the case is in reality trying to manage in absentia. The firm simply drifts without guidance and is in an industry which is no longer profitable to small independents absent constant attention.

TEACHING APPROACHES

The analysis is lacking complete financial information because of the owner's unwillingness to share that information with the consultants. Some industry information is given as well as some financial averages. The data in the case is sufficient to glean an understanding of key problems.

The case has several problems and these can be attacked in a variety of ways. Should Ms. Peters sell the business or can she save it? Are there strategies she can use to generate more business? Should she stay in business, but diversify? What are the strengths and weaknesses of the business?

The owner's answers to the telephone questions and the observations of the consultants can be used as a basis for evaluating management competency. As the questions and answers indicate, Ms. Peters wanted advice, but was unwilling to give any assistance to the consultants. In their recommendations, the consultants addressed the lack of stability, the lack of attention to image in a company which had just proven unsuccessful, and the difficulty associated with absentee management and decision making. Also mention was made of the target market. In a small town with perhaps less than 10,000 inhabitants and a college population of 6,000, should the students not be targeted?

QUESTIONS

1. **What is the main problem presented by the case and its attendant circumstances?**

The problem is that Ms. Peters had just reacquired a business in which she has little interest. She does not actively manage the firm but wants to retain decision making powers. She does not have an in-house manager and all decisions must wait for her attention. Her selections are not varied with an incredible number of videos on war and western themes, perhaps assuming that small-town farmers like those types of videos. She has made no changes in the store image or policies. The only noticeable difference is the name change back to Movies R Us. There is not even an announcement made indicating that the store is back under its original more successful management.

2. **What situation gives you a clue that the consultants are going to have a difficult time with this client?**

Ms. Peters makes two appointments for which she does not show and then tells the clerks not to give out any financial information when they talk to the consultants.

3. **What should Movies R Us be able to track with a state of the art computer system? What seems to be the problem?**

All inventory and sales information should be tracked as well as a breakeven and a profit/loss indication for each video in stock. Particulars about the membership and their interests could also be tracked. A reservation system could also be used effectively by producing a daily listing of what is available and what is requested by whom with their phone numbers. The problem seems to be lack of training on the system by the users as evidenced by Cindy's surprise at the reports capability of the system. The information may well be available, but the staff is using the system like an automated cash register.

4. **The owner was asked about the strength of the company and the response was that stability was its strength. What do you think about that response?**

How can stability be a strength when the company has just failed under the interim owner? Ms. Peters sold a profitable company to an individual and was forced to repossess it one year later. Now she herself is experiencing some problems which may well be a holdover from the previous management but what has she done to differentiate herself from Mr. Cuthbert? It would seem that she has done nothing.

5. **The owner was asked about the bases of competition for the firm. Do you agree from the response that the bases of competition are service, selection and prices?**

The answer seems to be one given without much thought. The service is clearly not a component because of the shorter hours, the lack of a night deposit for rentals, and the unavailability of a reservation system. Prices seem to be the same or higher and the selection is questionable. Does quality of selection mean multiple copies of a few tapes or two or three copies of many tapes?

6. **Based on the information on the supporting documentation, do the personnel have the qualifications to make critical decisions about the firm?**

Perhaps the bookkeeper could make some educated guesses about the inventory, if the information were available. Those persons working more often in the store might also be able to make decisions based upon observation and requests, but they have no authority to make decisions even about policies such as running specials.

7. **Based on the information given about Beverly Hills Cop 2, did the store make a profit? Why or why not?**

Using the cost of $89.95 for 9 tapes, the expense was $809.55. The total revenue from rentals of the 9 tapes was $499.49, meaning that there was a loss of $310.06 on one of the best-selling videos of that year. If other inventory decisions were similar, which appears to be the case, then purchases as well as selection needs to be investigated.

8. **Examine the supporting information of the partial inventory. What would you do about the selection process?**

There are extreme numbers of expensive movies. Perhaps the rental has fallen off, because there are now fewer customers. It appears that multiples of expensive films are not meeting the desires of the target market. By contrast, the multiples of less expensive movies seem to be performing better. Could this be an indication of the competition? Multiples which have low checkout rates versus single copies always rented can be tracked by the computer and should be. Even an eyeball count would reveal an entire shelf of Platoon still in inventory on this given day. Obviously, the inventory needs to be tracked.

9. What would be some recommendations for this company if it stays in business?

In order to be competitive on the bases indicated, Movies R Us must modify their operating procedures. Store hours should be revised to capitalize on late-night business. A reservation system should be adopted and its use promoted to all customers.

The company could promote service by placing an employee on the floor to offer assistance and recommendations to shoppers rather than just responding to requests. The bit-screen television should also be utilized to attract attention and generate interest in available movies not just as an entertainment for the clerks.

Actual price is less important that the consumer perception of a bargain. Changing the specials periodically creates an image of value. One method might be to promote specials on movies with a particular theme, actor, or character. A new section of the store could be dedicated to these weekly specials creating an opportunity to generate rentals that would not otherwise occur.

Availability of movies is important. Purchases should be based on record keeping and historic data to minimize unrented movies. Guesswork is dangerous and should not play a role in purchasing decisions.

When the movies arrive, they should be grouped, clearly defined and labelled for each access. A section labelled New Releases would also be appropriate and maintained so that movies popular for many years would not be so shelved.

If the manager is going to be absent, then decision making and planning should involve the employees who are on site. Those involved with daily operations are cognizant of facts often overlooked by management. Staff meetings and brainstorming sessions are valuable source of ideas for management. A managerial position might well be developed for decision making, assessing competition and planning for success. Most importantly, the manager needs to be actively involved, concerned and willing to implement necessary changes.

10. Should the business be sold?

The owner/manager is not even interested enough to participate in a review of the store's position. Given this level of disinterest, the best option is to sell the business if possible. Managerial behavior change is required for success and the present owner seems disinclined to make any significant changes.

11. If the business cannot be sold, what are the prospects?

It is unlikely that the business can be sold as a video store. There are already six proclaimed video stores in this small town not counting the rentals which take place in department, grocery and convenience stores. The best solution may be the liquidation of the inventory, equipment and fixtures through sales to customers and/or competitors and the subleasing of the store for the duration of the lease.

12. Notice that the industry contains material through 1988. Bring that information up to date through an industry analysis using Standard and Poors, Moodys, Valueline or other sources. What is happening to the industry? Can small independent outlets continue to be successful? Why or why not?

This answer may well depend on the timing in which the case is studied. We suspect that chains such as Blockbuster and increased sales through mail order and department stores will squeeze the small independents out of the major market areas.

In the smaller market areas, proliferation of video stores has intensified the competition. The smaller market combined with the larger number of competitors makes survival ever more difficult.

CASE H

CAMPGROUND FOR SALE! -- SOLD!

OVERVIEW

This is an actual case. The names and locations have been changed to disguise the identity of the people involved, but the details are accurate. The dialogue has been dramatized, but is a close representation of the actual interview.

The case requires the student to extract from the interviews and exhibits relevant information for an evaluation of the worth of a small business. The case is an excellent representation of the American dream faced with harsh reality. Like most people who start and manage small businesses, the Calvins have little business experience and have failed to consider the prospects for success or failure in this venture. They are ready to invest their life savings and yet they have no conception of what is required for the business to survive nor the probability of that survival.

TEACHING APPROACHES

The case is lacking complete financial information because of its lack of availability. This is a typical problem in consulting or working with small business ventures. Nevertheless, the data in the case is sufficient to assess the prospective purchase.

Students may be assigned to determine what information is required to assess the purchase decision and to investigate whether that information is contained in the interview or exhibits. Questions listed in the following section may be assigned as part of a written case report or used as a basis for class discussion. Further, a written assignment could require students to critique the interview from the perspective of questions which should have been asked. Finally, the case lends itself to a role playing situation because it deals with plans and dreams which are emotional as well as financial.

QUESTIONS

1. **The principal question asked by the client is whether the campground is worth its asking price, however, that is not the client's real question. What is the real question and why is the distinction important?**

The client's real question is, "Can we be successful if we purchase this campground for the price quoted?" This question incorporates the stated one but goes far beyond in that it deals with the probability that the client will have the financial, managerial and marketing expertise to make the venture successful. Worth simply deals with the issue of whether the prospective return is sufficient to justify the price, while the larger issue treats the purchase as a component affecting the cash outflows.

2. **Given that data is incomplete how would you approach the idea of evaluating the quoted price of the business?**

The best approach is to begin with a cash based break-even analysis which uses the first and second mortgage payments as part of the fixed requirements. The analysis should be reported in terms of occupancy capacity required for break-even during the camping season.

3. **Prepare a break-even analysis on the case basis with and without an owner's draw. Express the answer in terms of occupancy ratio considering a camping season of six months and subjectively evaluate the resulting ratios.**

The major component of the variable expenses is electricity, but that, like other variables is so small that it can be ignored and treated as though it were fixed. The sales of the campground store have been insignificant based on the size of the 'cost of goods sold' reported on the income statement. Historic labor costs will be irrelevant as will be depreciation. In fact, the only relevant significant costs will be payments on the first and second mortgage, repairs, utilities, advertising and insurance. From the interview data, mortgage payments will be $1,335 ($460 + $875) per month or $16,020 per year. If utilities are forecast at $3,000 per year, repairs at $2,000, insurance at $1,500, and advertising at $2,000, total cash expenses without considering labor or owner's draw will be $24,520. If we assume that the owners will wish to take a draw equal to their present income of $40,000, the total cash expenses will be $64,520.

There are 64 camp-sites available during the 180 day camping season, or 11,520 potential revenue nights. If the average income produced by those sites is $10 per day as forecast by the client, the break-even will be as follows:

BEP = $24,520/$10 = 2,452 nights
2,452/11,520 = 21% average occupancy
BEP = $64,520/$10 = 6,452 nights
6,452/11,520 = 56% average occupancy

Clearly, these break-even forecasts are less than desirable because the data upon which they are based is so rough. Nevertheless, the analysis permits some initial conclusions to be drawn.

First, the analysis would indicate that the campground can probably support itself if no labor costs or owner's draw is required and if there are no hidden or unexpected costs or renovations. A draw for the owners is required in the near future. The analysis leads to deep concern about the ability of the campground to support the owners. It seems highly improbable that a small, unknown campground operated by total neophytes could expect to be over half full on every single night of a six month camping season.

4. What would be the result of a lower price?

The mortgage payments are the principal component of the fixed costs. A little investigation will show that the second mortgage, to be carried by the present owner, is being amortized over 10 years at 10%. Should the purchase price drop by 10% ($112,500) and all other components remain the same, the new second mortgage payment would be $8,484 ($112,500-$39,000-$20,000 = $53,500; $53,500 @ 10% for 10 years = $707/month). The new cash outflows would be $44,484 and $62,484. The new break-evens would be 20% and 54%. A 10% drop in price does not dramatically affect break-even. A much higher, and therefore improbable, price break would be required.

5. What significance does a year-to-year lease on the surrounding property have for this venture?

There can be no assurance of the availability of the land beyond a single year. If the availability of the land is crucial to the success of the venture, the short term nature of the lease is probably sufficient to make the purchase undesirable.

6. What would you recommend to the client?

Given the managerial inexperience of the couple, the fact that the campground is not now functioning and will require an unknown amount of work and marketing to bring it back into operation and given the fact that the business has never generated sales close to those required to support the clients, and considering that the clients will be risking their life savings, the recommendation should be "Do not purchase this business."

CASE I

CHRISTIAN'S

CASE SUMMARY

This case provides the teacher with a useful tool for introducing students to the process of evaluation and analysis of an investment opportunity. The realism of the case is reflected by the questionable figures provided by the current owners. The student must be able to discern fact from fiction when coming to an investment decision. The case incorporates the use of several financial tools in the analysis stage, however, the student is also required to examine several environmental factors and place a value on their weight in the final decision.

CASE OBJECTIVES

1. To expose the student to the thinking process and work needed to evaluate a business investment opportunity.

2. To carry the thinking process to the final stage of either accepting the plans or abandoning such investment opportunity.

3. To examine environmental factors and determine their value in the final decision.

4. To understand that financial data is not always accurate and to recognize these inaccuracies in information.

SUGGESTED CLASSROOM APPROACHES TO THE CASE

The case offers a high degree of flexibility to the instructor. It could be handled with emphasis on the financial aspects or on other issues with less emphasis on the financial aspects. The recommended approach is to consider, but not to overemphasize, the calculations due to the lack of sufficient data to make these figures highly reliable. The instructor's notes are provided as suggestions for the instructor: to be supplemented and tailored to the specifics of the class.

The figures obtained in the case are presented here with few changes. These figures include many assumptions, inconsistencies and numbers that are difficult to explain. However, this adds to the realism. Following are some examples of questionable figures.

Exhibit 2, Profit and Loss Statement, contains errors and raises many questions. For example, the operating expenses should include only depreciation and interest on business loans, equipment payments and car payments. The full payment amounts are not deductible expenses. Payments include return of principal that cannot be deducted as an expense, even if we agreed with treating all these items as business related.

Also on Exhibit 2, the period from June 13, 1983 to October 31, 1983, has advertising expenses of $2,750 even though the case states that $2,750 represents advertising expenses for a full year. Obviously, this profit and loss statement is not accurate and reflects the owners' ignorance of accounting principles.

The balance sheet in Exhibit 9 lists fixed assets as $22,300 even though the accountant estimated their market value at $11,175.

QUESTIONS

1. Describe the nature of the restaurant industry.

2. What methods of valuation should be used in the decision process by the group of students?

3. How significant is the value of Goodwill in the decision? How will this affect financing of the venture?

4. What incongruencies do you see in the provided figures? What should they be?

5. What weight should be placed on the environmental factors affecting the restaurant?

6. Can such a venture be successful under absentee ownership? How vital is the entrepreneurial spirit of the original owners to the success of Christian's?

7. What are the Pros and Cons of the investment proposal?

Issues

The issues involved in this case include valuation of a going concern, determination of market potential, estimating sales, preparing pro forma statements, determining the needed financing and selecting sources of financing, negotiating the purchase and balancing the risk and return considerations associated with the venture.

Several questions may be asked before the decision to undertake the project is made. They are: (1) Is Christian's a good investment? (2) Is Christian's a good bargain in terms of return on investment at the $57,750 asking price? (3) Is it possible to convince the owners to sell it at a lower price? (4) How can the needed funds be raised? (5) Are the expected returns worth it in terms of the risks involved? (6) What form of organization would be the best to use in terms of legal responsibility, in reduction in the tax burden? (7) Can the group handle unforeseen circumstances? (8) Is this investment viable under the most likely events without undue optimism and wishful thinking? (9) Can the group of investors work harmoniously to manage the investment without undermining their other objectives such as school or work?

Pros and Cons of the Investment

Christian's as an investment seems to be promising for the following reasons: (a) The business is profitable. (b) The restaurant has a developed group of loyal customers. (c) Charlottesville seems to be an expanding area with regard to income. (d) If the apparently popular seafood is introduced, the business could be even more successful. (e) The business seems to run itself without much need for constant monitoring. That makes the investment congruent with the objectives of the prospective owners. (f) The expected return on investment seems to be adequate and immediate. (g) The inexpensive food business in general seems to offer a business that is less vulnerable to economic downturns. (h) The determination, persistence, energy and open-mindedness of the students would give a chance for the business to grow. (i) The existence of well-established business organization is vital.

Some of the unfavorable arguments include the following. (a) If the business opportunity is so great, why would the owners be willing to sell it? (b) Present owners are planning to open a new restaurant that may draw customers from Christian's. (c) The asked price for Christian's far exceeds the net assets which results in payment for goodwill. This goodwill is hard to measure and may disappear shortly after the old owners leave. Additionally, the goodwill figure could not be depreciated for tax purposes and would deprive the owners of the additional depreciation associated with paying the extra costs for depreciable assets. (d) The students lack the experience in the restaurant business. This inexperience may prove to be a handicap. (e) Absentee ownership in a restaurant business is viewed by many to be a guarantee for failure. (f) While 25% required return may seem high, it is before taxes and based on doubtful estimates. (g) The students do not have their own resources. Most of the funds will be borrowed from the bank or from relatives. This would result in placing extra burdens on the new managers. Also, it will make it difficult for them to withstand any difficulties that may be encountered in the beginning. (h) Dealing with employees in the restaurant business is usually a frustrating experience. It is a highly labor intensive business with much dependence on unskilled, usually less reliable (absenteeism and turnover), pool of potential employees.

Price and Return

The total investment will be $57,750. The $500 organization expense was ignored because it can be paid from income from operations and is included in current liabilities. Additional working capital may be needed for business. Also, an allowance must be made for unforeseen circumstances.

Even though the market value of the fixed assets as listed by the CPA is $11,175, the relevant figures in buying a business are the expected earnings and cash flow. Capitalization of earnings is the right approach to use.

The sales figures for years 1, 2, 3, 4 and 5 can be adjusted as follows to estimate related cash flows.

	Years of Operation (000's)				
	1	2	3	4	5
Sales	240.0	264.0	272.0	272.0	272.0
Variable Expenses 68%	163.2	179.5	185.0	185.0	185.0
Operating Margin (32%)	76.8	84.5	87.0	87.0	87.0
Fixed Expenses (see Ex. 8)	42.0	40.8	40.9	42.4	42.4
Earnings before interest & taxes	34.8	43.7	46.1	44.6	44.6
Interest	6.0*	5.1*	4.1*	2.9*	1.6*
Earnings before bonus & taxes	28.8	38.6	42.0	41.7	43.0
Bonus 10%	2.9	3.9	4.2	4.2	4.3
Taxable Earnings	25.9	34.7	37.8	37.5	38.7
Add Back Depreciation	4.4	4.4	4.4	4.4	4.4
	30.3	39.1	42.2	41.9	43.1
Add Back Interest	6.0	5.1	4.1	2.9	1.6
Est. Cash flows ignoring loan	36.3	44.2	46.3	44.8	44.7
Loan Service	-12.0	-12.0	-12.0	-12.0	-12.0
Salvage					+20.0
Revised Cash Flows	$24.3	$32.2	$34.3	$32.8	$52.7

*Interest is based on the following amortization schedule, for a $40,250 loan at 15% annual interest rate with five year life and five annual payments at the end of each year.

End of Year	Remaining Loan Balance	Annual Payment	Interest	Reduction Principle
0	40,250	0	0	0
1	34,281	12,007	6,038	5,969
2	27,416	12,007	5,142	6,865
3	19,521	12,007	4,112	7,895
4	10,442	12,007	2,928	9,079
5	1*	12,007	1,566	10,441

*Error is due to rounding

The internal rate of return for this investment project based on the cash flows listed above can be computed two ways.

1. The IRR based on an investment of $57,750 and the estimated cash flows ignoring the loan is 66%. The $57,750 investment covers both the loan and the students' own investment, so to compare this investment to its related cash flows, we add back depreciation and interest.

2. The IRR based on the $17,500 equity investment in the business and the revised cash flows is 158%. The $17,500 equity investment does not include the $40,250 bank loan, so the annual loan payment was subtracted in order to compare the equity investment to its related cash flows. The IRR computed on the equity investment shows the effect of financial leverage.

(A calculator was used to compute the IRR. Manual calculations may result in a slightly different answer.)

It seems from a quick examination that the price is very reasonable. The sales estimates used assume a 10% increase in Year 2 over Year 1, 3% increase in Year 3 over Year 2, and no increase in Years 4 and 5. These estimates are very conservative. Care must be taken in studying the cash flow estimates to insure that the net cash flows reflect all cash outflows. There is a tendency to underestimate costs and overestimate benefits. Comparisons can be made between Christian's experience and cost ratios in similar restaurants as found in various services such as local businesses, associations or Robert Morris Associates or Dun & Bradstreet Key Business Ratios. This comparison may reveal areas where costs are underestimated and revenues are over-estimated.

Another way of looking at the situation is to ask the following question: If it costs approximately $58,000 to acquire the business, if the minimum required return before taxes is 25%, and if the business could be sold at various prices, what is the minimum annual cash flow required to satisfy these conditions? The answers, depending upon salvage value are:

Salvage Value Before Taxes	Minimum Annual Cash Flows that Would Yield 25%
$-----0	$21,567
10,000	20,349
15,000	19,739
20,000	19,130
25,000	18,521
30,000	17,912
35,000	17,302
40,000	16,693
45,000	16,084
50,000	15,475

(A calculator was used to compute these figures. Manual calculations may result in slightly different figures.)

Can the Price be Reduced

The price for any business depends upon the circumstances surrounding the transaction and the bargaining skills of the involved parties. An evaluation should be made of the likelihood that present owners could settle for a lesser price.

Financing by Owners

To reduce the dependency on bank credit and to get the present owner's interest in future success of the business, the students should explore the possibility of asking present owners to receive part of their payment on a cash basis and the other as a loan payable with interest comparable to the bank rate and as a percentage of future earnings. However, tying the new business closely to old owners is not advisable in the management area since it reduces the chances of implementing innovative ideas.

The students should also satisfy themselves that they have explored enough financing sources to get the best loan possible with regard to interest rate, loan life, and other terms. Contrary to public opinion, it pays to shop around for loans.

Harmony Among the New Investors

The investors should study themselves and take a hard look at their interests and personalities. Needed work and areas of responsibility must be divided in advance. Partners in small corporations are similar to partners in a partnership. They must be able to get along and agree on direction and approach to managing the business. Agreements should be made in writing and details should be stated as much as possible prior to entering into such a joint venture. What would happen if a partner wants to get his money back? How will differences in philosophy be resolved? Who will decide on general management, marketing, operations, and financing issues? Also, how much distribution of income will be expected and how will failure or success and growth be handled?

Time Element

The students were asked to make up their minds within ten days because other individuals were interested in the business. Accordingly, the analysis must be quick yet complete as possible.

Forecasts

The provided figures are fundamental to the analysis. Therefore, a careful examination of the underlying estimates is needed. Do the cost estimates include all elements of costs and do they allow for inflation? Are sales estimates reasonable? What is the effect of future competition on these estimates? Are menu prices competitive? What is the effect of the increasingly popular fast food business on Christian's price structure and cost factors? Are fixed assets in good condition? What additional investments are needed in this area?

Other factors that could affect the success of the business include the reaction of the current employees to the change in management. Also the cook is a key individual in the success of a restaurant. What are the chances that the cook would like the present changes? Would the cook be willing to accept new changes in the menu?

With regard to the new manager to be hired, how can management insure his interest and attention to the business? How would old employees react to the new manager? How would the customers react to the new manager?

What about thefts in restaurants and lack of internal controls? Would the new manager be able to handle the situation?

Variable Versus Fixed Costs

Fixed expenses amount to about $42,000. With variable expenses of 68%, the contribution margin is 32%. Accordingly, a minimum sales level needed to cover fixed costs is about $131,250 (42,000/0.32). This amounts to average monthly sales (ignoring the seasonal nature) of about $11,000.

Concluding Remarks

The students are faced with various alternative courses of action. They can go ahead and acquire Christian's as planned or they can forget about this opportunity and look for another investment. They can also elect to make a counter-offer to the current owner that is less than the asked price for the business. Conversely, the price could be raised if the owners would be willing to sign a no competition agreement within a range of 100 miles for a five-year period.

Several pro forma financial statements could be prepared using varying assumptions to determine the effect on earnings and cash flows. This would help in making a better decision.

Based on the information provided above, Christian's restaurant business is a good investment. However, due to the lack of sufficient historical data, the uncertainties involved in the restaurant business with regard to competition and volume of business and due to the rather vague notion why the owners are willing to sell such a great business, the investment should be classified as a speculative venture.

In the real situation, due to the pressure involved to make a quick decision and due to the school situation, the deal fell through and the students decided to let this opportunity pass by.

CASE J

MARTIN ENTERPRISES
"WHAT ARE WE WORTH?"

CASE SUMMARY

The CEO and the board of directors of Martin Enterprises are struggling to determine just how much their company is worth. This situation was precipitated when two major shareholders became dissatisfied and indicated that they wanted to liquidate their interest in the company. The two dissatisfied shareholders own over 25% of the common stock. An investment banking firm was employed to determine the value of the company for the purpose of establishing a fair purchase price for the stock. Then three unsolicited offers to purchase the entire company were received from outside investors. The case contains a detailed description of the process for estimating the value of a business conglomerate. The actual valuation performed by the investment banking consultant is included as an exhibit in the case. One of the prospective purchasers takes exception to the valuation process used by the investment banker and this is also included as an exhibit.

Students are asked to assume the CEO's role and (1) evaluate the criticism of the valuation process, (2) put the three purchase offers into a common framework and evaluate them, and (3) make a recommendation for acceptance or rejection. This case can be used in an undergraduate or graduate level business policy course or in a senior level financial management course. A working knowledge of the net present value methodology is assumed.

TEACHING OBJECTIVES

The basic objectives of the case is to provide the student with the experience of determining what a company is worth. The case presents summaries of the actual reports that were available to the decision-maker and used to arrive at a recommendation to the board. An opportunity is provided to use financial analysis (NPV) to compare the purchase offers. In addition, the availability of the actual valuation and critique provide a real-world experience that should aid the student in understanding the process and analysis used in determining what a shareholder's equity is worth. Since one of the prospective purchasers takes significant exception to the valuation performed by the investment banker, this must be dealt with. There is a shareholder issue that lurks beneath the surface; namely, how does the CEO and the board prioritized the needs of the two groups of shareholders (those who wish to sell and those who wish to keep their stock)? If they act to serve the interests of one group, will this create an inequity to the other group? Does one group deserve more consideration than the other? Can the issue be avoided?

The author recommends that these issues be dealt with in the following order: First, consider the criticisms of the Armstrong & Cochran Report that are made by Westcor. This will require that the student study and understand both the A&C report (Exhibit 1) and the Westcor reply (Exhibit 2). If all or some of the criticisms are valid, then perhaps the price that shareholders should expect to receive for their stock should be reduced.

Second, place the three offers into a common framework so that they can be fairly compared. Third, prioritized the two stockholder groups; that is, decide which group management must strive to serve when a conflict arises. When these sub-issues have been dealt with, a recommendation can be made to the board of directors.

QUESTIONS

1. **Don Choice, representing Westcor Holdings, makes several criticisms of the valuation of ME calculated by the investment banker firm, Armstrong & Cochran. Are some or all of these criticisms valid? Do you believe that the A&C valuation should be adjusted downward? Substantiate your recommendation.**

    The thrust of the criticism made by Westcor is that the valuation of ME by A&C is too high. The instructor may wish to raise the following points and/or others before making the assignment. Or, the instructor can defer comment until the assignment has been completed and raise these points during the case discussion.

a.   While it is possible that A&C has made some mistakes in analysis or that its assumptions are unrealistic, it is a reputable investment banking firm and has experience in making valuations of businesses.

b.   A&C has nothing to gain from overvaluing ME.

c.   If A&C made mistakes or unrealistic assumptions, it is unlikely that all of these would produce errors in the same direction; that is, to systematically overvalue ME. More likely, mistakes or the effects of questionable assumptions would balance out.

d.   Westcor is a prospective purchaser. It has a vested interest in making its offer look attractive to Walka and the ME board of directors. The A&C valuation is significantly higher than what Westcor has offered. This difference has to be explained away.

Given these cautions, it is still the CEO's responsibility to evaluate the Westcor criticisms in a rational, systematic manner and make his opinion available to the board. Below is a brief evaluation of each of the criticisms raised:

The scope of the A&C report is limited. A&C responded to the request by Walka board. This is a difficult issue to evaluate and is the subject of Question 3. Briefly, the author's position is that the request made by Walka and the board was entirely appropriate. The particular issue of concern is how to buy out those shareholders who are adamant to sell.

A&C did not highlight the cyclicality of the whole portfolio of businesses. This is a weak argument, at best. Virtually all businesses are harmed by recessions. Is there evidence to suggest that department stores, home centers, ranches, tourism (i.d., Bryce Canyon Division) will suffer more than the general economy? To a small extent, yes. But should not this be the responsibility of the buyer to determine? Should the agent performing the valuation assume the worst case in making his analysis? This argument does not weaken the A&C valuation.

The A&C valuation methodology is incomplete:
The discount rate use in the study is too low. Westcor shows that the value of the company to both the buyer and the seller depends on the discount rate used. While this is unarguably true, it is virtually always a point of contention in the buying/selling of a business. The author's position is that while one could make an argument that 13.5% is too low for a conglomerate with the problems of ME, any risk premium above 5% will be difficult to substantiate to the selling shareholders. In addition, the primary trouble spot in the company, the Department Store Division, is being marketed for sale or liquidation. There is no basis for

lowering the valuation because of the discount rate. Interestingly, the discount rate used has a significant impact on the present value of each of the three offers.

The valuation of the building materials division is excessive.
One must deal with the following argument to assess this criticism.
The liquidation value of the retail stores fails to properly estimate the actual liquidation proceeds. The author agrees with Westcor on this point. Liquidation costs (ongoing overhead, severance, legal, and least costs) appear to be ignored or underestimated. The cumulative impact on the valuation is estimated to be in the neighborhood of $1 million.

A&C states that selling stockholders should take a 30%-40% discount on their stock for lack of marketability. The block of stock should be valued as control stock. Only two shareholders, who control 2% of the stock, have voiced a strong commitment to sell. It is highly improbable that another 26% of the stock is in the hands of "silent" dissatisfied shareholders. The author believes that A&C is on very solid ground with its analysis and that the discount is appropriate. In making this argument, Westcor appears to be attempting to make the selling stockholders strong advocates for a sale of the company to a third party. Westcor is saying on the one hand that the stock is not worth as much as A&C has calculated, but on the other hand, the price that the dissatisfied shareholders should receive is substantially higher than the A&C recommendation.

If the criticism of Westcor that has merit is taken into account, then a downward adjustment of approximately $1 million in the ME valuation should be considered. However, Westcor had no vested interest in making an evenhanded critique of the A&C report. It is very possible, even likely, that the businesses would be shown to be undervalued in other areas if all the assumptions are subjected to a complete critical review (See "Postscript" below). The author recommends that Walka and the board be sensitive to these possible overstatements of value in any counteroffer negotiations that might take place. It is recommended that Walka and the board not agree to any reduction in the sales price based on the Westcor criticism.

2. **Construct a common analytical framework for comparing the purchase offers by B.J. Jennar, Joe F. Conn, and Westcor. This should be in a format that would be easily understood by the members of the board of directors. On the basis of your analysis, put the purchase offers in a rank order (from best to worst).**

A common framework is necessary to compare the three different offers. Since each offer involves the payment of a stream of money over time in addition to the cash down payment, the author recommends calculating the net present value of each.

Since A&C has used a discount rate of 13.5% in its valuation calculation, it would be evenhanded to use this same discount rate in calculating the net present value of the offers. The purchase of preferred stock is not dealt with, since each potential purchaser is making an identical cash offer of $100 per share to be paid at close. The revenue streams that would be generated by each offer are shown below:

Time Period	B.J. Jennar	Joe F. Conn	Westcor
At close	$4,000,000	$9,650,000	$6,674,375
After 1 year	960,000	1,750,000	2,025,000
2 year	1,080,000		275,000
3		1,080,000	275,000
4		1,080,000	275,000
5		1,080,000	3,025,000
6		1,080,000	
7		1,080,000	
8		1,080,000	
9		6,681,000	

The revenue streams from the Arthur and Webb offers are specified in their offers. The revenue stream for the Westcor offer was calculated as follows: After one year, the interest on the five-year, $2,75 million note is paid. Since the interest rate on the note is 10 percent, this amounts to $275,000. The same revenue stream occurs after two, three, and four years. After five years, the interest and the principle are paid:

$275,000 + $2,750,000 = $3,025,000.
(interest)   (principle)

The net present value and price per share (based on 266,471 shares of common stock) for each offer is shown below:

Offer	Net Present Value	$Per Share
B.J. Jennar	$11,126,792	$41.76
Joe F. Conn	11,191,850	42.00
Westcor	10,632,781	39.90

Based on this type of financial analysis, the offer by B.J. Jennar is best, followed by Westcor, and Joe F. Conn. None of the offers comes very close to the valuation made by A&C. If a $1 million reduction in the A&C valuation is acknowledged (based on the Westcor criticism), the valuation of ME is approximately $15 million. This would still be almost $4 million higher than the best offer.

If a higher discount rate is used, as suggested by Westcor, the valuation of A&C declines, but so does the net present value of the three offers. For example, if a 15 percent discount rate is sued in the calculations, the net present value of the three offers is:

Offer	Net Present Value	$Per Share
B.J. Jennar	$10,984,537	$41,22
Joe F. Conn	11,171,739	41.93
Westcor	10,714,000	40.20

There is an additional complexity to resolve with the Joe F. Conn offer, the down payment at close is not in cash, but in stock. It would be appropriate to attach a discount to this value if one assumes that selling almost $10 million in stock would depress its price significantly. As soon as a discount of 5 percent or more is used, the Joe F. Conn offer drops to the bottom of the group, and perhaps out of consideration.

3. **Anticipate that a conflict of interest will eventually face the CEO (and board of directors) involving the shareholders who desire to sell and those who have expressed no such desire. Can management serve both groups equally? If not, whose interests should receive a higher priority? Substantiate.**

From a financial perspective, the general responsibility of management and therefore the CEO and the board is to maximize the value of shareholder's equity. Ignoring the issues concerning risk and net present value considerations, there is a difficult shareholder issue to be dealt with by Walka and the ME board of directors. First, a potential conflict must be recognized. The value of shareholders' equity does not appear to be maximized by accepting any of the three offers being considered. While accepting one of the offers may well suit the interests of those shareholders who are dissatisfied, it almost certainly will not serve the interests of those "loyal" shareholders who have not expressed a desire to sell. An offer to purchase stock at, or very near, the value calculated by A&C may create a "neutral" situation for the majority of shareholders. Lower offers fail the test of maximization of shareholder value.

By expressing a desire to sell their stock, the dissatisfied shareholders have removed themselves from the highest priority position with respect to management's actions. Management's responsibility is to first ensure the maximization of the value of loyal shareholders who wish to keep their equity in ME. If, and only if, the interests of these shareholders coincide with those of the dissatisfied shareholders, can management treat them with equal priority.

Walka and the board of directors specified to A&C the appropriate objective, which was to determine the fair value of ME and recommend an objective, fair purchase price for the stock of those who wished to sell. Westcor's criticism is off base when it suggests that the proper objective is "to maximize the value for all shareholders today."

The dissatisfied shareholders can only be happy with a purchase of their stock, either by ME or a third party. There is simply no evidence that the loyal shareholders will find their value maximized by the sale of the company to a third party. Furthermore, Walka and the board should not be pressured into a sale of ME at substantially less than the A&C valuation simply to accommodate the dissatisfied shareholders. To do so would acknowledge their interests as having highest priority.

4. Based on your analysis of Questions 1-3 above, what is your recommendation to the board? Substantiate.

The author recommends that Walka make the following recommendation's to the ME board of directors.

a. Take only those actions that recognize the interests of the loyal shareholders as having the highest priority. Shareholders who wish to sell their stock will be dealt with in an honest and equitable manner. However, the purchase of their stock will not be done in any manner that creates any reduction in value for the loyal stockholder group.

b. Reject all prospective offers. When considered in a net present value framework, the offers are significantly below the valuation determined by A&C.

c. Discuss with the board the alternative of "countering" one or all of the offers. If a counteroffer is made, it should be at or near the valuation made by A&C. For reasons mentioned above, this still may not best serve the interests of the loyal stockholders. However, it would serve to get important issues on the table for discussion if a counteroffer alternative were considered.

d. Assuming that the board rejects the counteroffer alternative, proceed with the strategy to sell/liquidate the Department Store Division. Pursue actions that will allow the company to repurchase the stock of the dissatisfied shareholders (i.e., sell off other low-priority assets, seek funding from a lending institution, etc.).

e. If sufficient funding can be obtained, make an offer to repurchase the stock at the price recommended by A&C ($37 to $42 per share). If funding cannot be obtained, continue to operate ME with present management and live with the difficult situation. It would be better to operate with dissatisfied shareholders than to sell or liquidate the company in order to accommodate these shareholders.

EPILOGUE

The CEO recommended that all of the offers be rejected. The board agreed. In a rather complicated situation that followed, a leveraged buyout of the dissatisfied shareholders' stock was accomplished. ME offered two options to all shareholders for the purchase of their stock:

1. $37.50 per share, in cash,

                    or

2. $42.50 per share - $32.50 in cash and a $10, five-year note bearing interest at 10 percent.

The response to the offer surprised the CEO and the board. Approximately 40 percent of ME shares were rendered for sale. About half of these (20 percent) were offered for cash and the rest for cash plus the five-year note. The total cost of the leveraged buyout was approximately $4 million. The company did not have to liquidate productive assets to accomplish the buyout. Instead, the financing was arranged through a bank in Denver. Undervalued assets essentially provided the collateral for the loan. In the judgment of the bank, the valuation made by A&C underestimated (rather than overestimated as was argued by Westcor) the value of ME.

Martin Enterprise attempted to sell the ailing Department Store Division but could not attract a buyer. The division was liquidated within a year at an approximate loss of $2 million.

By the end of 1988, just eighteen months later, the ME management team had turned the situation around. For the year 1988, ME achieved record performances in sales revenue and net profit. As it turned out, shareholders were well rewarded for the decision to hold their stock.

CASE K

MAIL ORDER PHARMACY

CASE SUMMARY

This is a general marketing management case which also illustrates and examines the evolving use of direct-response strategies and techniques as marketing tools in the health care industry. To deal with the problem that is presented, students will be challenged to bring to bear their knowledge of general marketing as well as direct-response marketing theory and communications. Their understanding of what works in direct marketing, i.e., the established "rules" regarding what generally works best, will also be directly challenged. This case works well in either senior level or graduate level marketing strategy courses, and especially well in direct response marketing courses.

TEACHING OBJECTIVES

1. To give students experience in defining and analyzing strategic marketing options in a setting involving products, services, and the relatively new marketing application area, the health care industry.

2. To enable students to determine the conditions under which direct marketing is the preferable marketing method.

3. To provide students with insights into and greater facility with direct-response problem solving technologies.

4. To provide students with an opportunity to deal with a direct-response marketing problem containing a variety of direct-response strategy elements.

QUESTIONS

1. Given the facts Mr. Grabarth has assembled, what are his overall marketing strategy options?

Grabarth has begun with direct marketing as his strategy of choice. Students should be asked to identify, given the environment and trends that exist in the industry, any other options he might have for entering the retail pharmaceutical business. Someone might come up with a viable way to enter this already very crowded industry, other than direct marketing, but it's unlikely. The direct response channel is where the fast growth is, and it's the channel that can be the most responsive to the price and convenience demands of consumers. Direct response channel marketers of prescription products are also ideally suited and situated, due to their reliance on databases, and sophistication in using them, to meet insurance company demands for detailed monitoring of the behavior of health care delivery system participants and prescription drug users.

2. How viable does the mail-order option Mr. Grabarth has selected appear to be?

This case (and this question) allows the instructor to engage students in a good discussion of "what is direct marketing?" The direct marketing field is usually misunderstood. Too often, it is seen as "junk" mail sent to disinterested prospects, or as "junk" calls" made to unwary phone service subscribers.

Direct marketing is a strategic approach to doing business which can involve a large combination of tools which work very well when they are matched, singly or in combination, with the marketing tasks for which they are well suited. Usually this is not the total sale. Rather, direct marketing is most often used to accomplish a piece of the sales task -- lead generation, for example. Likewise direct marketing can fail utterly when it is not used appropriately -- that is, used to do a task which it is incapable of doing.

Using it properly, Grabarth can very likely make the direct response channel work for him, but it will not be easy. Normally students will quickly recognize that direct marketing is very probably a cost-effective way to address a part of the pharmaceutical product market, either directly to consumers or through health insurers. What they may not recognize is that there are many ways to fail. Many consumers, even at the expense of paying more, will not be willing to do business by mail, or phone. Thus, all people on health insurance company lists or other lists of people who have bought prescription drugs, are not good prospects. Only a percentage of them are likely to be. In other product-market areas, marketers find that only about one-third or less of all buyers are direct response prospects. The rest want to see and talk directly with a person in a store, and many of these are very resistant to direct response approaches.

Direct response is a "personal" business. CPS will have to learn how to personalize its communications with prospects and customers. "Personal" means such things as writing marketing communications to prospects and customers in a me-to-you way rather than company-to-audience way. For example, Grabarth, himself, may need to become the "author" of communications with customers. "Personal" also means finding out through analysis of database data that certain customers are prime prospects/users for certain things or are responsive to certain types of promotions, and using this information in the development of message and mailing strategies.

Assuming he has the intelligence and resources to set up the company, Grabarth should also have the intelligence and resources to set up a direct response company that can do the things that are necessary if he is to prosper. This means hand holding the customer, even when the customer is wrong. It also means a variety of other things some people do not like to do, such as creating order forms designed to increase prospect or customer desire for the product rather than designed to serve the computer center's desire for easy-to-process forms. If he doesn't have the proper attitude about this and other related aspects of direct response, he should stay out of the business.

Grabarth should also realize that the telephone is a major part of direct response, especially in his type of business, and he must be ready to create a telemarketing operation structured to permit it to be cost effective. Misuse of the telephone is one of the most common mistakes in all of marketing. Telephone mismanagement often destroys otherwise viable companies. The telephone is not merely a sales tool. It is a marketing medium, and must be very carefully managed if it is to be truly effective.

Since CPS will be sending catalogs, the company will have its "store" open all the time and can, therefore, be said to be making a continuous offer to sell. The trick for CPS will be to conceive of special offers to sell to overcome procrastination, or to keep people from switching to another source of supply. Such offers can be made in mailings that are supplementary to catalog mailings. They can also be made via the phone. The number and variety of offers that can be conceived are limited only by the imagination of the marketer's staff.

3. What appears to be the direct response marketing strategy options available to Grabarth?

Strategy is driven by the market place position a company wants. Grabarth wants to serve health insurance clients and also the general consumer pharmaceutical market. These markets present him with very different problems.

Insurance companies will first have to be sold on CPS as the prescription drug supply source they endorse for the clients they insure. Most will no doubt be picky about which company they choose to recommend, and this will turn on whether or not CPS can deliver low prices and the monitoring services they are increasingly needing. Furthermore, most will want to deal with only one company, as more than one would mean two databases and reduced effectiveness of the monitoring of health care system participants and individual drug purchase behavior.

CPS can probably also serve the general pharmaceutical consumer market. In fact, some insurance companies will demand that he have a successful program with the general public underway before insurance companies will find his company of much interest. Selling the consumer market directly will require a detailed direct response program including catalogs, telemarketing programs, solo mailings, etc. These tools and programs will also be required to service the insurance company client market. Thus, this will not necessarily be a duplication of effort. However, the company will have to be much more aggressive in this market.

4. **Delineate an offer or set of offers that CPS might make to the general consumer market for prescription drugs (as opposed to the insurance company client market).**

Typical of what CPS might do is select a list of either insurance company clients or a direct response list (list of persons who have bought some kind of pharmacy product by mail, if such a list is available) and offer them the opportunity to qualify for permanent additional discounts if they will agree to buy a minimum of products from CPS during a specified period of time. CPS might pick out all diabetes sufferers and make them a separate special offer because they are diabetes sufferers. It is important to note that when offers are being changed, the dollar price need not be changed. The offer has a variety of elements, e.g., product or products, price, guarantee, payment methods, time limits, etc. Changing any one of these changes the offer and usually changes the market's response to the offer.

5. **What, if any, are some of the major legal issues that must be dealt with if Mr. Grabarth is to use the direct response marketing channel for medical products marketing?**

The entire range of anti-trust legislation is applicable to this case: conspiracy, price discrimination, unfair competition, etc. Quasi-legal issues such as privacy are also relevant. Deception in advertising is the area that will probably affect the company most, because it will be doing a lot of promoting, and its copywriters may be tempted to make extravagant claims. Health care industry marketers must offer more scientific proof of whatever claims are made than is required in most other industries. This is more true of product/drug efficacy claims than of marketing factor claims such as low price or convenience, etc.

Privacy is an issue in the case because of the database information the direct response marketer must have in order to sort out the best customers for greater emphasis, and in this case, to perform the monitoring of the industry players desired by the drug companies. Many people say that using data in a database to select prospects for additional marketing effort is an invasion of privacy. As of this writing the courts have not endorsed this view, but they are under heavy pressure to do so and many observers feel they will to some extent at least. Whether the courts will condone monitoring drug user behavior with detection of drug abusers in mind is an even more open question.

The industry's argument, which is a valid one, is that marketing cannot be efficient without information, and that the information is not used to invade privacy but to limit marketing efforts to those persons most likely to be interested in being served by the company.

CASE L

TeleSell™

CASE SUMMARY

This case realistically outlines an entrepreneurial opportunity in mid-length form. This type of presentation would be likely as a second round written presentation to potential investors of their screening experts. (Ordinarily the initial written presentation is a one-page affair.)

TeleSell™ builds on the enduring popularity of motivational and expert speakers for salespeople, especially among salespeople who spend most of their time out in the field. Keeping such individuals highly motivated is seen as key to their success and satisfaction. Since they operate alone, sales managers and peers can offer little support, and that lack can partially be filled in by Telesell™.

TEACHING OBJECTIVES

1. To introduce the student to mid-length business proposals.

2. To focus student attention on the integration of imagination and facts which are the hallmark of the opportunity analysis.

3. To provide the student with a mix of qualitative and quantitative data for use in opportunity analysis.

QUESTIONS

1. What are the strengths and weaknesses of TeleSell™?

Like all opportunities, this one is hardly an open-and-shut case. While the telephone costs are well-known, the cost of licensing materials and readings from the top-selling sales experts is an unknown. There are few standards established for pricing such uses of intellectual property, so estimates of cost in this area are particularly weak. Some preliminary information on the openness of sales experts to TeleSell™ and their initial monetary demands would be in order.

In addition, there is the whole area of image. While the use of proprietary 1-800 (WATS) lines carries little negative onus, some of the authors may be bothered by having their names associated with a 1-900 pay-per-minute line. Since "adult" talk lines and other unsavory services use the 1-900 approach, this projected expansion of the business in year two might meet with resistance.

Other potential areas of concern include: (1) Experts preferring a one-expert-per-day approach rather than sharing their audience with their competitors, (2) Experts taking this idea and starting their own lines catering to their established clients and thus skimming the "cream" of the market, (3) Lack of specification of a "critical mass" of sales experts needed to make the business work, (4) No testing of the idea with currently active sales managers, and (5) Inadequate consideration of motivational tools applicable across distances such as mailgrams, cards, overnight packages, sales manager phone calls, etc.

The strengths of the proposal is its uniqueness, its consideration of competitive issues in the narrow scope of telephone delivery of services, its consideration of multiple rounds of growth, its attention to the skills of the start-up advisors, and its detailing of the target market and estimation of relatively reasonable targets for market penetration.

2. What intellectual property issues have a major impact on the case?

There are two issues: licensing of the materials from the experts, and protecting TeleSell™ from competition.

Licensing quotes (read by actors and the authors themselves) for telephone delivery is a relatively new idea. The likely approaches to licensing would be paying a fixed licensing fee (useful to licensor in start-up situations because if the idea is poor, the licensor still receives its money up front), and/or a royalty for use of each quote (great for the licensee, since only what is used is paid for, but a problem for the licensor unless careful record keeping of use is possible).

Other issues in this arena is whether to grant an exclusive (preferred by TeleSell™) or nonexclusive license (generally preferred by licensors), and whether the licensor or Telesell™ would hold the copyright on the scripts and tapes used on the network itself. Telesell's™ goal is to be the only firm with permission to distribute the information via telephone. Potential licensors, unsure as to future growth of this market (by other firms or as an expansion of their own distribution channels) may want to preserve as much freedom as possible. They will weigh this potential against the hard dollars and exposure offered by TeleSell™ to arrive at their decisions.

The second issue is competition from potential licensors and from third-party entrants, such as publishers and other telephone network service providers. The Tele-Sell™ *idea* is not protectable. The specific authors and quotes used is subject to protection through copyright, and license agreements with the authors themselves. But there is nothing to prevent someone else from amassing a stable of competing best-selling authors and starting a competing service to TeleSell™.

As noted in the case, only through getting the big names, getting them first, and pursuing any infringements, can TeleSell™ keep the market to itself. A major threat to this is the potential defection of authors when licensing periods end.

3. What technology issues play a major role in the case?

TeleSell™ generally uses existing telecommunication technology. The WATS lines (1-800 numbers) and pay-for-service 1-900 numbers already exist, and can be obtained from telephone companies or remarketers, who buy large numbers of 800 and 900 lines and resell them to customers such as TeleSell™. There is considerable price and service competition, and also considerable expertise to assist in the evaluation of telecommunication offerings, over and above the expert already recruited.

The voice technology for the quotes is also well-established. The preferred method today uses computer based digital sound, which is less likely to fall prey to mechanical problems common with tapes. The method is widely used in voice mail systems and produces a very high fidelity, and permits easy editing using a personal computer on-site of via modem from remote locations. Additionally, the computer-based method permits detailed accounting records to be kept of quotation use, and permits an easy upgrade path to future versions where users with TouchTone℠ phones can input their credit card number or select the kind of TeleSell™ help they want.

The key concept for opportunity analysis here is that neither the telephone, voice or billing via touchtone technologies pose a threat to the analysis since all are well established, well documented, and subject to considerable competition. No new inventions or even adaptations of existing technologies are needed.

4. Overall how would you rate the opportunity presented in this case? Would you recommend investing $600,000 in the start-up? Why or why not?

The market projections are easily verified, and the market share seems reasonable. The costs (outside of licensing fees) are known and the service price is competitive. The technology is known and offers no surprises.

Panels of experts reviewing this proposal have suggested that it is likely to meet the profitability estimates projected, assuming licensing fees can be kept to the initial estimates. By more directed targeting of sales managers and approaching them in smaller segments, rather than all 22,000 at once, marketing costs could be decreased from $325,000 to approximately $125,000 for the year, thus speeding breakeven and minimizing investment.

It is unclear how much capital Katz is putting into the start-up, whether debt or equity capital is being sought, and what financial conditions (ownership percentage investors get; collateral for creditors) are being supplied.

Overall, the opportunity appears worth pursuing. The next steps recommended include clarifying licensing opportunities and costs (including providing a list of the key authors and their current sales in other media), conducting a preliminary market study (e.g., focus groups) with sales managers who would be the primary market for TeleSell™ initially, providing detailed financial projections and listings of start-up capital already available to the principals, and preparing a demonstration version of TeleSell™ which potential investors and customers could use.

ACKNOWLEDGEMENTS

This case was developed by Professor Jerome Katz for use in classroom discussions. The author wishes to thank Rich Pisani and Greg Upchurch for their advice.

CASE M

COMIC RELIEF

<u>CASE SUMMARY</u>

This case describes the setting in which two brothers, Joe and Patrick, discuss the possibility of starting up a mail order business that deals with comic books and original comic art. The setting primarily revolves around an annual comic convention where Joe, who is in his mid-thirty's brings up the business idea to Patrick, who is in his mid-forty's.

With the exception of a love of comics and a lifelong history in collecting them, the situations of the two brothers differ. Patrick, the elder brother, is a recent widower who appears to be somewhat depressed in contemplating his future. He has no children, is employed with the post office, and has extra time that he could devote to the business. While Patrick did not attend college, Joe recognizes Patrick's enthusiasm for collecting comics and the fact that Patrick has developed contacts with several comic artists over the years. Joe is married to Linda, has two children, and is employed with the State Department of Revenue; he attended college and is more comfortable with the business aspects and is computer literate.

While the relationship between the brothers is a good one, the facts of the case provide a situation of uncertainty due to the recent changes in Patrick's life. Thus the motivation issues of the individuals involved should be addressed by students in responding to the questions of the case. The brother's individual knowledge levels with regard to comic collecting are roughly equivalent; Joe is more knowledgeable of business issues but

Patrick has more knowledge and contacts with the original comic art area of the business. The financial investment issue is not a strong factor in the case as the brothers have an existing inventory that would command little cash outlay and the emphasis on a mail order business would preclude the necessity of additional capital. The investment of personal time and energy, however is an issue.

TEACHING OBJECTIVES

1. To identify issues associated with the decision to start up a business entity.

2. To apply the advantages and disadvantages of the various legal forms of business organizations to the facts of a given case.

3. To determine the most appropriate legal form of a business organization for the given facts.

4. To assess the differences, both limitations and resources, that potential partners bring together in the establishment of a business venture.

5. To view the importance of an organized plan for new business formation relevant to a typical situation involving family members.

APPROPRIATE APPLICATIONS OF THE CASE

Business start-up strategies
Family business - the new venture
The legal form of the venture
An understanding of sales on consignment

QUESTIONS

1a.   What are the relevant choices of legal forms of business organization available to Joe and Patrick?

There are three relevant choices of legal forms of business organization. The first is a sole proprietorship, with Joe as owner and Patrick either serving as an employee and/or Patrick selling inventory on consignment. The limitations of financial capital and unlimited liability normally associated with a sole proprietorship formation have been minimized in this case through the facts that have been provided pertaining to an existing inventory and the mail order aspect of operation.

The second, although notably a weaker option, is partnership. While a partnership is viable, the conflict aspects should be addressed due to the current uncertainty of Patrick's situation. The partnership option becomes more viable if considering one in which Joe has a greater than 50% ownership interest in the business, as he is currently contributing the most in terms of getting the business started up.

Finally, a Subchapter-S is a viable option. This has the advantage of being tailor-made for a family type operation and minimizing the potential of conflict once the business is operating due to the legal work performed initially. It allows for the protection of limited liability and ongoing life of the business in the event that either brother has changes in their personal circumstances or interest levels in the business. It also allows for ownership to be doled out among other family members over time, such as Joe's children.

1b. **What are the relevant issues for Joe to consider in this case regarding the formation of the described business venture?**

A. A primary issue for Joe to consider is the motivation and commitment level for the business. Is he really motivated to start this business from his own desire and therefore sufficiently committed to the business? Has he merely conceived of starting the business in an effort to help out Patrick during his transition period? The determination of these issues would speak to the appropriate legal form of business entity due to the expected length of life for the business.

B. Do the brothers possess sufficient knowledge and background to start a business of this sort?

C. Is there a need in the market for this type of business?

D. Would the retail or mail order form be more appropriate?

E. Will the brothers' existing resources (time, inventory, and network capabilities) be sufficient to enable the business to meet the market demand?

F. Has the issue of financial capital been fully addressed?

G. What are the brothers' realistic short-term and long-term aspirations for this venture?

2. **What liabilities and strengths are each of the brothers bringing to the start-up?**

LIABILITIES:

Patrick:
    A. The timing places Patrick in an uncertain position in terms of his future. For example, is Patrick emotionally able to take on anything at this point? A second question involves whether he will marry again, which could lead to future location issues.
    B. The case alludes to Patrick's lack of business knowledge; does he fully comprehend the implications of the business formation?

Joe:
    A. The investment of available time to devote to the business. Joe is up front in the case that this is an issue. He has a full time job and a family.
    B. The motivation issue is questionable in the case. Is Joe considering the venture for appropriate reasons?

STRENGTHS:

Patrick:
    A. Time to devote to the business.
    B. Inventory to contribute.
    C. Knowledge and enthusiasm for comics.
    D. Specialized knowledge of the original comic art market.
    E. Spare garage to contribute for inventory storage.

Joe:
    A. Desire for more challenge.
    B. Inventory to contribute.
    C. Knowledge and enthusiasm for comics.
    D. Knowledgeable of business, legal, and finance related issues.
    E. Computer literate.

3. Determine whether Joe should propose the business be established as retail or mail order. What are the issues?

Joe should propose the mail order proposal. This is the preference that both brothers have expressed. It contains several benefits: low start-up costs, requiring less capital due to no physical plant required, allows the brothers to work at the hours of their choosing, allows them to choose how quickly to grow, allows for seasonal kinds of involvement through their timing and choice of mailings and advertisement, allows for their market to be more expansive than a shop would allow.

4. What would be the favored form of business organization from Joe's standpoint? ... from Patrick's standpoint?

Joe would likely prefer the Subchapter-S option. The advantages are the limited liability and unlimited life, with the ownership of shares readily transferrable to other family members. The taxation aspect of a Subchapter-S likely precludes the overriding disadvantage of double taxation normally associated with a corporation. The only disadvantage is that a Subchapter-S is the most difficult of the three options to organize, but once formed, it should allow for a reduction of conflict, and the ability to expand to allow other interested individuals to participate. Various policies and responsibilities could be aligned or distributed according to the brothers' strengths and interests.

Patrick would likely prefer at this time that Joe establish the business as a sole proprietorship in which Patrick could participate with little responsibility. He could help his brother as needed and sell inventory on consignment. With time, Patrick could determine the degree of commitment he could make to the business venture. However, this places the initial burden of organization and liability on Joe.

CASE N

ENVIRONMENTAL SYSTEMS

CASE SUMMARY

This case deals with a hard-working, conservative entrepreneur, Terry Dobbs, who initiated a successful waste disposal company and subsequently formed a partnership with the well-connected, but much less conservative Alan Archer.

The case attempts to illustrate the entrepreneurial personality and the difficulty of forming viable partnerships. Someone (who, himself, was a partner in a law firm) once said, "A partnership is like a marriage and just as difficult to dissolve. So, choose your partners very carefully." The case addresses the need for a written partnership agreement and illustrates provisions of such agreements.

TEACHING OBJECTIVES

1. To illustrate entrepreneurial personality.

2. To provide an example of an entrepreneurial opportunity.

3. To provide an example of a partnership that has soured due to personality differences between the partners.

4. To illustrate the need for a careful selection of partners and the need for a written partnership agreement.

ISSUES IN THE CASE

1. The ability of successful entrepreneurs to recognize business opportunities.

2. The type of financing entrepreneurs can pursue.

3. The type of growth strategies entrepreneurs can pursue.

4. The hazards encountered in selecting a partner.

5. The difficulties of partnership dissolution.

QUESTIONS

1. What characteristics of an entrepreneur does Terry possess?

Terry is a risk taker, but he is a conservative risk taker. He looks for prudent ventures with easy, owner-financing. He is a leader and likes to do things in his own way. He is able to mobilize rather meager resources.

2. What events triggered Terry's venture? What opportunities were captured by Terry?

Terry worked for United Chemical and witnessed that company's need for professional waste disposal. As a chemist familiar with waste problems, he was in a position to initiate a waste disposal firm. He recognized the general trend toward environmental protection.

3. Should Terry dissolve the partnership?

There is no easy answer to this question. Ideally, perhaps, he should continue the partnership in order to capitalize upon Alan's contacts, but continuation of the partnership would require that Terry and Alan reach agreement on financial issues. Such agreement depends upon the willingness of both parties to change their behavior. The case does not present Alan's point of view, so we really don't know too much about him.

If financial agreement is impossible, Terry needs to dissolve the partnership and face the consequences, which include a rather large guarantee of partnership debt. We don't know if Alan will pay his share of the debt.

4. In selecting a partner, what should Terry have looked for?

Terry wisely selected a partner with the ability to generate business, but unwisely chose one who had far different financial goals. Terry should have looked for:

a. knowledge of the business.
b. similar attitudes toward risk and financial management.
c. ability to generate business.
d. similar attitudes toward business planning.
e. comparable contributions toward the partnership capital.

Of course, partners do not always arrive with such qualifications; therefore, Terry should have identified the characteristics he most desired in a partner.

ACTUAL OUTCOME OF THE CASE

Terry Dobbs and Alan Archer dissolved the partnership. As a result, Terry lost business in Texas because he and Alan signed a non-compete agreement. However, he and Alan amicably divided the assets. Alan kept his state-of-the-art assets and their accompanying debt, which he was able to pay off. Terry contributed his share of partnership assets to a wholly-owned corporation and suffered minimal, negative tax consequences. Terry's corporation has prospered. He has not sold any of his stock.

CASE O

THE FAB LAB

CASE SUMMARY

This case deals with the actual experiences of a couple who have started their own business and are now facing some of the difficulties of business ownership. They must make decisions regarding the future direction of business growth, decisions which are mutually exclusive and will impact the business for years to come. The main challenge for John and Lisa Schroeder is to evaluate the alternatives and choose the best option which allows the business to grow while working within the limited financial resources of the Fab Lab.

TEACHING OBJECTIVES

1. To show the inter-related business functions and how financial resources influences marketing decisions.

2. To demonstrate the impact of inadequate capitalization.

3. To show the transition process from employee to employer.

4. To illustrate an owner's decision-making process.

ISSUES IN THE CASE

1. Growth - How can John continue to develop sales growth given financial and personal constraints?

2. Adequate capitalization - What was the impact of receiving $30,000 less than expected?

3. Planning - How did John transition into owning his business?

4. Decision making - In addition to the financial considerations, what factors will affect John's decision? How much importance should the financial constraints affect his decision?

QUESTIONS

1. As a consultant to John, how would you advise him to develop his business?

Discussion should initially focus on the constraints John faces -- financial and personal. Students should be encouraged to develop solutions which fit within the constraints. The astute student will recognize the low probability of borrowing additional funds since the business is new and there is not enough collateral for further debt.

Students may want to discuss the possibility of the sales representative becoming a partner in the business and putting up cash. Instructor should discuss John's reasons to start the business initially (i.e., to run his own shop) and the impact a partnership would have.

It may be helpful to use a force field analysis technique for each alternative developed by the students. They should be reminded it is generally easier to remove barriers that hinder growth than to push harder on the forces for a particular alternative.

They should be encouraged to think of other alternatives than those listed in the table.

2. What impact does receiving $30,000 less than expected have on John's decision?

Discussion should focus on the limitations the decreased loan amount places on the business, i.e., the decreased amount preventing John from immediately hiring a salesperson, and entry into the government contracting market. Another point to bring out is that having cash flow difficulties shortens a business owner's decision-making cycle. Instead of being able to implement plans for the long term growth, the owner must be concerned with ensuring short term cash needs are met.

3. How did John make the transition from being an employee to an owner?

This is a particularly good question to ask an entrepreneurship class. The discussion should focus on the progressive steps John took to separate himself from his employer.

These steps include:

a.　Attaining a management position with his former employer.

b.　Approaching his former employer about ownership in the firm and waiting for his answer.

c.　Discussing his idea to start his own business with customers.

d.　Receiving positive encouragement from customers.

e.　Obtaining the support of his spouse.

f.　Starting a business where he had strong technical knowledge and significant customer contact.

g.　Identifying a significant market niche -- small jobs not profitable for his former employer.

h.　Putting together a business plan -- which aided him in evaluating the feasibility of start-up.

i.　Obtaining a bank loan.

Students may question the ethics of John discussing starting his own business with customers while employed. If this occurs, it would be good to emphasize that this does not appear to be a serious problem since his former employer subcontracted work to him after Fab Lab's start-up and John had discussed possible co-ownership in the company with his employer.

The purpose of the question is to show the systematic progression John took in starting the business. Each succeeding step was a natural movement toward starting up his business.

4. Did John make the right decision to buy the additional machinery, even though he probably could have succeeded without them, and without putting the company in a tight cash flow situation?

The discussion could be centered around evaluating the pros and cons of purchasing the additional equipment.

Pros:	Cons:
Additional capability and capacity.	Puts Fab Lab in tight cash position, i.e. Fab Lab must be self-sufficient.
May be unable to find the equipment at such a reasonable price in the future.	Doesn't strictly need right now.

Students should be encouraged to discuss the impact of cash flow upon business decisions. Cash can be an influencing factor, but generally not the deciding one. If a purchase makes sound business sense, and has the potential for quickly replacing needed cash, then the business owner should strongly consider making the purchase. Students should recognize the extremely fortunate event of the pre-payment.

ACTUAL OUTCOME

Sales began to pick up after the case write-up. John decided to pursue government contracting at a slow pace and to finance the growth from the business. He also recognized his weakness to develop new sales, and began development of his sales abilities. These efforts have paid off. Fab Lab has gone from the two part-time employees to four full-time employees and one part-time employee, excluding John. Sales have increased from between $3,000 to $4,000 per month, to over $15,000 per month.

CASE P

THE CREATIVE MIND

CASE SUMMARY

Dr. John Reilly, a successful psychologist, envisioned The Creative Mind as a self-improvement supermarket where individuals, businesses, and other mental-health professionals could find a wide range of materials dedicated to self-improvement subjects, from dealing creatively with death to improving their backhand or overcoming public-speaking anxiety. He also saw the store as a rich referral source for his practice and a place where he could send his patients who, along with therapy, wanted to pursue self-improvement projects.

Dr. Reilly was a perfectionist who was compulsive about doing things right; therefore, when he began to develop his concept he consulted with professionals -- financial people, lawyers, and accountants, as well as his wife and his father, himself a failed entrepreneur. With their input he developed an extremely professional business plan. With the plan in hand and with his passionate dedication to his vision and his natural persuasive ability, he had little trouble getting investors. The first The Creative Minds store opened in Johnson County, Kansas, an affluent suburb of Kansas City, in the fall of 1987.

By 1990 the store was grossing about $350,000 annually -- near break-even. The financial situation did not allow for the required funds for franchising efforts, however, so Dr. Reilly recruited additional investors to provide the capital for franchise promotion in exchange for part of his ownership interest. The additional funds were used for mailings, advertisements, and trade shows. Although two franchises were eventually

mailings, advertisements, and trade shows. Although two franchises were eventually sold, neither was successful and fees collected covered only a small part of the investment required to start them. A change of location to a more desirable site and expansion into a trendy local shopping area did little to improve the financial picture. The Christmas season of 1991 was the crucial period. If extensive sales increases were not realized, the business could not survive.

TEACHING OBJECTIVES

1. To give students an opportunity to analyze the process of recognizing the signs of success and/or failure.

2. To provide a vehicle for studying the hazards of implementation.

3. To show that passion, creativity, and vision alone cannot lead to success -- a measure of objectivity and significant managerial skill is also required.

4. To demonstrate the critical differences between creating and implementing.

QUESTIONS AND EXERCISES

1. **Assuming that The Creative Mind survives the new year, what options can you see to make this a profitable venture? Explain.**

   Students' answers may vary. Answers should include such options as:

   consolidating all operations into one good location of appropriate size, based on analysis of current and expected customer base.

   Dr. Reilly should concentrate his time and effort into making this one business profitable and successful. He could develop the corporate business which was originally an integral part of the plan but was not attended to.

   promotion activities with other mental-health professionals, schools, health clubs, civic organizations, local businesses etc. to increase customer base and referral base. The list of promotion possibilities is extensive.

   public relations efforts with local news programs and newspapers to increase awareness of what the store has to offer.

getting professional management help, both for the current operation and to develop the franchise program. This could be achieved in exchange for an ownership interest.

2. Was "The Creative Mind" a good name for the venture? Why or why not?

The name does not adequately reflect the range of products available nor the audience which Dr. Reilly was trying to reach. A name that encompassed a larger range of the products and customers would have been better. A large percentage of people do not consider themselves to be creative; the name may have been a deterrent to them.

3. When would you recommend selling franchises?

Franchising can be successful only when there is a successful going business enterprise to serve as a sales tool and a model for development of franchises. Not only did the Reillys have no expertise in franchising, they did not know how to make the core business successful. They could not therefore train franchisees how to manage a successful business -- one of the main functions of a franchisor.

4. What should Dr. Reilly do before trying to expand?

After three years and failing to make a profit, Dr. Reilly should reassess his concept and its execution. The key question before attempting expansion is whether even one store can be profitable. The first step to assessing this is a market study to determine demand. Additionally, he should assess the availability of the products available in the market which could differentiate this venture from mere bookstores. Another key is to determine the buying habits of purchasers of this type of material. Is walk-in business an important contributor or must some developmental work be done to draw customers to the store?

He might also try experimenting with the parameters of the business: for example, a secondary location at a lower rent may have produced equivalent sales. He should experiment with advertising, the sales format, and the pricing structure to derive an optimal profit formula.

5. How could The Creative Mind's product or image be changed to decrease its susceptibility to competition from general purpose and discount bookstores?

Theme advertising and promotion could help to differentiate the store from mere bookstores. An example might be recreating Sigmund Freud's office as a selling display or holding theme events in the store. Another approach along the same line might be promotions centered on unique holidays, such as Einstein's birthday.

Creating a unique shopping experience through decor and displays as well as selling approach and attire of salespeople is another way to differentiate. Hiring artists, psychology students, advertising majors, sculptors, writers, athletes, etc. as sales and demonstration staff would also serve this purpose.

Differentiation of product line is a must. Dr. Reilly should carry difficult-to-find products: books from specialty publishers with limited distribution, a broad selection of academic journals and reprints dealing with the many subjects addressed in the store, output of local creative people. This network can then help him expand to carry output of artists from other parts of the country, especially if and when franchises are sold.

6. Consider key decision points: opening the store, changing locations, undertaking the franchising effort, moving to The Plaza. Would other options have been feasible at those times? Explain.

Opening the store: examples -- delay, go upscale, go downscale, locate in a professional building with a lot of psychologists in its, do it by mail, sell materials only at seminars, sell direct to professionals for their in-office point of sale displays, hire a professional retail expert.

Changing locations: examples -- reduce size, stay in same location, change format of the business a la one of the above, expand inventory, sublease an existing location or locate with another business.

Undertaking the franchising effort: this clearly should not have been done at this point. If he was determined to franchise, he could have hired a franchising expert.

Moving to The Plaza: examples -- change the format of the business, consolidate space with another niche store catering to a similar audience, grow in current location -- do not expand.

7. What problems can you identify from the case which might have led to the crisis described at the end?

Lack of experience. The two primary owners had no experience in running a retail business or in franchising.

Lack of a unique product. The company ended up being a specialty book store, unable to defend against the encroachment of national book chains and discounters.

Failure to execute the plan. Dr. Reilly did not spend time learning the business nor using his selling skills to assure the success of the original venture.

Franchising without a plan. Dr. Reilly was not prepared to support the franchisees with a success-proven model. Also, the franchises were located too far away from the mother store to be serviced economically.

Inappropriate location. The location was too expensive. Dr. Reilly's selection of location was based, not on criteria rationally tied to key success factors but on his subjective and grandiose vision for the venture.

Expanding before ready. The second location was opened without giving sufficient attention to basic questions of demand and viability of the venture.

EXERCISE: Planning to Avoid Failure. Make a list of all the things that could have gone wrong with The Creative Mind concept implementation, including those that did go wrong that you find in the case. Make a plan that shows how to identify and avoid the most likely events.

This list will vary. Students should be encouraged to develop as long a list as possible. The point is that dealing with the possibility of having made a poor decision up front can help entrepreneurs avoid mistakes, thus increasing the chances of success.

The list of problems in Question 7 can be a good starting point. Each problem identified should be followed by a detailed plan consisting of at least three steps which could be taken to avoid the problem. Again, students should be encouraged to list as many steps as they can think of. They should also be encouraged to collaborate in developing the list of possible problems.

EXERCISE: Entrepreneurial Ethics. Some studies have shown that ethical lapses may be more common in entrepreneurial organizations. Identify at least two possible ethical problems in this case and tell why you think these are ethical issues.

Referring patients to purchase materials at a business owned by the therapist could be construed as an ethical lapse. Doctors who have an interest in drug stores to which they refer patients or who own interest in nursing homes or other types of facilities to which they refer patients are roundly criticized. In some states doctors are forbidden to own an interest in such facilities. It could be seen as a violation of the trust relationship between doctor and patient/client.

Bringing in new investors may represent an ethical lapse, depending on the understanding of the original investors and on the kind of information given to potential investors, especially as the venture began to draw closer to crisis. If Dr. Reilly misrepresented information in any way or failed to disclose relevant information, this would constitute taking money under false pretenses, if not fraud.

The sale of franchises may have been done in an unethical manner. The usual franchise arrangement calls for extensive "how to" management training for franchisees, as well as advertising and marketing expertise. Since The Creative Mind had no one who was qualified to do this and since the business itself was not profitable, one must wonder what information was given to potential franchisees and how the current picture of the business was presented to entice franchisees. If Dr. Reilly failed to be completely upfront in the presentation of the expertise or availability of support staff and materials, this would represent a serious ethical lapse.

TEST BANK

CHAPTER 1

Multiple Choice

C   1.   The psychological need most satisfied by starting one's own venture is:
- A.   Social.
- B.   Status.
- C.   Self-actualization.
- D.   Esteem.

B   2.   The belief that America is moving toward a more entrepreneurial society is justified by which of the following fundamental changes?
- A.   The recognition that larger organizations fulfill basic needs for autonomy and security.
- B.   A growing belief that entrepreneurship is not just for the rich and famous.
- C.   Increasing entry costs and other start-up barriers.
- D.   The absence of programs to study, teach, promote, and accelerate entrepreneurship.

D   3.   The fact that a two-income family is becoming a standard in America has what effect on entrepreneurial ventures?
- A.   Decreases the number of ventures due to more financial stability.
- B.   Decreases the number of ventures because most new ventures require significantly more investment.
- C.   Has no effect on entrepreneurship.
- D.   Encourages entrepreneurship due to more available capital.

A   4.   Which of the following will not have a continued positive effect on the total number of new ventures started?
    A.   Increased education of the population regarding the perils of new ventures.
    B.   A shift in women's roles in economic life.
    C.   An increase in the cultural diversity of the workforce.
    D.   Changes in the tax structure supporting new ventures.

C   5.   Which of the following does not reflect the significance of entrepreneurship?
    A.   New inventions
    B.   The sheer number of new ventures being started
    C.   A net increase of new jobs in Fortune 500 firms
    D.   Job creation in small and new firms

A   6.   The percentage of businesses having less than 100 employees is:
    A.   Almost 100%
    B.   75%
    C.   15%
    D.   70%

C   7.   Which of the following is true about most new ventures?
    A.   Most will experience modest, but continued growth.
    B.   Most will become high-growth ventures.
    C.   They will stay quite small.
    D.   They are in highly technical areas.

B   8.   If a new venture goes quite well and achieves rapid growth as planned by the entrepreneurial team, then the primary challenge is:
    A.   Obtaining more capital to achieve even greater growth.
    B.   Maximizing growth without losing control.
    C.   Finding a buyer for the business.
    D.   Entrepreneurship is no longer a challenge.

D   9.   The probability that a new venture will be successful is dependent:
    A.   Solely on previous experience and management skills.
    B.   On how well the opportunity was researched prior to the launch.
    C.   Solely on the amount and availability of capital.
    D.   On a host of factors, including those outside the entrepreneur's control.

A   10.   Which of the following is not a factor cited in studies investigating why new ventures fail?
- A.   The amount of capital invested
- B.   The industry the new venture is in
- C.   The education of the entrepreneur
- D.   The size of the venture

B   11.   The fact that a significant portion of new ventures fail within the first few years suggests that:
- A.   It's strictly a function of underestimating capital requirements.
- B.   New entrepreneurs must be as well prepared as possible.
- C.   America should experience a decreasing number of new ventures due to the learning curve.
- D.   The dynamics of the industry are solely to blame.

B   12.   Gustavus Swift's successful meat shipping operation can be traced to a number of factors typical of 19th century entrepreneurs. Which of the following is not one of those factors?
- A.   A drive to cut unit costs of operations.
- B.   The aid of the federal government in capitalizing new ventures.
- C.   Close personal control of the operations.
- D.   Increasing the capital base through employee ownership.

A   13.   Sam Walton's overriding objectives characterizing his entrepreneurial drive were to:
- A.   Cut costs and provide customer service.
- B.   Solicit and utilize employee suggestions.
- C.   Delegate authority and decision making to employees.
- D.   Provide a superior product and charge appropriate prices.

C   14.   A key principle which became a driving force behind the success of Mary Kay Cosmetics was:
- A.   Expanding the product line available to each "Beauty Consultant".
- B.   Emphasizing the importance of selling techniques.
- C.   Belief in the golden rule as a guide to conducting business affairs.
- D.   Limiting inventory and overhead costs.

A   15.   The role that ethics plays in new ventures compared to larger, established firms is:
- A.   Ethics are particularly crucial in entrepreneurial ventures.
- B.   Just as important as in larger firms.
- C.   Not as important for new ventures due to the lack of publicity.
- D.   Ethics in the new venture is important, but cannot affect the financial status of the venture.

D   16.   In combination with vision and dedication, which of the following is becoming a necessary ingredient for new venture success?
- A.   Large amounts of capital
- B.   A superior product or service
- C.   An existing market for the product
- D.   The ability to plan

C   17.   The fact that entrepreneurial firms have more freedom of movement concerning ethical decision making can be attributed to several factors. Which of the following is NOT one of those factors?
- A.   Since most ventures are small, there is less publicity accorded them.
- B.   The SEC fails to monitor non-publicly traded firms.
- C.   The involvement of government agencies in new ventures prevents severe problems from developing.
- D.   Small ventures are exempt from many laws and regulations.

D   18.   Which of the following is true regarding written ethical codes and entrepreneurial ventures?
- A.   Most entrepreneurs have a written ethical code in place prior to launching a venture.
- B.   All entrepreneurs will have some form of code in place since it is required by law.
- C.   Entrepreneurs need not concern themselves with ethical codes since there are no financial consequences.
- D.   Most entrepreneurs have no written ethical code prior to launching a venture.

C   19.   The belief that life's priorities should be God first, family second, and work third came from which entrepreneur's culture?
- A.   Gustavus Swift
- B.   J.W. Marriott
- C.   Mary Kay Ash
- D.   John Johnson

C   20.   George Orwell's quote that "all animals are equal, but some animals are more equal than others" means that:
          A.   There's equality in the animal kingdom after all.
          B.   New ventures started by minorities have a higher survival rate.
          C.   Anyone can start a venture, but some have a higher probability of succeeding than others.
          D.   Ventures that have more access to capital will ultimately be successful.

D   21.   Gustavus Swift had to overcome several obstacles to attain success in his meat shipping operation. The foremost obstacle was:
          A.   Overcoming opposition by eastern butchers.
          B.   The high rail rates for shipments of dressed beef.
          C.   Assembling the needed capital to set up cold storage facilities.
          D.   The technological problem of developing a refrigerated rail-car.

B   22.   Paul Galvin's success with the Motorola venture was largely due to:
          A.   Mass merchandising
          B.   Innovation and diversification
          C.   Focusing on efficiency and, therefore, lowering unit costs
          D.   Increased mechanization of the production line

C   23.   Cutting costs and developing customer relations are prime objectives most associated with:
          A.   Richard Sears
          B.   John Johnson
          C.   Sam Walton
          D.   J.W. Marriott

A   24.   Roy Speer is known primarily for launching the:
          A.   Home Shopping Channel
          B.   Roy Rogers Food Chain
          C.   Cabletron Cable Network
          D.   Hot Shoppes Food Chain

C   25.   The belief that the golden rule is a practical guide to conducting one's business affairs is associated with which of the following entrepreneurs?
          A.   Sam Walton
          B.   Bob Levine
          C.   Mary Kay Ash
          D.   Richard Sears

True/False

F   26.   The growth rate of new ventures created by men is considerably higher than the rate for ventures created by women.

T   27.   A growing appreciation that the risks of new venture failure have been overstated has a positive effect on the number of new ventures created.

T   28.   Uncovering new venture opportunities is a benefit of the computer and information revolution.

F   29.   The number of ventures started by minorities is decreasing due to the "buy American" theme.

F   30.   The number of new ventures has been decreasing from year to year due to corporate downsizing and spin-offs.

F   31.   Changes in tax structures will hinder, not foster entrepreneurial ventures.

T   32.   In recent years, the significance of entrepreneurship has been in the area of job creation.

T   33.   Most new ventures are in manufacturing and service-related industries.

F   34.   The number of new entrepreneurs is decreasing each year due in part to the financial risks involved.

F   35.   Ventures must be started with the intent of making the business a full time career for them to be successful.

T   36.   The kinds of ventures created are subject only to the entrepreneur's vision.

T   37.   Some ventures require virtually no capital to launch.

F   38.   Once a venture is launched, the "entrepreneurial" tasks decrease in importance.

F   39.   One of the reasons the number of new entrepreneurs increases each year is that most new ventures achieve high growth rates.

T   40.   The survival rate of new businesses has been distorted by the media and others.

F 41. The industry the new venture is in has little effect on the survival of the new venture.

F 42. Successful entrepreneurship is nothing more than just finding an idea today and opening the doors tomorrow.

T 43. A characteristic of successful entrepreneurs which is just as important as hard work and drive is the ability to find a need and fill it.

T 44. Regarding the successful entrepreneurs portrayed in this chapter, there is little evidence to suggest they had formal, written business plans.

F 45. Increased education of the general population will not have any effect on the failure rate of new ventures.

Essay Questions

1. Evidence suggests that America is moving toward an entrepreneurial society. Discuss five fundamental changes occurring in the U.S. that encourage this entrepreneurship.

2. Discuss the significance of entrepreneurship in terms of its historic and recent impact. How was the significance changed over the years?

3. Discuss the need for entrepreneurial vision and dedication in the launch and success of a venture. Have the two characteristics increased or decreased in importance? Why?

4. What is the role and importance of ethics in entrepreneurial ventures? Why are ethics important to the entrepreneur?

5. Sam Walton and Mary Kay Ash are two "visionaries" portrayed in the chapter. What are the similarities in their management style and corporate culture?

CHAPTER 2

Multiple Choice

E   1.   Which of the following is often considered to be outside the realm of entrepreneurship?
A.   Being creative and innovative in developing new products or services.
B.   Managing an existing venture in such a way that it grows rapidly and consistently.
C.   Starting a business.
D.   Accepting risk in the development of a new or growing venture.
E.   Running the day-to-day operations of a small company.

A   2.   Innovation can best be thought of as:
A.   The introduction of a new product, service, or process.
B.   The driving force behind creativity.
C.   The only link between imagination and the introduction of an innovative product, service, or process.
D.   An ingredient sufficient by itself to establish entrepreneurship.

D   3.   Which of the following is most true about starting a new business?
A.   It necessarily involves creativity and innovation.
B.   It must be highly entrepreneurial in nature.
C.   The amount of planning involved is about the same for all new businesses.
D.   It is not necessarily highly innovative.

B   4.   Which of the following is a possible problem of administrative structure?
- A.   It ties an organization and its people to its overall mission.
- B.   Too much of it hinders the introduction of innovations in the marketplace.
- C.   It provides direction, policies, controls, and supervision.
- D.   Some structure is needed to control performance.

C   5.   Which of the following is true of venture capital?
- A.   It is available for both high risk and medium risk ventures.
- B.   New ventures cannot succeed without it.
- C.   It is associated with high potential ventures.
- D.   The venture capitalists primarily make loans that banks will not make.

D   6.   A key distinction between entrepreneurship and corporate management is the issue of risk management versus risk minimization. In this regard, which of the following is true?
- A.   Entrepreneurship deals primarily in risk minimization
- B.   Corporate management deals in risk management
- C.   Risk management attempts to minimize risk
- D.   Entrepreneurship is risk assuming

B   7.   Using multiple sources of financing and building an entrepreneurial team with different but compatible skills are both examples of:
- A.   Risk minimization
- B.   Managing assumed risk
- C.   Attempting to eliminate risk
- D.   Disinvestment

A   8.   Investing resources after first identifying opportunities is:
- A.   A characteristic of entrepreneurship.
- B.   Most commonly associated with corporate management.
- C.   An example of resource-driven investment.
- D.   The same as looking for opportunities that fit within the limit of the available capital.

D 9. Intrapreneurship can best be thought of as:
   A. A formal structure within a corporation in pursuit of the benefits of entrepreneurship.
   B. A joint agreement between two ventures to invest resources in a particular project to minimize risk.
   C. A process with little potential because of the excessive management layers in today's corporations.
   D. An attempt by corporations to instill the process of entrepreneurship within the corporate frameworks.

A 10. Of the five components of entrepreneurial ventures, the one that is perhaps the most significant key to success is:
   A. Managerial skill
   B. Having a great opportunity with high potential
   C. Adequate financing
   D. The legal structure of the new venture

C 11. The entrepreneurial process begins with the_____ and ends with the _____.
   A. Opportunity, structure
   B. Opportunity, resources
   C. Entrepreneur, strategy
   D. Resources, opportunity

D 12. The term for the variables which represent situations or characteristics that cause the individual to consider launching a new venture is:
   A. Precipitating
   B. Triggering
   C. Enabling
   D. Antecedent

B 13. A specific event or situation that occurs prompting an entrepreneurial act is the:
   A. Enabling variable
   B. Precipitating variable
   C. Antecedent variable
   D. Background variable

A 14. Antecedent variables are commonly thought of as:
   A. Stage-setting variables
   B. Triggering variables
   C. The variables sufficient to cause a new venture creation
   D. Situations or events

C   15.   The motivation to launch a venture is a function of:
         A.   Background, antecedent, and precipitating variables.
         B.   Antecedent, precipitating, and triggering variables.
         C.   Antecedent, triggering, and enabling variables.
         D.   Background, antecedent, and enabling variables.

B   16.   The two variables which, by themselves, comprise the potential entrepreneur's motivation to launch a venture are the:
         A.   Antecedent and enabling variables.
         B.   Antecedent and triggering variables.
         C.   Background and antecedent variables.
         D.   Precipitating and enabling variables.

D   17.   The willingness or motivation to start a venture is illustrated in which of the following equation forms?
         A. $M = \Sigma A_i + \Sigma T_j$
         B. $M = \Sigma A_i \times \Sigma E_k$
         C. $M = \Sigma E_k \times \Sigma T_j$
         D. $M = \Sigma A_i \times \Sigma T_j$

C   18.   Which of the following is not true of the entrepreneurship motivation equation?
         A.   If either factor is zero, the motivation to launch a venture will be zero.
         B.   As the number or strength of the variables increases so will the motivation to launch a venture.
         C.   As the number or strength of the variables decreases, the motivation to launch a venture will increase.
         D.   Each of the variables can only be subjectively measured.

C   19.   Which of the following would be considered an antecedent factor?
         A.   Job dissatisfaction
         B.   A missed promotion
         C.   Past experience
         D.   Loss of job

D   20.   Which of the following is true of a person who possesses strong amounts of antecedent and triggering factors only:
         A.   A venture will be launched.
         B.   There is not sufficient motivation to launch a venture.
         C.   The enabling factor is no longer important.
         D.   There will be a desire to launch a venture, but the venture will probably not be launched.

A 21. The two components of entrepreneurship which comprise the enabling factor are:
    A. The resources and opportunity
    B. The resources and strategy
    C. The opportunity and strategy
    D. The structure and resources

B 22. The primary reason for different rates of growth for new ventures is:
    A. Simply the nature of the product or opportunity
    B. The degree of entrepreneurial behavior in the venture
    C. Some ventures have more access to capital than others
    D. The enabling factors for some ventures are much stronger

D 23. The amount of entrepreneurship present in a new venture is primarily a function of:
    A. The size of the market for the product
    B. The amount of competition that exists
    C. How much funding is available to the entrepreneur
    D. The desires and skills of the founder

D 24. The factor that differentiates the low growth from others is:
    A. Low growth ventures necessarily have weaker enabling variables
    B. Low growth ventures are limited by their financial resources to begin with
    C. Low growth venture entrepreneurs have weaker background variables
    D. Low growth ventures are not intended to grow beyond limits set by the owner

A 25. Low growth ventures are most significantly characterized by:
    A. Concentration on operational issues
    B. Strategic innovation
    C. A high amount of entrepreneurship
    D. High growth goals

D 26. Which of the following is not true of low growth ventures?
    A. Use of small amounts of market research
    B. They generally only serve a single market
    C. Lack of strategic innovation
    D. Use of multiple sources of financing

C   27.   Absorption periods are usually longer for:
- A.   Growth oriented ventures because of the size of the venture
- B.   Low growth ventures because of the large number of prior entrepreneurial thrusts
- C.   Low growth ventures because of limited experience
- D.   Growth oriented ventures because of the prior learning experiences

B   28.   The prior number of entrepreneurial thrusts and the venture's growth level are determining factors in:
- A.   The level of strategic innovation
- B.   The length of the absorption period
- C.   The success of implemented strategies
- D.   Increasing amounts of innovation activity

C   29.   Which of the following is a way of managing assumed risk?
- A.   Using a single source of financing rather than several sources
- B.   Purchasing fixed assets to eliminate rent payments
- C.   Undertaking multiple ventures simultaneously
- D.   Assembling an entrepreneurial team with identical skills

A   30.   Identifying opportunities that fit within the limits of available capital is:
- A.   Most commonly associated with corporate management
- B.   A characteristic of entrepreneurship
- C.   An example of opportunity-driven investment
- D.   A method of risk management

D   31.   Factors such as the loss of a job, inventing a new product, or being approached to become a partner in a new venture are all examples of:
- A.   Antecedent factors
- B.   Enabling factors
- C.   Stage-setting variables
- D.   Triggering factors

True/False

F   32.   Entrepreneurship can only occur with the launch of a new venture.

F   33.   Because a new business is started means that it is entrepreneurial.

F   34.   The introduction of a new product or service to a market is creativity.

F   35.   Innovation is the link between imagination and the introduction of a new product, service, or process.

T   36.   Administrative structure is needed in order for innovations to be introduced into the marketplace.

T   37.   Maintaining growth requires as much entrepreneurial activity as launching a venture.

T   38.   Managing growth is part of entrepreneurship.

F   39.   The use of multiple sources of financing is a characteristic of low growth ventures.

T   40.   Many ventures are successful without infusions of venture capital.

T   41.   Venture capital involves an exchange of funding for a share of ownership.

T   42.   Internally generated funds may be sufficient to achieve desired growth.

T   43.   All ventures contain a degree of entrepreneurship.

T   44.   Corporate management's goal is to minimize risk while being as productive and profitable as possible.

T   45.   Risk management does not attempt to eliminate or even minimize risk.

F   46.   An entrepreneur will often prefer to produce the product himself instead of subcontracting in order to maximize internal investment.

F   47.   Determining where an investment should be made after determining the amount of available capital is opportunity-driven investment.

F   48.   Action versus analysis is a distinction made when comparing types of new ventures.

F   49.   Contributing capital to selected ventures outside the corporation is an example of disinvestment.

Essay

1. Explain how entrepreneurship differs from corporate management in regards to risk, investment, and other characteristics or philosophies.

2. Explain the five components of entrepreneurial ventures with regard to how they form an entrepreneurial process. How does the process begin and end?

3. Explain how the decision to launch a venture is determined in terms of what factors, or variables, are present as motivating forces in the decision. Give examples for each variable and express venture launch likelihood as a function of these variables.

4. Explain how different amounts of entrepreneurship exist in various ventures.

5. Explain how the amount of entrepreneurial activity varies over time and across the different levels of ventures. What activities can cause the levels to change for each type of venture?

CHAPTER 3

Multiple Choice

C   1.   Defining an entrepreneur strictly as an individual who is primarily responsible for gathering together the necessary resources to initiate a business?

     A.   Purposefully excludes innovation because it is inherent in initiating a business.

     B.   Recognizes that initiating a business is the primary function of the entrepreneur.

     C.   Focuses on venture launch.

     D.   Is the definition used by the author.

A   2.   A popular definition for entrepreneur is an individual who gathers the necessary resources to launch and/or grow a business focusing on innovation and development of new products or services. Which of the following is not implicit in this definition?

     A.   There exists a tie between venture success and innovation.

     B.   The recognition that entrepreneurs may exist in both large and small ventures.

     C.   Individuals are not entrepreneurs simply because they have started a business.

     D.   There is a link between innovation and entrepreneurship.

A   3.   The limited success of studies aimed at determining similarities among entrepreneurs can be attributed to:
     A.   The fact that all entrepreneurs exhibit certain and absolute characteristics.
     B.   The lack of a common setting in which to study entrepreneurs.
     C.   Researchers use differing numbers of people in their samples.
     D.   Entrepreneurs have so many differences that trying to categorize them will be impossible.

C   4.   The characteristics entrepreneurs exhibit are typically:
     A.   Similar to those of corporate managers.
     B.   Clearly identifiable in comparison with other groups.
     C.   Tendencies rather than absolutes.
     D.   Not much different from those of the general population.

B   5.   The largest percentage of new ventures are launched when the entrepreneur is between the ages of:
     A.   20-29
     B.   30-39
     C.   40-49
     D.   50+

D   6.   The time span during which a particular entrepreneur is likely to launch a new venture is:
     A.   Dependent on the background and precipitating variables.
     B.   A function of how strong the enabling factors are.
     C.   Commonly called the window of opportunity.
     D.   Referred to as an entrepreneurial window.

C   7.   The push/pull hypothesis regarding entrepreneurial behavior has what effect on the antecedent and precipitating variables?
     A.   Allows both variables to be positive or negative.
     B.   Causes the antecedent variable to have a negative effect while the precipitating variable may be positive or negative.
     C.   Allows the precipitating variable to have either a positive   or negative effect.
     D.   The hypothesis has an effect on the antecendent and enabling factors but not the precipitating factor.

B   8.   The contention that most entrepreneurs are displaced persons supports:
- A.   The fact that entrepreneurs are "pulled" into starting a business.
- B.   Negative events playing a key role in new venture creation.
- C.   A strong relationship between the type of business started and the entrepreneur's work background.
- D.   A positive event triggering a displaced person's venture launch.

C   9.   Factors such as risk-taking propensity, need for achievement, need for autonomy, and a willingness to work long hours:
- A.   Determine the ultimate success or failure of the new venture.
- B.   Are examples of the entrepreneurial window.
- C.   Are components of the entrepreneurial personality.
- D.   Are all necessary personality traits for a person to be considered "entrepreneurial."

B   10.   To say that an entrepreneur is a risk assumer means that:
- A.   They assume the high levels of risk normal for a venture launch without concern.
- B.   They are moderate or calculated risk takers.
- C.   The entrepreneur is risk seeking.
- D.   They seek out high risk ventures with the greatest potential.

A   11.   If a person considering launching a new venture has just been dismissed from a job, which of the following is true?
- A.   The relative risk may be much smaller.
- B.   The relative risk may be much greater.
- C.   The absolute risk may be much smaller.
- D.   The absolute risk may be much greater.

D   12.   The concept of opportunity cost or opportunity risk is most associated with:
- A.   Risk assumption
- B.   Absolute risk
- C.   The entrepreneurial personality
- D.   Relative risk

B   13.   The popular conception that entrepreneurs are independent individuals who
           are willing to assume risks in order to be in control:
           A.   Is dissimilar to research findings
           B.   Is supported by research findings
           C.   Cannot be substantiated through research
           D.   Contradicts the internal locus of control concept

D   14.   Entrepreneurs' belief that their personal success or failure is a result of
           their own actions:
           A.   Reflects a high need for achievement
           B.   Is the same as autonomy
           C.   Is atypical of how most entrepreneurs feel
           D.   Is the internal locus of control concept

C   15.   Along with the need for autonomy, which of the following explains the
           decision to leave a job and risk personal capital in a venture?
           A.   High risk-taking propensity
           B.   Internal locus of control
           C.   Need for achievement
           D.   Need for power

A   16.   The primary personal goal of small business entrepreneurs is:
           A.   Technical proficiency
           B.   A profitably harvested venture
           C.   An extravagant lifestyle
           D.   Growth of the venture

D   17.   A key distinction between small business entrepreneurs and growth
           entrepreneurs is that:
           A.   Small business entrepreneurs are goal directed rather than means
                 oriented.
           B.   Growth entrepreneurs are means oriented rather than
                 goal directed.
           C.   Growth entrepreneurs are both means oriented and goal
                 directed.
           D.   Small business entrepreneurs are means oriented rather than goal
                 directed.

B   18.   Being less concerned with structure and control is a characteristic typical of:
- A.   Small business owners not concerned with growth
- B.   Growth entrepreneurs
- C.   Autonomy-driven entrepreneurs
- D.   A "means" rather than "goals" orientation

C   19.   Which of the following is true regarding the personality type of growth entrepreneurs?
- A.   They focus on operations duties.
- B.   They are more concerned with structure and control than small business entrepreneurs.
- C.   They tend to be more intuitive thinkers than small business entrepreneurs.
- D.   They have a lower tolerance for ambiguity.

A   20.   One of the differences between small business entrepreneurs and growth entrepreneurs is their view of risk. In that regard:
- A.   Small business entrepreneurs are risk avoiders while growth entrepreneurs are calculated risk takers.
- B.   Small business entrepreneurs are risk assumers while growth entrepreneurs are risk seekers.
- C.   Small business entrepreneurs are risk assumers while growth entrepreneurs are moderate risk takers.
- D.   Small business entrepreneurs are risk avoiders while growth entrepreneurs are uncalculated risk takers.

D   21.   It is well known that there are many differences among entrepreneurs as a group. Knowing this, which of the following is true?
- A.   There are more differences between men and women entrepreneurs than there are between entrepreneurial women and non-entrepreneurial women.
- B.   The degree of risk taking propensity between male and female entrepreneurs is the primary difference.
- C.   Women in general have a more internal locus of control than female entrepreneurs.
- D.   There are more differences between entrepreneurial women and non-entrepreneurial women than there are between men and women who are entrepreneurs.

B   22.   Research studies focusing on entrepreneurial differences between men and women indicate that:

    A.   Women are psychologically less effective than men in managing and growing business ventures.

    B.   Entrepreneurial tendencies are pervasive in both genders.

    C.   Women generally have both a higher energy level and greater risk-taking propensity than men.

    D.   Though there are many differences among entrepreneurs, they are more widespread than one might think.

A   23.   One of the problems women face in obtaining financing for a new venture is:

    A.   Their propensity to launch service or retail ventures.

    B.   Evidence suggesting that ventures launched by women have a higher failure rate than those launched by men.

    C.   The difference in the educational level of men and women.

    D.   Women don't possess as many of the "entrepreneurial" characteristics leading to a potentially successful venture.

A   24.   Which of the following statements is true regarding business ownership and family stress?

    A.   There is considerable overlap between the demands of the business and the demands of the family.

    B.   The amount of family stress is directly related to the number of hours spent with the business.

    C.   The amount of family stress is a unrelated to the number of hours spent with the business.

    D.   Women business owners experience more stress than do women in corporations.

D   25.   The primary reason why women business owners experience more life satisfaction and less stress than women corporate managers is that:

    A.   Less stress is a function of greater financial stability.

    B.   Normal management situations in corporations are more stressful.

    C.   Women business owners have more supportive husbands.

    D.   Women business owners have more control and flexibility.

D   26.   The number of minority-owned enterprises increased dramatically in the 1980's due at least partially to:
  - A.   Demand in both the construction and financial sectors.
  - B.   The decline in defense spending.
  - C.   The overall decline in the domestic economy.
  - D.   Government utilization of minority suppliers.

A   27.   In which of the following industries are minorities well represented in terms of number of enterprises?
  - A.   Transportation
  - B.   Manufacturing
  - C.   Construction
  - D.   Mining

C   28.   Jointly owned ventures run by a husband/wife team are referred to as a:
  - A.   Family owned business
  - B.   Family business enterprise
  - C.   Co-preneur ventures
  - D.   Co-venture

B   29.   Co-preneur, or husband/wife-run ventures, are particularly risky if:
  - A.   It's a low growth venture
  - B.   The marriage is new
  - C.   Each spouse has professional or managerial experience
  - D.   There's a stable marriage relationship

D   30.   The primary value an advisory board has to an entrepreneur comes from:
  - A.   Directing the entrepreneur toward sources of funding.
  - B.   Locating suppliers or customers.
  - C.   Generating sales leads.
  - D.   Advice given to the entrepreneur

C   31.   Co-preneurs should pay particular attention to:
  - A.   Separating their own capital from that of the business.
  - B.   The decision-making process.
  - C.   Having a clear understanding of the role each will play.
  - D.   Ensuring that they work on all tasks together.

A   32.   The definition of entrepreneur to be used throughout this course is:
          A.   An entrepreneur is an individual who launches a venture and/or
                significantly improves it through innovative means.
          B.   An entrepreneur is the individual who is primarily responsible for
                gathering together the necessary resources to initiate a business.
          C.   An entrepreneur is an individual who marshals the resources
                necessary to launch a business that focuses on innovation and
                development of new products or services.
          D.   An entrepreneur is an individual who runs a business at his/her own
                financial risk.

D   33.   Regarding displaced persons, which of the following statements is true?
          A.   Most displaced persons start a business similar to the person's
                previous work background.
          B.   Most start a venture because of the occurrence of some positive
                event.
          C.   Most displaced persons are "pulled" into launching a
                venture.
          D.   There is little relationship between the type of business started and
                the person's previous work background.

A   34.   The popular conception that the entrepreneur is a high risk taker:
          A.   Is refuted by research findings
          B.   Is similar to research findings
          C.   Cannot be substantiated or refuted through research
          D.   Is primarily attributable to women having higher risk
                levels

C   35.   The willingness of an entrepreneur to begin a venture without knowing
          whether it will succeed is an indication of:
          A.   Absolute risk
          B.   Internal locus of control
          C.   Tolerance for ambiguity
          D.   Opportunity risk

True/False

F   36.   Entrepreneurs have been studied a great deal with much success.

F   37.   A small percentage of entrepreneurs come from families with
          entrepreneurial experience.

T   38.   The educational backgrounds that entrepreneurs possess are as varied as their ages.

F   39.   The push/pull hypothesis focuses on the likelihood of a new venture launch.

F   40.   Potential entrepreneurs are "pushed" into beginning their own venture when some positive event happens to them.

T   41.   In the case of displaced persons, there is little relationship between the type of business started and the entrepreneur's previous work background.

T   42.   Both the "push" and "pull" forces may be at work in a given situation.

F   43.   Entrepreneurs are inherently high risk takers.

F   44.   Entrepreneurs are willing to assume a high amount of risk that would be normal for a venture launch.

T   45.   Autonomy and internal locus of control typify the entrepreneur perhaps more than any other characteristics.

T   46.   Tolerance for ambiguity is the acceptance of uncertainty as a normal part of one's life.

T   47.   There is no single set of characteristics that defines a successful entrepreneur.

F   48.   Low growth owners are generally less concerned with structure and control than growth owners.

T   49.   Family stress is not a strong function of the number of hours spent with the business.

F   50.   Though an entrepreneur may be defined several different ways, all definitions focus on the initiation of a business.

T   51.   There is no one best age in which to launch a venture.

T   52.   The time period during which a particular entrepreneur may launch a venture is referred to as an entrepreneurial window.

F   53.   Research has shown that the "push" rationale for starting a business is stronger for women than men.

T   54.   High growth entrepreneurs tend to be goal directed rather than means directed.

Essay Questions

1.   Differentiate between the characteristics of entrepreneurs who own low growth ventures and those who own higher growth firms in terms of background, education, view of risk, etc.

2.   Though there is no one particular personality type representative of all entrepreneurs, there does appear to be four components of the personality common to most entrepreneurs. Identify and discuss those components and how they play a role in the decision to leave the safe confines of a corporation and launch a venture.

3.   Why have studies aimed at determining entrepreneurial characteristics resulted in only limited success? Why is it particularly difficult to differentiate between successful and unsuccessful entrepreneurs?

4.   Discuss some of the unique problems facing women entrepreneurs, minority entrepreneurs, and family business entrepreneurs.

5.   Discuss how assembling the entrepreneurial team is a function of the nature of the venture and the amount of desired growth (i.e., apply your reasoning to both low- and high-brow ventures). Also, what are some of the functions an advisory board performs for a typical entrepreneur?

CHAPTER 4

Multiple Choice

B   1.   When speaking of new ventures, most people's discussions of business plans will be about:
A.   Strategic plans
B.   Financial plans
C.   The planning horizon
D.   Marketing plans

C   2.   The primary goal of the financial plan is to:
A.   Guide the new venture's strategy
B.   Project sales, expenses, profits, and losses
C.   Convince investors of the future potential of the company
D.   Analyze the venture's capabilities and identify distinctive competencies

A   3.   Which of the following is true of strategic plans?
A.   The plan is revised at least annually
B.   The plan is revised every 2-3 years as the economy and industry change
C.   The plan is revised whenever additional funding is needed
D.   The plan is prepared by the firm's financial staff

C   4.   Which of the following is true of financial plans?
        A.   The document is prepared by top management and key operating managers
        B.   The document is read by management and key employees
        C.   The document requires substantial amounts of information about the economy and industry
        D.   The plan should be revised quarterly.

B   5.   Objective information such as economic factors, trends in the industry, and a thorough competitive analysis:
        A.   Is considered part of the company's specific strategy
        B.   Are all important ingredients of a business plan
        C.   Is extremely expensive information to gather.
        D.   Should be revised every 2-3 years as the environment changes

A   6.   Potential investors want to see what the business is all about and what its financial projections are, but they are not particularly interested in the:
        A.   Operational details of the business
        B.   Marketing considerations
        C.   Investor considerations
        D.   The scope of the opportunities

C   7.   An important distinction between strategic plans and financial plans is that:
        A.   Financial plans should be reviewed and revised periodically whereas strategic plans are only prepared at the onset of the venture.
        B.   Strategic plans are often protected from being read by employees for competitive reasons whereas financial plans are read by top management and other key personnel.
        C.   The strategic plan should be revised periodically whereas the financial plan is prepared only when funding is needed.
        D.   Because strategic plans concern the direction of the venture, financial projections are included in financial plans only.

A   8.   The strategic planning process for entrepreneurial ventures:
        A.   Is not significantly different than it is for large businesses
        B.   Is significantly different than planning for a large business
        C.   Will result in the same type of strategies for both small and large businesses
        D.   Is not as important as the resulting document outlining strategies and objectives.

D   9.   Prior to identifying the venture's capabilities or its environment, which of the following must be determined?
A.   The venture strategy
B.   The amount of resources required
C.   The actions necessary to actually put the strategy into action
D.   The nature of the venture

C   10.   Which of the following is the proper sequence of stages for the entrepreneurial strategic planning process?
A.   Strategy development stage; premise stage; analysis stage; implementation stage
B.   Premise stage; strategy development stage; analysis stage; implementation stage
C.   Premise stage; analysis stage; strategy development stage; implementation stage
D.   Strategy development stage; analysis stage; premise stage; implementation stage

D   11.   An analysis assessing entrepreneurial opportunities should:
A.   Identify areas or fads with short opportunity windows warranting immediate action.
B.   Identify areas with small markets to allow for niche marketing.
C.   Focus on current opportunities and not future developments or trends.
D.   Determine the investment return for an exploitable strategy.

A   12.   A firm that has no distinctive competencies will:
A.   Benefit from a large market
B.   Never be able to exploit a given opportunity
C.   Never be able to develop an effective venture strategy
D.   Necessarily fail in competition with firms possessing competencies

C   13.   Which of the following is true of distinctive competencies?
A.   They are necessary for new venture success.
B.   They are usually sustainable over an extended period of time.
C.   Eventually, other firms will counter the competency.
D.   They are supported by a competitive advantage.

B   14.   Purchasing instead of leasing facilities has what effect on an venture's level of risk and working capital?
- A.   Decreases risk, increases working capital.
- B.   Increases risk, decreases working capital.
- C.   Decreases risk, decreases working capital.
- D.   Increases risk, increases working capital.

C   15.   The first step of the implementation stage of the planning process is to:
- A.   Establish controls to ensure that the venture's strategies work as planned.
- B.   Start the "actions" dictated by the supporting strategies.
- C.   Assemble the necessary resources.
- D.   Monitor the environment for changes which may have occurred that may alter the venture's strategy.

A   16.   In writing a financial plan, entrepreneurs should know that the most important part is the:
- A.   Executive summary
- B.   Financial analysis section
- C.   Operations and strategy section
- D.   Environmental analysis section

D   17.   In writing a financial plan, entrepreneurs should remember to:
- A.   Include a substantial, detailed financial analysis.
- B.   Describe the technical aspects of the product/service.
- C.   Emphasize operational issues.
- D.   Substantiate sales projections.

A   18.   The format for the strategic plan is:
- A.   Not as critical as for the financial plan.
- B.   Just as critical as for the financial plan.
- C.   Heavily market-oriented.
- D.   Heavily quantitative.

C   19.   Perhaps the most significant mistake an entrepreneur can make regarding the financial plan is to:
- A.   Emphasize market orientation over financial orientation.
- B.   Include financial projections for at least three years.
- C.   Use one plan for all types of investors.
- D.   Not focus on the technical aspects of the product/service.

A   20.   From a long-term perspective, perhaps the most critical part of the
            financial plan is to:
            A.   Determine the amount of capital needed.
            B.   Match expenses with sales projections.
            C.   Document sales projections at least five to ten years in the future.
            D.   State objectively what the risks are.

D   21.   When considering the types of items included in the financial plan, which
            of the following is true?
            A.   A financial plan is less restrictive than a strategic plan because
                  financial plans must be tailored to specific types of investors.
            B.   A financial plan is less restrictive than a strategic plan because it
                  focuses primarily on the financial aspects of the venture.
            C.   A strategic plan is more restrictive because it focuses on the more
                  complicated strategic direction of the firm.
            D.   The outline for a financial plan is more restrictive than the strategic
                  plan.

B   22.   Which of the following is not a common ingredient of financial and
            strategic plans?
            A.   Identification of cash flow
            B.   Break-even analysis
            C.   Income and expense projections
            D.   Sales forecasts

D   23.   Extrapolating historical data into the future to forecast sales:
            A.   Is the most correct way of forecasting sales for existing
                  firms.
            B.   Will be optimal but only if historical sales are not uniformly
                  increasing.
            C.   Is the only way new ventures can forecast sales.
            D.   Will be incorrect unless trends or patterns in the data are accounted
                  for.

B   24.   Interviewing other entrepreneurs in the industry as a way of projecting
            sales is:
            A.   Unwise, both ethically and pragmatically.
            B.   Particularly useful for new retail businesses.
            C.   Never reliable because no entrepreneur would honestly provide that
                  information.
            D.   Only useful if entrepreneurs in the same location and industry are
                  interviewed.

C   25.   The primary purpose of the strategic plan is to:
- A.   Convince investors of the future potential of the company.
- B.   Analyze the venture's capabilities and identify distinctive competencies.
- C.   Specify actions necessary to achieve goals.
- D.   Identify sources and uses of funds

B   26.   The two aspects of the financial plan that investors are particularly interested in are the investor considerations and:
- A.   Operational considerations
- B.   Marketing considerations
- C.   Human resource considerations
- D.   Competitive considerations

D   27.   The communication of strategic plans to employees has a(n):
- A.   Effectiveness benefit
- B.   Planning benefit
- C.   Resource allocation benefit
- D.   Motivation benefit

C   28.   A financial plan will not be accurate or well documented unless the planning process is completed and:
- A.   A financial strategy is determined
- B.   Objectives and goals are identified
- C.   A sales forecast is developed
- D.   A baseline comparison has been made

A   29.   The analysis stage of the strategic planning process involves:
- A.   The venture's capabilities and its environment
- B.   Primary and supporting strategies
- C.   Analyzing the nature of the venture
- D.   Determining which actions are necessary to put the strategy into action

D   30.   Establishing controls and assembling the necessary resources are steps in what phase of the strategic planning process?
- A.   Premise
- B.   Strategy development
- C.   Analysis
- D.   Implementation

D   31.   An analysis of the venture's capabilities must be in relation to:
            A.   Distinctive competencies
            B.   The entrepreneurial team's skills
            C.   The financial resources available
            D.   The opportunities being considered

True/False

F   32.   Financial plans are intended to be read primarily by management and other key employees.

F   33.   The financial plan is designed to be an internal guide of actions necessary to achieve the firms goals.

T   34.   The strategic plan is not intended to be read by outsiders.

F   35.   Investors are not particularly interested in the marketing aspects of the business plan.

T   36.   The financial plan is revised only when additional funding is needed.

T   37.   Many of the benefits derived from developing a business plan come from the planning process itself.

T   38.   The distance to the planning horizon is not as important as the fact that some planning horizon exists.

T   39.   Business plans cannot be developed without first developing the firm's strategy.

F   40.   The strategic planning process for entrepreneurial ventures is significantly different than it is for large businesses.

F   41.   All new ventures must have some type of distinctive competency in order to survive.

T   42.   The stronger the opportunity/capability match the easier it is to develop strategies.

F   43.   Risk can be better managed by owning rather than leasing facilities.

T 44. All business plans must contain a financial strategy.

F 45. The implementation stage of the strategic planning process consists of four steps.

F 46. Since the financial plan is an external document, the format for the plan is not as critical as for the strategic pan.

T 47. A thorough assessment of venture capabilities should be made before determining the strategy.

T 48. The executive summary is the most important part of the financial plan.

F 49. The outline for a strategic plan is somewhat more restrictive than the financial plan because of the items that must be included.

T 50. If enough data is available, an extrapolation of the data into the future is the prime method of forecasting sales.

T 51. Distinctive competencies are seldom sustainable over an extended period of time.

Essay

1. What are some of the differences between strategic plans and financial plans? How is the focus of each plan different?

2. Identify and describe some of the benefits of developing business plans. Is there an inherent benefit in the planning process itself? Why?

3. Describe the strategic planning process as it relates to entrepreneurial ventures. What are some important considerations, or steps, in each of the four phases?

4. Present a comprehensive strategic plan outline such as the one suggested in the chapter. What are some useful guidelines to follow in the writing of the plan?

5. Suppose you are considering opening a small sporting goods store. How would you collect data in order to forecast sales? Specify steps you would take to determine an estimate of the total market and obtain a "ballpark" sales projection.

CHAPTER 5

Multiple Choice

D   1.   In regard to how early American pioneers evaluated the westward opportunities they sought, which of the following is likely?
A.   If there had been more uncertainty, fewer would have ventured forth.
B.   Evaluating opportunities today is drastically dissimilar from the early years.
C.   If more were known about opportunities and roles, more would have ventured forth.
D.   More certainty would have led to greater preparation.

A   2.   Which of the following most accurately expresses the relationship between the degree of uncertainty and the proliferation of new ventures?
A.   If more were known, fewer entrepreneurs would start a venture.
B.   If more were known, more entrepreneurs would start a venture.
C.   Greater uncertainty leads to greater preparation.
D.   Since uncertainty is inherent in new venture launches, there is no relationship between levels of risk and the proliferation of new ventures.

C   3.   The key to successfully pursuing an entrepreneurial opportunity is:
A.   In coming up with the right idea.
B.   Having previous experience in the new venture's industry.
C.   Dependent on the analysis of the opportunity.
D.   Having enough funding available.

B 4. The term "baby boom" referring to the significant increase in the number of people born in the 15-year period following WWII is an example of a:
   A. Social trend
   B. Demographic trend
   C. Business trend
   D. Technological trend

D 5. Demographic trends can involve:
   A. A decline in the number of smokers
   B. Shifts in co-habitation patterns
   C. The number of dual career families
   D. Changes in number of people in an age group

A 6. Which of the following is an example of a social trend?
   A. The number of single parent families
   B. Increases in the level of education
   C. Changes in earning of population classes
   D. Changes in spending patterns

B 7. The most pervasive single trend in American society over the past twenty years is that of:
   A. Increased interest in environmental issues
   B. Women entering the labor force
   C. The increased growth in the number of teenagers
   D. Increases in levels of education

C 8. Which of the following is a consequence of the social trend of more women entering the labor force?
   A. Changes in education
   B. Changes in marriage and divorce rates
   C. Proliferation of women into professional occupations
   D. The number of single parent families

D 9. Which of the following is an example of a business trend?
   A. Computer-related trends
   B. Increases in medical diagnostic equipment
   C. Increased medical claims processing services
   D. Technology consultants

B 10. The "launchpad" concept is particularly prevalent in the _____ area.
   A. Manufacturing
   B. High-tech
   C. Service
   D. Retail

D 11. Which of the following is true regarding "launchpad" jobs?
   A. They are responsible for many entrepreneurs being "pushed" into starting their own ventures.
   B. They are responsible for many new ideas in the manufacturing industry.
   C. Studies show that a small percentage of entrepreneurs got their idea from a prior job.
   D. They are the base from which many new ventures are launched.

C 12. A person who attempts to produce and market an invention is sometimes referred to as a(n):
   A. Co-preneur
   B. Market-oriented innovator
   C. Inventrepreneur
   D. Market-preneur

A 13. Which of the following is the first step in exploiting "non-obvious" opportunities?
   A. Recognize the possibilities
   B. Create a product that can meet some untapped need
   C. Identify an obvious need and create a product that meets that need
   D. Marshall the resources to exploit them

D 14. Which of the following is a way of recognizing a not-so-obvious opportunity?
   A. Create a product that can hopefully meet some untapped need.
   B. Identify an obvious need and fill it by creating a product or service.
   C. Marshall resources to exploit current opportunities.
   D. Look for other uses of existing products.

A   15.   An objective evaluation of venture opportunities is critical because:
          A.   Investors require documentation on the venture's probability of success.
          B.   It increases the intuitive ability of the entrepreneur.
          C.   An objective assessment increases the probability that the decision to pursue a venture will be based on intuition.
          D.   It will result in tunnel vision toward goal achievement.

C   16.   The window of opportunity is the period of time during which:
          A.   A particular entrepreneur is likely to launch a new venture.
          B.   The new venture has protection from competition.
          C.   An investment has maximum potential for success.
          D.   An acceptable return is provided for a logical investment.

B   17.   Depth of the market for a product refers to:
          A.   How many uses a particular product has.
          B.   How intensive a product is used by its customers.
          C.   How many "similar" products exist in the marketplace.
          D.   The total number of customers to buy a particular product.

D   18.   Breadth of the market refers to:
          A.   How intensive a product is used by its customers.
          B.   How many "similar" products exist in the market-place.
          C.   The total number of customers who buy a particular product.
          D.   The number of different uses for a product.

D   19.   Which of the following statements about the size of the total market is true?
          A.   The larger market is always preferred.
          B.   The size of the market has little to do with the amount of investment required.
          C.   Size of the total market is synonymous with depth and breadth of the market.
          D.   A larger market often invites competition.

A   20.   The key to insulating a product from competition is:
          A.   To have some aspect of the product that is not easily duplicated.
          B.   Obtain patents.
          C.   Safeguard trade secrets.
          D.   Delay the obsolescence of the product.

C   21.   The risk of a venture will be higher if:
- A.   The window of opportunity is extraordinarily long.
- B.   The market is extremely broad or deep.
- C.   The product is totally new.
- D.   There is not much capital investment in fixed assets.

A   22.   The risk of a venture will be lower if:
- A.   The market for the product exhibits great depth or breadth.
- B.   There is a long payback period.
- C.   There are no alternative uses of the product.
- D.   The product is easily copyable.

B   23.   The first stage of the analysis process for a new venture is:
- A.   An objective analysis that determines growth possibilities.
- B.   To determine whether the overall idea is sound.
- C.   Determining how much capital is needed to launch the venture.
- D.   Composition of the entrepreneurial team.

C   24.   Regarding the venture evaluation process, an unfavorable <u>entrepreneur's</u> perspective coupled with a favorable <u>investor's</u> perspective should result in:
- A.   Venture-launch
- B.   Downscaling the venture
- C.   Reformulating the management team
- D.   Scrapping the venture

A   25.   Regarding the venture evaluation process, an unfavorable <u>investor's</u> perspective coupled with a favorable <u>entrepreneur's</u> perspective should result in:
- A.   Downscaling the venture
- B.   Venture launch
- C.   Scrapping the venture
- D.   Reformulating the management team

B   26.   Which of the following is an item typically used in the informal venture analysis stage?
- A.   Total market size determination
- B.   The 10/1 ratio
- C.   Cash flow analysis
- D.   Type of equipment needed to make the product/service.

D   27.   The first part of the formal analysis stage to be completed is the:
A.   Financial feasibility
B.   Technical feasibility
C.   Operational feasibility
D.   Marketing feasibility

D   28.   Which of the following most accurately describes fatal flaws?
A.   They represent conditions or events which reduce the possible returns.
B.   They are a necessary part of the informal analysis stage.
C.   Fatal flaws are defects in the design, durability, or reliability of the product.
D.   They are negative events or conditions which override all favorable results.

C   29.   If a fatal flaw is encountered, then:
A.   The venture must be abandoned.
B.   The entrepreneur must realize that practically all new ventures are characterized by fatal flaws.
C.   The venture must at least be revised significantly.
D.   The entrepreneur should attempt to override this condition by finding a favorable result which will help in rationalizing away the fatal flaw.

A   30.   Which of the following is an example of a demographic trend?
A.   Increases in levels of education
B.   A decline in the number of smokers
C.   Shifts in political persuasion
D.   An increase in the number of women entering the workforce.

B   31.   An example of a social trend that can affect opportunities include:
A.   Computer-related trends
B.   The number of dual career families
C.   Changes in racial percentages with the population
D.   Increases in levels of education

D   32.   How intensively a product is used by its customers is in reference to:
A.   Breadth of the market
B.   Size of the total market
C.   Market feasibility
D.   Depth of the market

A   33. A product with a number of different uses would be considered to have:
- A. Breadth of market
- B. Depth of market
- C. Large market size
- D. All of the above

C   34. Regarding the venture evaluation process, an unfavorable <u>investor's</u> perspective coupled with a favorable <u>entrepreneur's</u> perspective should result in:
- A. Reformulating the management team
- B. Abandoning the venture idea
- C. Locating other types of investors
- D. Venture launch

D   35. An entrepreneur's ability to lower venture risk will be enhanced by:
- A. Developing a product that is totally new
- B. Fully devoting resources to one and only one product
- C. Investing in fixed assets rather than leasing
- D. Developing extensive uses for the product

True/False

F   36. If more were known about the opportunities and risks that lay before entrepreneurs, more entrepreneurs would start a venture.

T   37. The key to successfully pursuing an entrepreneurial opportunity is in analyzing the opportunity well to maximize the probability of success.

F   38. The "baby boom" is an example of a social trend.

T   39. General increases in the levels of education is an example of a demographic trend.

F   40. The demand for technology consultants is an example of a technological trend.

T   41. The launchpad concept is especially prevalent in the high-tech area.

T   42. A person who attempts to produce and market a product they have invented is referred to as an inventrepreneur.

T   43. An objective assessment reduces the probability that the decision to launch a venture will be based on a hunch.

T   44.   The window of opportunity is the period of time during which an investment has maximum potential for success.

F   45.   Breadth of the market for a product refers to how intensive a product is used by its customers.

F   46.   Depth of the market refers to how many different uses a particular product has.

F   47.   Patents and protecting trade secrets are the major key to insulating a product from competition.

T   48.   Having a product or service that is not easily duplicated is the key to protecting the product from competitors.

T   49.   The first stage of the new venture analysis process is to determine whether the venture idea is sound.

T   50.   The informal analysis serves as a screening device to quickly determine if an opportunity is worth the effort of further analysis.

F   51.   Examining the venture idea for "fatal flaws" completes the informal analysis stage.

F   52.   Determining if any fatal flaws exist is the first and foremost aspect to consider in the formal analysis.

T   53.   Fatal flaws are conditions or events which override all other favorable results of the analysis.

T   54.   The strength of the entrepreneurial team is the prime determinant in the decision to provide external capital to an entrepreneur.

Essay Questions

1.   Identify various sources of trends and give examples of the trends.

2.   What are some possible ways a potential entrepreneur may recognize a not-so-obvious opportunity? What methods can be used to recognize or generate ideas for opportunities?

3.   Identify and describe the criteria potential opportunities should meet in order to be worthy of pursuing.

4. Discuss the first stage of the new venture analysis process. Be sure to mention items typically included as a start on the analysis process and the various combinations of entrepreneur/investor perspectives and their likely result as it applies to the new venture idea.

5. Discuss the parts of the formal analysis including the concept of fatal flaws. Give examples of questions that need to be answered for each feasibility element and also give examples of fatal flaws.

CHAPTER 6

<u>Multiple Choice</u>

C   1.   Which of the following is an advantage of start-ups?
  A. Credibility
  B. Time to launch
  C. Flexibility
  D. Financing

D   2.   Which of the following is a disadvantage of start-ups?
  A. Inflexibility
  B. Image
  C. Staffing
  D. Credibility

D   3.   Which of the following is an advantage of buyouts?
  A. Flexibility
  B. Initial cost
  C. Image
  D. Trained employees

A   4.   Which of the following is often a disadvantage of buyouts?
  A. Cost of purchase
  B. Continuity of operations
  C. Location
  D. Financing

B   5.   Which of the following is an advantage of start-ups?
              A.   Time to launch
              B.   Initial cost
              C.   Credibility
              D.   Financing difficulties

A   6.   The greater potential and long run cost effectiveness of buyouts is often balanced by:
              A.   High initial cost
              B.   Financing difficulties
              C.   The fact that it's a going concern
              D.   An excessive "time to launch" period

D   7.   The benefit of flexibility as it applies to start-ups refers to:
              A.   The legal form of the venture
              B.   The time commitment the entrepreneur will devote to the venture
              C.   Maximizing returns on investment
              D.   All of the above

C   8.   A start-up's ability to create a desired market image in competitive strategy is primarily based on:
              A.   Flexibility
              B.   A lower intial cost
              C.   A lack of reputation prior to the launch
              D.   The legal form of the venture

B   9.   Startups are relatively more difficult to finance than buyouts because of:
              A>   The higher initial cost
              B.   The time it takes to establish credibility
              C.   The inherent inflexibility of startups
              D.   Staffing costs

D   10.   Which of the following is true regarding buyouts?
              A.   The process involved is not as entrepreneurial as for startups.
              B.   Investors perceive less benefits of buyouts than with startups.
              C.   Growth oriented entrepreneurs prefer buyouts less than startups.
              D.   Buyouts are as entrepreneurial in nature as a start-up.

C   11.   When considering the advantages of launching ventures via buyouts, it is apparent that the advantages revolve aroung the fact that:
A. Buyouts are substantially less risky than startups.
B. The impact on competition is greater for buyouts.
C. The venture is an ongoing business.
D. Financing is much easier to obtain for buyouts.

A   12.   The reason why financing may be more readily available for buyouts instead of startups is because:
A. Buyouts have a lower risk of failure.
B. Startups require more money to launch.
C. Entrepreneurs who need financing for buyouts have more experience than entrepreneurs associated with startups.
D. Investors are always willing to lend higher sums of money to buyouts.

D   13.   Which of the following is not a method used in the buyout search process?
A. Industry search
B. Location-based searches
C. Advertised intentions
D. The leveraged buyout

B   14.   One of the significant differences between the LBO and other buyouts is:
A. The price of the purchased venture.
B. The impact the LBO has on the new venture's ability to compete.
C. LBO's do not "create" new ventures.
D. Investors will only approve LBO's if the venture is a partnership.

D   15.   Which of the following is true regarding LBO's?
A. The financing is similar to that of other buyouts.
B. There is no competitive impact affecting the venture's ability to compete.
C. Owners utilizing LBO's have more debt in their personal name
D. The purchase places a high percentage of debt on the venture, more so than for other buyouts.

A   16.   The key to the LBO is that:
  A.   The firm assumes the debt rather than the individual owners.
  B.   The purchased firm must be newly created and is a high growth market.
  C.   The owners must insure that the buyout doesn't have a competitive impact on the venture.
  D.   Management of the existing firm becomes the new owners.

B   17.   The primary disadvantage of utilizing a franchise as a way of creating a new venture is:
  A.   The amount of operating restrictions placed on the entrepreneur.
  B.   Cost of the franchise
  C.   Financing the venture
  D.   The lack of management training

D   18.   The primary issue for an entrepreneur considering beginning a franchise is:
  A.   Location
  B.   The amount of training and support provided by the franchisor.
  C.   How the franchise will be financed.
  D.   One of cost versus benefit.

C   19.   A new concept in entrepreneurship that shows promise in successful new venture creation and management is the:
  A.   Franchise
  B.   Family business
  C.   Incubator startup
  D.   Leveraged buyout

D   20.   Sharing administrative support such as copiers, mail processing, and computers is a characteristic of:
  A.   Small business development centers
  B.   Franchises
  C.   Family business groupings
  D.   Incubator startups

D   21.   Which of the following is not one of the three forms an incubator may take?
    A.   Privately held
    B.   For-profit
    C.   State sponsored
    D.   Tenant sponsored

A   22.   Which of the following is true regarding the success rate of incubators in relation to new ventures in general?
    A.   Evidence has been thus far inconclusive.
    B.   Incubators are not as successful as new ventures in general.
    C.   Incubators are as successful as new ventures in general.
    D.   Incubators have a better success rate than ventures in general.

C   23.   Over two-thirds of all new ventures are organized as:
    A.   Partnerships
    B.   Corporations
    C.   Sole proprietorships
    D.   S corporations

D   24.   From a new venture perspective, which of the following is the biggest advantage of the sole proprietorship?
    A.   The sole proprietorship can obtain financing easier than a partnership or corporation.
    B.   Having only a one-person management expedites the planning process.
    C.   The limited liability of the single owner.
    D.   Ease of venture launch

A   25.   Which of the following is a shared disadvantage of sole proprietorships and partnerships?
    A.   No continuity on death of an owner
    B.   Difficulty in raising capital
    C.   Managerial weaknesses
    D.   Limited liability of owners

C   26.   Having a low cost of venture formation is an advantage associated with:
    A.   Sole proprietorships only
    B.   Partnerships and corporations
    C.   Sole proprietorships and partnerships
    D.   Corporations only

A   27.   Unlimited liability on the part of the owner(s) is a disadvantage of:
- A. Both sole proprietorships and partnerships
- B. Sole proprietorships only
- C. Partnerships only
- D. Corporations

B   28.   The primary distinction between a partnership and a limited partnership is the:
- A. Limited liability of the general partner
- B. Limited liability of the non-managing partners
- C. Fact that limited partners are allowed only to manage the firm but not invest in it.
- D. Number of partners allowed to make managaement decisions.

D   29.   The preferred form of new venture launch from the investor's perspective is the:
- A. Sole proprietorship
- B. Partnership
- C. Limited partnership
- D. Corporation

A   30.   A primary reason why many entrepreneurs prefer the corporate form of ownership is the:
- A. Limited liability
- B. Low cost of formation
- C. Shared earnings
- D. Ease of corporate dissolution

C   31.   A Subchapter S corporation has all the characteristics of a corporation except that it:
- A. Reduces administrative requirements
- B. Reduces the liability of the owners
- C. Is taxed as a partnership
- D. Makes exchange of ownership more difficult

B   32.   The tax status of Subchapter S corporations or regular corporations is of primary concern for:
- A. High growth entrepreneurs
- B. Low growth entrepreneurs
- C. Venture capitalists
- D. Creditors

A   33.   Low growth entrepreneurs who wish to avoid double taxation of profits would not organize a new venture as a:
    A.   Regular corporation
    B.   Sole proprietorship
    C.   Partnership
    D.   Limited partnership

True/False

T   34.   If the venture is built around a new product or service, there may be no alternative to the startup.

T   35.   It is much easier to develop an image and competitive strategy from the beginning than it is to alter that of an existing firm.

T   36.   Buying an existing venture will usually cost more than starting a venture from scratch.

F   37.   An advantage of startups is that the time to launch is shorter.

F   38.   Startups are relatively easier to finance than buyouts.

F   39.   Startups are more entrepreneurial in nature than buyouts.

T   40.   Buying an existing firm effectively eliminates part of the competition.

F   41.   The startup offers significantly greater competitive possibilities than does the buyout.

T   42.   Financiers are generally more willing to go with existing firms than they are a startup.

T   43.   Buyouts typically are less risky than startups.

F   44.   Buyouts are generally less cost effective over the long run because of the high initial cost.

T   45.   The leveraged buyout is a means of creating a new venture.

F   46.   The LBO typically has little effect on the new venture's ability to compete.

F   47.   A firm purchased via a LBO is purchased with a high percentage of equity.

T   48.   Debt used in purchasing an existing firm is in the firm's name and not the owners'.

T   49.   Incubators thus far have not had much effect on economic development.

F   50.   Similar constraints exist between taking over an old family business and starting a new family business.

F   51.   The majority of all ventures are organized as partnerships.

T   52.   The partnership shares many of the characteristics of the sole proprietorship.

T   53.   A key distinction between sole proprietorships and corporations concerns the issue of owner liability.

Essays

1.   Identify and describe the advantages and disadvantages of both startups and buyouts.

2.   What is the difference between a LBO and other buyouts? Describe the leveraged buyout process and the importance of the firm-assumed debt.

3.   How are incubators significantly different from other forms of startups? What forms do the incubators normally take? What do you think the input of incubators will be and why?

4.   Describe some of the control and ownership issues which must be addressed when taking over an established family business. Do these issues differ from those of initiating a new family business? Why?

5.   Describe the three primary forms of business and the variations, if they exist, within each category. What are some advantages and disadvantages of each of the forms?

CHAPTER 7

<u>Multiple Choice</u>

C   1.   Which of the following is true regarding the degree of difficulty in obtaining capital for a new venture versus an existing venture?

    A.   Obtaining capital for a new venture is less difficult because there is no record of failure.

    B.   Obtaining capital for an existing venture is more difficult because of the large amounts of past startup cash needed.

    C.   Obtaining capital for new ventures is more difficult than for an existing venture because there is no history of successful performance.

    D.   There really is no difference in the financing degree of difficulty.

C   2.   Research and development activities as well as prototype development are typically in what stage of venture development?

    A.   Startup

    B.   Post-startup

    C.   Pre-startup

    D.   Growth

B   3.   Acquisition of inventory and plant and equipment are typically activities in what stage of venture development?

    A.   Pre-startup

    B.   Startup

    C.   Post-startup

    D.   Growth

A   4.   The cost of underwriting more financing for the business is an activity normally associated with the _____ stage of development.
A.   Growth
B.   Startup
C.   Pre-startup
D.   Post-startup

D   5.   Which of the following is not an activity typically in the venture's pre-startup stage of development?
A.   Site acquisition
B.   Prototype development
C.   Research and development
D.   Plant and equipment acquisition

C   6.   The two basic sources of financing for a venture are:
A.   Venture capital and non-venture capital.
B.   Bank loans and initial public offerings.
C.   Debt capital and equity financing.
D.   Personal funds and publicly funded stock.

A   7.   The primary distinction between equity financing and debt capital is:
A.   The ownership provision
B.   Equity financing is typically not useful in financing small ventures.
C.   Larger ventures utilize more debt financing than equity financing.
D.   Debt capital is provided to the venture in exchange for a given amount of decision making authority.

C   8.   Financing obtained through family and friends is considered:
A.   Equity financing
B.   Debt capital
C.   Either debt or equity
D.   Neither, since it doesn't involve interest payments or ownership provision.

B   9.   A non-institutional investor who may, as an individual, invest in a given venture is considered a source of:
A.   Debt capital
B.   Equity financing
C.   Venture capital
D.   All of the above

D   10.   Of every 1000 plans submitted for review to venture capital firms how many will ultimately meet the financial expectations of the capitalists?
   A.   10
   B.   50
   C.   6
   D.   2

B   11.   An important characteristic shared by most venture capitalists is that:
   A.   Most will only invest in ventures returning dividends less than three years from startup.
   B.   Capitalists usually have potential equity participation in the venture.
   C.   Most will not actively monitor the performance of the venture.
   D.   The rate of return is not as important as the length of time it takes to receive the return.

C   12.   Venture capital firms tend to be located in areas that support:
   A.   Second stage venture financing
   B.   Startup venture financing
   C.   High technology startups
   D.   Manufacturing-intensive industries

A   13.   The most important factor for corporate venture capital firms in deciding to underwrite a venture is:
   A.   The degree of corporate fit with the present company.
   B.   Low total investment
   C.   High rates of return
   D.   A quality entrepreneurial team

C   14.   An advantage for a large corporation in having a corporate venture capital firm is that:
   A.   There's generally low total investment required.
   B.   Large corporations have high quality management teams.
   C.   The welfare of the sponsored venture does not substantially impact the parent firm.
   D.   Some corporations are highly risk sensitive; they will only invest in projects with high rates of return.

A   15.   Small firms which speculate in private investment placements for small companies are called:
   A.   Boutiques
   B.   Small business investment companies
   C.   Investment bankers
   D.   Enterprise investment companies

D   16.   Which of the following is true regarding initial public offerings?
- A.   Few large ventures are launched without IPO.
- B.   With IPO's come the advantage of increased funding and control of the corporation.
- C.   The amount of funds raised through an IPO is regulated by the SEC.
- D.   IPO's subject the venture to substanting more regulations and reporting requirements.

B   17.   Using little or no debt to finance a venture is:
- A.   Justified because it reduces taxes by eliminating interest expense.
- B.   Unwise because of the limitations placed on the firm.
- C.   Wise because full ownership then rests with the entrepreneur.
- D.   Bad because the firm is more vulnerable to cyclical downturns.

C   18.   The most common source of debt funds besides friends and family is:
- A.   Small business administration loans
- B.   Supplier capital
- C.   Banks
- D.   Economic development funding

C   19.   Taking advantage at credit terms such as 2/10, net 30 as a way of accumulating small amounts of capital is known as:
- A.   Customer capital
- B.   Non-interest debt
- C.   Supplier funding or trade credit
- D.   Resource-based capital

A   20.   Entrepreneurs who sell major products or services requiring deposits before the product is shipped are utilizing:
- A.   Customer capital
- B.   Supplier capital
- C.   Internal cash management procedures
- D.   Customer credit terms

D   21.   The impetus behind economic development funding in the 1980's was:
- A.   The need for more high technology enterprises.
- B.   The need to make industry profitable again
- C.   The need to create more minority-owned enterprises
- D.   The need to create local jobs

B 22. Developing a sound accounts receivable policy as a way of impacting financing needs is an example of:
   A. Customer capital
   B. Internal cash management
   C. Supplier funding
   D. Debt capitalization

D 23. Which of the following is not a source of debt capital?
   A. Family and friends
   B. Small Business Administration
   C. Banks
   D. Informal investors

B 24. Which of the following is primarily a source of equity capital?
   A. Economic development programs
   B. Small business investment companies
   C. Government-secured investment
   D. Banks

D 25. Low growth ventures typically will not utilize which of the following sources of financing?
   A. Family and friends
   B. Small Business Administration loans
   C. Banks
   D. Small business investment companies

B 26. Rapid growth ventures typically will not significantly utilize which of the following sources of financing?
   A. Private venture capital firms
   B. Family and friends
   C. Small business investment companies
   D. Informal investors

D 27. The use of personal funds as the <u>primary</u> source of financing is most prevalent in which type of venture?
   A. Low growth
   B. Moderate growth
   C. High growth
   D. Moderate growth ventures making an acquisition

D   28.   Initial public offerings are most often used in:
           A.   The pre-startup stage for high growth ventures
           B.   The startup stage for high growth ventures
           C.   The post-startup stage for low growth ventures
           D.   The post-startup stage for high growth ventures

A   29.   The use of bank financing is the primary source of external funding in:
           A.   The startup stage of low growth ventures
           B.   The pre-startup stage of low growth ventures
           C.   The startup stage of high growth ventures
           D.   The post-startup stage of high growth ventures

B   30.   Which of the following is not an activity typically in growth stage of venture development?
           A.   Facility expansion
           B.   Determining cyclical cash flow needs
           C.   Acquisitions
           D.   Geographical expansion

A   31.   Which of the following is an activity typically in the startup stage of venture development?
           A.   Acquisition of plant and equipment
           B.   Prototype development
           C.   Underwriting of additional financing
           D.   Redistribution of cyclical cash flow needs

B   32.   Which of the following is not considered a source of equity funding?
           A.   Personal funds
           B.   Banking institutions
           C.   Friends and family
           D.   Informal investors

C   33.   Which of the following time periods is typical of the duration for which venture capitalists will invest before receiving returns?
           A.   1-2 years
           B.   3-5 years
           C.   5-10 years
           D.   10+ years

True/False

T   34.   Low growth small businesses typically do not need substantial funding once the initial launch and stabilization occurs.

F   35.   Equity financing is providing capital in exchange for interest payments.

T   36.   All ventures will have some equity funding since all ventures are ultimately owned by someone.

T   37.   The investment of equity funds means financial ownership.

F   38.   An informal investor is any institutional investor who invests in a given venture.

F   39.   For every 1000 business plans submitted for review to venture capitalists, approximately 50 actually receive funding.

T   40.   Venture capitalists usually invest for a five to ten year period before receiving their returns.

T   41.   Virtually no "first launches" are done with public offerings.

T   42.   The advantage of debt financing for the entrepreneur is that full ownership remains with the entrepreneur.

T   43.   Virtually all firms use a combination of debt and equity to finance the venture's growth.

F   44.   Using little or no debt is advantageous to the venture because there is no interest expense associated with the debt.

F   45.   Investment bankers are the most common source of debt funds beside friends and family.

T   46.   The Small Business Administration primarily makes guaranteed loans through commercial banks.

T   47.   A primary objective of economic development funding is to provide jobs for local residents.

T   48.   Family and friends can be a source of both debt and equity capital.

T 49. Low growth ventures will never use venture capital because they don't need it.

T 50. The type of financing used is dependent to a large extent on the stage of development of the venture.

F 51. Initial funding for moderate growth firms will come largely from small business investment companies and investment bankers.

T 52. Some amount of equity capital will be required regardless of the type of venture.

Essay Questions

1. What are some of the typical venture needs that require financing for each of several stages of development?

2. Identify and differentiate between the types of venture capital firms. What is the primary purpose of venture capitalists? What common characteristics do they share?

3. Identify and differentiate between the various types of investment bankers as to size, type of clientele, etc.

4. Identify various sources of debt capital and other non-equity sources of venture financing. What are some advantages and disadvantages of these sources?

5. What are the most common sources of financing for the various venture stages of development and growth rates?

CHAPTER 8

Multiple Choice

C   1.   The most important task for the new or emerging venture is:
- A. Product maturity
- B. Obtaining financing
- C. Strategy development
- D. Hiring personnel

D   2.   Entrepreneurial strategies which are distinctly different from others in existence are:
- A. Evolutionary
- B. Convergent
- C. Parallel
- D. Divergent

D   3.   Strategies which result from perceived new opportunities because of major changes in the industry or market are:
- A. Cost leadership strategies
- B. Focus strategies
- C. Evolutionary strategies
- D. Divergent strategies

B   4.   Which of the following statements concerning venture strategies is true?
         A.   Strategies appropriate for emerging industries apply to all types of ventures.
         B.   There is no single best strategy for a venture or for a given situation.
         C.   Divergent strategies, because they focus on market changes and new opportunities, are generally more successful than evolutionary strategies.
         D.   The stronger the opportunity/capability match, the more difficult is the strategy determination process.

B   5.   Which of the following is a generic venture strategy?
         A.   Deterrence
         B.   Differentiation
         C.   Offensive
         D.   Defensive

D   6.   Strategies that create value beyond that available from competing products are known as:
         A.   Focus strategies
         B.   Divergent strategies
         C.   Cost leadership strategies
         D.   Differentiation strategies

B   7.   From the entrepreneur's perspective, a primary benefit of employing a differentiation strategy is:
         A.   Higher quality products are generally cheaper to produce.
         B.   Protection against price pressure by customers
         C.   Being able to charge a lower price.
         D.   Once a product is differentiated, future market share growth is assured.

A   8.   Typically, employing a low cost leadership strategy requires:
         A.   Large market share
         B.   Non-commodity products
         C.   Differentiated products
         D.   High quality

C   9.   The key to employing a successful focus strategy is:
         A.   Focusing on obtaining market share.
         B.   Serving the entire market, but focusing on customer service.
         C.   Serving a small target market.
         D.   Providing additional generic services to smaller markets.

A   10. Which of the following is a <u>primary</u> competitive "wedge" for new ventures?
         A.   Parallel competition
         B.   Tapping unutilized resources
         C.   Joint ventures
         D.   Supply shortage

B   11. The reason why the new product or service "wedge" is rarely used is because:
         A.   The success rate of this strategy isn't high due to the difficulty of new entering markets.
         B.   Most new ventures aren't associated with totally new products or services.
         C.   The proliferation of new products/services in recent years has resulted in market fragmentation and fierce competition.
         D.   Most entrepreneurs lack experience in marketing new products/services.

C   12. The nature of a new product compared to existing products when using the parallel competition wedge is:
         A.   Quite different
         B.   Similar, but the new product has several value added features.
         C.   Marginally different.
         D.   Not comparable since no similar product exists.

D   13. The type of entry wedge utilized to take advantage of a market where demand for a product is unmet is:
         A.   Untapped resource
         B.   Demand shortage
         C.   Parallel competition
         D.   Supply shortage

A   14.   The type of entry wedge utilized which assures an entrepreneur of having significant business before the venture is launched is:
- A.   Contracting with a customer
- B.   Additional supplies
- C.   Joint venture
- D.   Franchise

D   15.   When an existing company forms a new venture partially owned by that company and partially owned by an entrepreneur, the entry wedge used is:
- A.   Licensing agreement
- B.   Franchise
- C.   Becoming a second source
- D.   Joint venture

B   16.   The entry wedge utilized by a large company which negotiates with existing managers or other interested entrepreneurs to take over production of the product is:
- A.   Selloff of a division
- B.   Market relinquishment
- C.   Licensing
- D.   Joint venture

C   17.   One of the two entry wedges which reflect government sponsorship rather than corporate sponsorship is:
- A.   Becoming a second source
- B.   Geographical transfer
- C.   Favored purchasing
- D.   Supply shortage

A   18.   Strategies for high-tech ventures virtually always revolve around:
- A.   A new product/process
- B.   A superior marketing effort
- C.   High quality products
- D.   Low priced products

B   19.   Which of the following is a type of strategy often used by high-tech firms?
- A.   Product protection strategy
- B.   Derivative product strategy
- C.   Cost control strategy
- D.   Parallel competitive strategy

D   20.   A type of strategy employed by high-tech firms which emphasizes developing a product similar to one which currently exists is the:
- A.   Support product strategy
- B.   Licensing strategy
- C.   Product innovation strategy
- D.   Derivative product strategy

C   21.   The entrepreneurial strategy similar to the parallel strategy suggested by Vesper is the:
- A.   High-tech differentiative strategy
- B.   Derivative product strategy
- C.   Product variation strategy
- D.   Cost control strategy

B   22.   Computer manufacturers who produce and market IBM-type equipment are utilizing what strategy?
- A.   Product protection strategy
- B.   Derivative product strategy
- C.   Support product strategy
- D.   New product innovation strategy

A   23.   In high-tech industries, the product differentiator focuses on:
- A.   Making higher quality products
- B.   Cost savings
- C.   Developing low price strategies
- D.   Producing similar products at competitive prices

D   24.   A critical key to success for ventures producing products in low-tech industries is the ability to:
- A.   Combat the quick rate of product obsolescence
- B.   Make variations of products which are better than existing products
- C.   Obtain large market share
- D.   Protect products from duplication by competitors

C   25.   Because low-tech products are often easily copyable, it is important that the entrepreneur focus on:
- A.   Product differentiation efforts
- B.   Obtaining patents
- C.   Producing the product cost effectively
- D.   Serving large markets instead of target markets

C   26.   The niche strategy used by entrepreneurial firms breaking into a market for the first time is similar to which strategy suggested by Porter?
    A.   Differentiation
    B.   Cost leadership
    C.   Focus
    D.   Parallel competition

B   27.   A captive supplier is a producer of either a product or component of a larger product who sells the product to:
    A.   A target market segment
    B.   Only one customer
    C.   A large portion of the total market
    D.   Equipment manufacturers

D   28.   Which of the following is not a benefit of the captive supplier strategy?
    A.   Lower risk
    B.   Elimination of the need to market the product(s)
    C.   Reduced costs
    D.   Dependency on the larger firm

A   29.   An entrepreneurial firm which provides the majority of its output to a single buyer and the remainder to other customers is known as a:
    A.   Partial captive supplier
    B.   Franchisor
    C.   Customer's contractor
    D.   Turnkey producer

A   30.   Which of the following venture categories has a higher failure rate than any other?
    A.   Retail
    B.   Wholesalers
    C.   Service firms
    D.   Manufacturing firms

A   31.   The most important key to a successful service venture is to:
    A.   Provide a cost effective service of sufficient quality.
    B.   Locate the venture in a prime traffic area.
    C.   Provide a high quality service and command a premium price.
    D.   Undercut the competition in price.

B   32.   An advantage of pursuing a niche strategy in that:
               A.   Large firms are hesitant to enter niche markets even if there is high growth potential.
               B.   The entrepreneur can become an expert in a narrow market.
               C.   Niche strategies are necessarily lower risk because of the smaller market.
               D.   It requires less investment since the market is smaller.

C   33.   Utilizing mail advertisements, electronic advertising, and catalog mailing are strategies employed by what type of venture?
               A.   Retail
               B.   Service
               C.   Direct marketing
               D.   High-tech

A   34.   Joint ventures, licensing, and the franchises are all examples of:
               A.   Competitive entry wedges
               B.   Generic strategy types
               C.   Focus strategies
               D.   Niche strategies

D   35.   The new venture entry wedge which is used to produce the product utilizing the name and trademark of an existing company is:
               A.   Joint venture
               B.   Franchise
               C.   Favored purchasing
               D.   Licensing

True/False

T   36.   Evolutionary strategies are only incrementally different from existing strategies.

T   37.   Divergent strategies are those which are distinctly different from others in existence.

F   38.   There is usually a single best strategy for a venture or for a given situation.

T   39.   Differentiation strategies can allow the entrepreneur to charge a premium price for the product.

F   40.   Low cost leadership typically requires only a small market share.

F   41.   Low cost leadership strategies offer work best when the product can be differentiated.

T   42.   The focus strategy may combine parts of both the differentiation and low cost leadership strategies.

T   43.   The focus strategy is not market share oriented.

F   44.   Most new ventures utilize the new product or service wedge because they involve totally new products/services.

F   45.   The favored purchasing entry wedge is a corporate attempt to channel business to minority entrepreneurs.

T   46.   Strategies for high-tech ventures virtually always revolve around a new product/process.

T   47.   Computer stores are prime examples of the derivative product strategy.

F   48.   The disadvantage of the product variation strategy is that it is both higher cost and higher risk.

F   49.   There is a strong relationship between the quality of the product and the amount of technology used in its production.

T   50.   Virtually all high-tech strategies are product related.

T   51.   Patents are not particularly useful if the product is easily duplicated.

F   52.   A niche strategy provides products/services to a small segment of customers well served by major companies.

T   53.   A captive supplier sells the product to only one customer.

T   54.   The product variation strategy is similar to the low cost leader strategy suggested by Porter.

F   55.   The short demand entry wedge occurs when demand for a product or service exceeds supply.

<u>Essay</u>

1.   Identify and describe the three generic strategies suggested by Porter. What are some benefits of employing these strategies?

2.   Identify and describe various strategies for high-tech manufacturers. What are the risks and benefits of each strategy?

3.   What are some of the key strategic issues to be considered for low-tech manufacturing ventures? How are these issues different than for high-tech manufacturers?

4.   Describe how the niche strategy can be profitable if done well yet risky due to either too little or too much success.

5.   Identify and describe some key strategic issues tried by retailers. Why must all these factors mesh together and provide consistency?

CHAPTER 9

Multiple Choice

B   1.   _____ are the basic building blocks of a venture's financial plan.
      A.   Price estimates
      B.   Sales estimates
      C.   Market size
      D.   Supply costs

D   2.   The _____ strategy can have the most impact on the short run success of the venture.
      A.   financial
      B.   human resource
      C.   distribution
      D.   marketing

D   3.   The product should be researched during the development of the marketing/promotional strategy in order to:
      A.   choose a possible pricing strategy
      B.   see where excess product costs can be trimmed
      C.   assess quality
      D.   understand psychological reasons for consumer choices

B   4.   Market segmentation allows the entrepreneur to:
      A.   identify specific buyers in the market.
      B.   best reach the market with the desired product.
      C.   create direct mail campaigns
      D.   better develop product characteristics

D   5.   The fundamental key to effective advertising is:
A.   simple message
B.   good graphics
C.   quantity
D.   timing

A   6.   One measurement of advertising effectiveness is:

A. $\dfrac{\text{sales}}{\text{advertising dollars}}$

B. $\dfrac{\text{sales}}{\text{number of ads shown}}$

C. $\dfrac{\text{number of customers}}{\text{number of ads shown}}$

D. $\dfrac{\text{number of customers}}{\text{advertising dollars}}$

B   7.   Which of the following advertising media offers the widest exposure?
A.   Yellow pages
B.   Newspapers
C.   Radio
D.   Cable television

C   8.   One of the steps of the financial strategic process is to analyze the financial condition of the firm. What is the purpose of doing this?
A.   Determine the current condition and develop pro forma statements for investment purposes.
B.   Determine the current condition in order to appropriately value stock issues.
C.   Determine the current condition and outline necessary changes in the financial mix.
D.   Determine the current condition and compare progress with that of competitors.

A   9.   Which pricing strategy encourages discounting (which may result in losses)?
A.   Competitor based
B.   Demand based
C.   Penetration
D.   Cost based

A   10.   Which pricing strategy charges the highest possible prices when the product is first introduced?
- A. Skimming
- B. Prestige pricing
- C. Demand based
- D. Cost based

C   11.   Which pricing strategy is designed specifically to capture market share?
- A. Demand based
- B. Competitor based
- C. Penetration
- D. Cost based

B   12.   _____ pricing strategy cannot be used as a long run pricing method.
- A. Cost based
- B. Skimming
- C. Demand based
- D. Prestige

D   13.   When evaluating alternatives surrounding an ethical dilemma, certain practical constraints limit the choices available. Which of the following is simply a convenient excuse for eliminating an alternative rather than being a real constraint?
- A. Lack of time
- B. Lack of money
- C. Lack of a trained staff
- D. Lack of management support

B   14.   The first step in the ethical decision making process is:
- A. to determine the ethical issues
- B. to collect the facts
- C. to develop alternatives
- D. to determine practical constraints

A   15.   A budget analysis serves to:
- A. signal existence of a problem
- B. identify specific problem areas
- C. help control spending
- D. suggest problem solutions

B   16.   A _____ that is too low may suggest that a firm needs to add more long term debt or equity to increase the level of cash.
- A.   inventory turnover ratio
- B.   current ratio
- C.   debt to equity ratio
- D.   expense ratio

C   17.   Return on investment is measured by the:
- A.   debt/equity ratio
- B.   current ratio
- C.   net income/equity
- D.   net income/net sales

D   18.   A measure of operating efficiency, the _____ varies widely from one industry to another.
- A.   current ratio
- B.   operating expense ratio
- C.   inventory turnover
- D.   net income/net sales

C   19.   On-the-job training, or OJT, requires which of the following to be successful?
- A.   Classroom instruction in addition to OJT
- B.   Role-playing exercises
- C.   Various task experiences
- D.   Experienced workers

D   20.   The strategy which should lay the foundation for all other strategies is the:
- A.   financial strategy
- B.   marketing strategy
- C.   human resource strategy
- D.   ethical strategy

B   21.   The venture whose owners develop an aggressive _____ strategy will typically do better than those owners who are conservative.
- A.   financial
- B.   marketing
- C.   human resource
- D.   ethical

C 22. Which of the following is NOT included in the analysis of the human resource strategy?
   A. Number of employee hours worked
   B. Communication problems
   C. Number of vacation weeks per employee
   D. Company growth rate

D 23. The total number of individuals and skill types needed in the enterprise must be based on a relationship between _____ and the necessary human resources.
   A. possible mechanization of routine tasks
   B. projected wage increases
   C. size of the company asset base
   D. projected sales

B 24. Which of the following is a component of a human resource strategy?
   A. Number of weeks of vacation new employees receive.
   B. The skills and experience of new employees.
   C. Community involvement of employees.
   D. The number of employees in the human resource department.

B 25. Cost-based pricing strategy is based on the formula:

   A. $\dfrac{\text{variable costs}}{\text{expected \# units sold}}$

   B. $\dfrac{\text{total costs}}{\text{expected \# units sold}}$

   C. $\dfrac{\text{total costs}}{\text{breakeven price}}$

   D. $\dfrac{\text{fixed - variable costs}}{\text{expected \# units sold}}$

True/False

F 26. Employees play a less important role in small ventures than in bigger enterprises.

T 27. Functional strategies often require more time to develop than do overall strategies.

T   28.   Budgets and charts which compare expected revenue and expenses to actual amounts are a key component of any well-managed firm's planning process.

T   29.   It is important to research the competitors before developing the marketing plan.

F   30.   The distribution strategy deals with getting information to the customer.

F   31.   Yellow Pages advertising attracts casual buyers.

F   32.   Radio advertisements are easily remembered.

F   33.   When identifying who might be affected by the consequences of ethical decisions, relevant stakeholders are only those who will be directly involved.

T   34.   An ethical venture, when defining strategy, will usually consider both the pragmatic and conceptual benefits that may accrue.

F   35.   Though firms in some industries continue to require managerial employees to sign non-compete agreements, these documents have generally not been given full court approval.

F   36.   It is generally accepted that utilizing a single medium while concentrating advertising in relative short time periods is better than utilizing multiple media and spreading the advertising budget across a broader time frame.

F   37.   After the "ideal" medium has been selected, the need for research is no longer needed.

F   38.   Absolute size is more important than relative size in print advertising.

F   39.   Distribution refers to the channels used to transport goods or services.

T   40.   The distribution dilemma is the tradeoff between cost and   control.

F   41.   The cornerstone of effective advertising is having a simple, understandable message.

F   42.   The financial strategy can have the most impact on the short run success of the venture.

F 43. Receivables turnover is valuable for spotting overstocking, understocking, and product obsolescence.

F 44. The disadvantage of advertising on television is the high cost per person watching.

F 45. The distribution plan and promotion plan are two distinct systems that do not interrelate.

F 46. Because of price elasticity, sellers using prestige pricing must be prepared to sell a higher quantity of the product.

Essay Questions

1. Knowing the venture's environment is an important aspect of managing growth. What are some examples of economic variables and their impact on financial strategy?

2. What are the six specific areas the financial strategy or planning process should address?

3. Imagine a venture you would be interested in starting. Examine the components of a human resource strategy and how you would address these needs in your venture. (Develop an outline of an action plan.)

4. Consider how a firm's ethical strategy could impact its business in a small community versus in a metropolitan area. Are all ethical strategies alike? Discuss two different perspectives and how they would likely influence business actions.

5. Identify and give a brief rationale for the steps in developing a marketing strategy.

CHAPTER 10

<u>Multiple Choice</u>

B   1.   The percentage of retail sales in the U.S. attributed to franchised businesses is approximately:
     A.   23
     B.   33
     C.   50
     D.   67

B   2.   The number of people employed by franchisors in the U.S. is approximately:
     A.   2.6 million
     B.   6.2 million
     C.   2.6 billion
     D.   15.2 million

B   3.   A franchisee offers the following to the franchise arrangement: business
location, personal drive, and:
     A.   proven methods of operation
     B.   community goodwill
     C.   marketing resources
     D.   brand name

C   4.   A franchisor brings a trademark, technical advice, and _____ to the
franchise arrangement.
     A.   financial equity
     B.   community goodwill
     C.   marketing resources
     D.   business location

C 5. The greatest difference between starting an independent venture and starting a franchise is:
A. the quality of products or services offered.
B. the amount of the entrepreneur's commitment to the enterprise.
C. the amount of training for the entrepreneur.
D. the availability of funds for the venture.

C 6. Which of the following aspects of technical assistance is usually NOT provided by the franchisor?
A. Site selection
B. Inventory control
C. Capital acquisition
D. Store remodeling

D 7. The foremost challenge for the franchisor is:
A. communicating standards, procedures, and policies.
B. evaluating the market strategy.
C. testing new products.
D. maintaining control of expansion.

B 8. Which of the following is usually not a problem for the franchisor once the franchise has begun to grow?
A. Recruitment
B. Funding
C. Communication
D. Franchisor-franchisee relations

D 9. Product and Trade Name franchising recently accounted for approximately _____ percent of franchised sales.
A. 35
B. 47
C. 60
D. 71

C 10. Product and Trade Name franchising appears in what phase of the industry life cycle?
A. Introduction
B. Growth
C. Maturity
D. Decline

A   11.   By setting high quality standards, a franchisor helps the franchisee do all of the following EXCEPT:
    A.   develop a better product offering
    B.   present a consistent image
    C.   ensure return business
    D.   instill the value of teamwork

B   12.   One disadvantage of the franchise arrangement for the franchisee is:
    A.   decreasing service costs
    B.   dependence on the franchisor
    C.   greater freedom of operations than an independent would have
    D.   brand name association

C   13.   One aspect of communication which could potentially create an obstacle to a successful franchisee-franchisor relationship is:
    A.   an established hierarchy
    B.   a well written contract
    C.   personal differences
    D.   defined meanings

C   14.   A disclosure document is sometimes called a prospectus or a/an:
    A.   requirement contract
    B.   habeas corpus
    C.   offering circular
    D.   noncompetition covenant

C   15.   Which aspect of investing in a franchise is different from investing in stocks or bonds?
    A.   Money
    B.   Risk
    C.   Time
    D.   Research

A   16.   Which of the following franchise examples is generally perceived as more risky than the others (so-called "blue chip" franchisees)?
    A.   Autotire
    B.   Burger King
    C.   KFC
    D.   Holiday Inn

A   17. Capital requirements for the franchisor include funds for:
      A.   Prototype development
      B.   Franchising fees
      C.   Equipment purchases for individual units
      D.   Inventory

C   18. Minimum capital requirements for the franchisor (excluding prototype development) can range from:
      A. $11,000 to $95,000
      B. $95,000 to $110,000
      C. $110,000 to $950,000
      D. $950,000 to $1,100,000

A   19. Many entrepreneurs would not start businesses with the same amount of new equipment, budgeted advertising, or _____ as new franchisees commonly do.
      A.   training expense
      B.   personal expense
      C.   inventory
      D.   real estate costs

D   20. One aspect of the franchise agreement which is generally not subject to negotiation is:
      A.   franchisee fee
      B.   products offered
      C.   location
      D.   hours of operation

C   21. Which of the following is NOT an element of the franchisee-franchisor relationship?
      A.   Legal agreement
      B.   Product delivery
      C.   Funding
      D.   Independence

A   22. What information does a disclosure document offer to the franchisee?
      A.   Franchisor expectations
      B.   Franchise hierarchy
      C.   New product ideas
      D.   Funding sources

B   23.   Which of the following is a financial concern for the franchisee?
- A. State licensing costs
- B. Franchising fee
- C. Promotions
- D. Operations development costs

A   24.   Which of the following is a financial concern for the franchisor?
- A. State licensing costs
- B. Franchising fee
- C. Rental costs
- D. Equipment costs

D   25.   Hidden costs for the franchisor can include research, legal, and _____ costs.
- A. franchisee recruitment
- B. blueprint development
- C. initial advertising
- D. accounting/bookkeeping

True-False

T   26.   The franchise agreement is usually written by a representative of the franchisor.

F   27.   If franchise earnings are below what the franchisor projected for the outlet, the franchisor will often decrease its franchise fee or royalty claims for first-year operations.

F   28.   The disclosure document is designed to provide all the information relevant to the business decision-making process.

F   29.   Franchising is a unique approach to business which originated in Germany.

T   30.   The franchise opportunity has three major components: trademark/logo, royalty fee, and marketing.

T   31.   Product and trade name franchising has historically had a geographical basis.

T   32.   The number of new franchisees entering product and trade name relationships has decreased in recent years.

F   33.   The explosion in franchising arrangements since the 1950's is primarily due to product and trade name franchising growth.

F   34.   As the relationship between the two parties in a continuing business transaction evolves, the familiarity with policies and procedures makes for a smooth partnership.

T   35.   Company-owned stores are more likely to implement policy and procedure changes than are franchised units.

F   36.   Legal problems tend to be more complex in a franchisor-franchisee relationship than in an integrated chain-store operation.

F   37.   Franchisee savings due to the bulk purchasing power of the parent company are limited to supply stock and other directly related equipment.

F   38.   If a parent company chooses to expand primarily through franchise assignment, it is able to "farm out" such operations as marketing research and sales.

F   39.   Companies in mature industries generally seek expansion through business-format franchising.

F   40.   When seeking potential venture partners, franchisors prefer those familiar with the industry so training can progress smoothly.

F   41.   Franchise expansion benefits the parent company financially solely through the sale of franchise operations.

T   42.   A franchisee might typically expect to recover the initial investment in 2-3 years.

F   43.   The franchisor is a helpful resource for the franchisee when deciding on local pricing and marketing issues.

T   44.   It can be difficult for the franchisor to modify the product/service when involved in a reciprocal franchise relationship.

F   45.   "Value added" refers to the superior product or service quality received by the consumer from a "known" seller.

<u>Essay</u>

1. Explain the difference between business format franchising and product and trade name franchising.

2. How does the franchisor benefit from the franchise arrangement? How does the franchisee benefit? Can a case be made that one party benefits more than the other?

3. Why might a combination of company-owned and franchisee-owned operating units appear to be the best business strategy? When might the exclusive use of one or the other approach be warranted?

4. When purchasing a "blue chip" franchise (such as McDonalds), why should the franchisee consider his or her own skills and aptitude?

5. What are some of the topics covered in a franchise agreement? What might happen if such aspects of the business were not clearly defined?

6. What are the capital requirements for someone wishing to start a franchise?

CHAPTER 11

Multiple Choice

B   1.   The United States recently accounted for _____ percent of the world's merchandise exports.
A.   8.7
B.   13.2
C.   23.2
D.   32.1

B   2.   Employment by exporting firms reached nearly _____ American jobs in 1989.
A.   1.7 million
B.   7 million
C.   17 million
D.   1.7 billion

C   3.   One alternative to international selling operations that is more readily available to larger companies is:
A.   licensing
B.   joint venture
C.   foreign investment
D.   exporting

B   4.   Some additional analysis of Gerber's intended foreign expansion markets could have revealed a solution to their now classic mistake in what area?

    A.   Translation
    B.   Packaging
    C.   Pricing
    D.   Distribution

B   5.   The most common method of moving into the international arena for emerging operations is:

    A.   joint venture
    B.   exporting
    C.   licensing
    D.   foreign investment

C   6.   The _____ phase of the international strategic planning process helps determine how to enter foreign markets.

    A.   premise
    B.   analysis
    C.   strategy development
    D.   implementation

D   7.   Controls are established in the _____ phase of the international planning process.

    A.   premise
    B.   analysis
    C.   strategy development
    D.   implementation

B   8.   Which of the following is NOT a good reason for exporting?

    A.   Greater fixed cost base
    B.   Serviceability
    C.   Create additional jobs
    D.   Availability of foreign comparisons

C   9.   Some possible obstacles to the internationalization effort include the additional legal costs, indeterminate demand, and:

    A.   greater fixed cost base
    B.   increased ROI
    C.   capacity utilization
    D.   availability of foreign comparisons

A   10.   When utilizing indirect exporting, the producer cannot control the marketing, distribution, or _____ of the product once it reaches the foreign market.
A.   serviceability
B.   greater fixed cost base
C.   capacity utilization
D.   availability of foreign comparisons

D   11.   A/an _____ acts primarily as an order-taker for the production company.
A.   commission agent
B.   foreign retailer
C.   export trading company
D.   export management company

B   12.   Which of the following is an example of indirect exporting?
A.   Distributor
B.   Commission agent
C.   End-user sale
D.   Foreign retailer

A   13.   Which of the following is an example of direct exporting?
A.   Distributor
B.   Commission agent
C.   Export management company
D.   Industry partnership exporting

D   14.   Serviceability concerns include which of the following?
A.   Excess capacity
B.   Label translation
C.   Additional foreign analysts
D.   Warranty language

C   15.   An export management company would most closely resemble a _____ in the United States.
A.   wholesaler
B.   distributor
C.   manufacturer's representative
D.   licensee

B   16.   Selling to a _____ consists of selling to wholesalers or brokers who break the shipment into smaller quantities for further dispensation.
- A.   commission agent
- B.   distributor
- C.   retailer
- D.   licensee

B   17.   Production companies who have an international distribution system benefit from a partnership with a new exporter because of the:
- A.   additional outlets
- B.   enhanced image
- C.   streamlined product offerings
- D.   price increases

B   18.   Which of the following involves the purchase of goods by the export intermediary?
- A.   Export management company
- B.   Export trading company
- C.   commission sales representative
- D.   foreign retailer

A   19.   Selling to _____ assures that the desired vendors carry the product.
- A.   retailers
- B.   distributors
- C.   export trade companies
- D.   end-users

C   20.   Which of the following is NOT a reason for selling directly to the end-user?
- A.   Complex product
- B.   Training needed
- C.   Higher profit margin
- D.   Institutional customer

C   21.   An obvious first target country for a new American exporter is:
- A.   Mexico
- B.   Japan
- C.   Canada
- D.   Great Britain

B 22. The primary source of exporting information is the:
A. U.S. Division of Export Services
B. U.S. and Foreign Commercial Service
C. International Trade Council
D. Association of Import-Export Companies

C 23. The Department of Commerce's _____ is a compilation of the best international trade and economic information and is available on CD-ROM.
A. International Trade Book
B. Business America
C. National Trade Data Bank
D. Guide to Exporting

A 24. Which of the following is NOT a key to successful international strategy implementation?
A. Internationally experienced managerial team
B. Intermediary relationship
C. Measures of control
D. Financing

C 25. One of the most significant concerns with the financial aspects of international transactions is:
A. Currency exchange
B. Intermediary markups
C. Time lag in receiving payments
D. Tariffs

A 26. General funding for financing payment lags can be obtained through some local banks, the Export-Import Bank, or:
A. the Small Business Administration
B. the Federal Reserve Bank
C. the World Bank
D. the International Trade Council

D 27. Which of the following is NOT an advantage of joint ventures?
A. Shared risk
B. Shared technology
C. Access to markets
D. Shared profits

True/False

F 28. An exporter's common mistake of "chasing orders" occurs when the exporter attempts to sell to a number of related areas of the world.

T 29. While direct export to foreign retailers may eliminate intermediate price markups, this alternative may suffer from a dearth of product carriers.

F 30. Companies who serve as the export intermediary do not produce goods or services. They only market them.

F 31. Direct exporting involves the use of different channels of distribution than does domestic marketing.

F 32. Because of their experience, larger firms rarely make mistakes in international expansion decisions.

F 33. Exporting is a viable alternative for any company when the domestic market turns sour.

T 34. When considering internationalization, the entrepreneur should first analyze domestic market opportunities.

F 35. The financial cost of doing the background research on international markets is often prohibitive.

F 36. Commission agents are hired by producers to "find" foreign markets for their goods or services.

T 37. One incentive for expanding into international markets is the potential to renew the product life cycle.

F 38. The primary difference between direct and indirect exporting is where the product actually leaves the possession of the exporting firm.

T 39. When engaging in indirect exporting, serviceability is the one area for which an international venture remains responsible once the product arrives in the target country.

F 40. Industry-wide trade shows are not utilized by those companies wishing to export indirectly because only industrial customers and international retailers attend.

F   41.   Joint ownership of a venture company is legally required to be split 50-50.

T   42.   Licensing to foreign interests is similar to franchising domestically.

T   43.   Direct investment means that the U.S.-based company begins a complete operation in a foreign country.

T   44.   The letter of credit is a commitment by the buyer's bank to pay the entrepreneur a sum of money upon compliance with the terms of shipment.

F   45.   The "letter of credit" process cannot be completed before the goods arrive in the foreign country.

F   46.   Licensing in the target country assures the entrepreneur's control over quality and distribution.

T   47.   One of the important ways an entrepreneur can maintain control over international sales is through on-site visits.

T   48.   The freight forwarder is an intermediary whose job it is to move the product from the plant to its overseas destination.

F   49.   Governments in capitalist countries can only restrict trade by economic means.

Essay

1.   What are some of the difficulties facing the entrepreneur who contemplates international operations? Give specific examples.

2.   As the owner of an _____ enterprise, you have decided that expansion into foreign markets might help alleviate your poor domestic outlook. Briefly step through the strategic planning process.

3.   In looking at the overall strategy of the firm, what are some specific questions or concerns the entrepreneur needs to answer in deciding whether an international effort "fits" the enterprise?

4.   How can utilizing the services of an export intermediary benefit the entrepreneur? How can their services limit or even hinder international success?

5. Consider exporting portable phones. Outline some concerns you as an entrepreneurial exporter would have when deciding whether or not to export (to country A?).

6. Using a diagram, describe the "letter of credit" process. Why is this form of payment valuable to the seller? to the buyer?

7. In what ways is licensing to foreign interests similar to franchising domestically? In what ways is it dissimilar?

CHAPTER 12

Multiple Choice

B   1.   Which of the following will least likely determine the structure of ventures with a parent company?
A.   Financing
B.   Marketing direction
C.   Legal issues
D.   Personal ego

B   2.   The primary basis of any firm's structure should be its:
A.   quality of personnel
B.   strategy
C.   present size of the business
D.   sales forecast

C   3.   Which of the following is NOT a way to arrange a divisional structure?
A.   Customers
B.   Geographical territories
C.   Functional skills
D.   Processes

D   4.   The _____ structure is particularly advantageous if one section is substantially more risky than the others.
A.   internal
B.   basic
C.   functional
D.   divisional

A   5.   One disadvantage of divisional structure is the:
  - A.   lack of coordination.
  - B.   lack of effective time management.
  - C.   confusion over decision making authority
  - D.   existence of freestanding units.

B   6.   One disadvantage of basic structure is the:
  - A.   lack of coordination
  - B.   lack of effective time management
  - C.   confusion over decision making authority
  - D.   managerial conflict

C   7.   One disadvantage of a functional structure in a new venture is the:
  - A.   lack of coordination
  - B.   lack of effective time management
  - C.   confusion over decision making authority
  - D.   existence of free standing units

A   8.   Lower cost is an advantage of which structure for a new venture?
  - A.   Basic
  - B.   Internal
  - C.   Functional
  - D.   Divisional

D   9.   Management levels should be added when the size of the venture increases and/or as:
  - A.   time passes
  - B.   the firm can afford to hire additional workers
  - C.   managers become more skilled
  - D.   the environment becomes unstable

C   10.   The _____ structure allows for quicker decision-making in a growing venture.
  - A.   basic
  - B.   internal
  - C.   functional
  - D.   organizational

B   11.   When a venture loses a sale even though the entrepreneur is prospecting
            for new customers, _____ concerns are the sign of inefficient operations.
            A.   administrative
            B.   customer
            C.   non-business
            D.   employee

D   12.   _____ concerns typically revolve around the inability to get definite
            answers from the owner/manager.
            A.   Administrative
            B.   Customer
            C.   Non-business
            D.   Employee

C   13.   When the entrepreneur tries to do all things for a new venture, _____
            is usually put on the "back burner."
            A.   managing
            B.   sales
            C.   planning
            D.   financing

C   14.   _____ refers to the arrangement of activities in order to produce more in
            the same amount of time.
            A.   Activity screening
            B.   Scheduling
            C.   Time management
            D.   Prioritizing

D   15.   Staff functions in an entrepreneurial venture tend to be:
            A.   less administratively oriented
            B.   highly regarded
            C.   over-specialized
            D.   more advisory than line functions are

D   16.   The merging of family norms and cultures with those of an enterprise is
            known as:
            A.   norming
            B.   culture merging
            C.   institutional overload
            D.   institutional overlap

A   17.   As the entrepreneur selects and develops the structure of a maturing family venture, the _____ must be considered.
      A.   complexity of relationships
      B.   family lifestyle
      C.   management succession
      D.   profitability of the venture

C   18.   If a newly acquired venture is small or is sufficiently related to the existing venture, the appropriate structure is:
      A.   a holding company
      B.   a subsidiary
      C.   absorption
      D.   two separate entities

C   19.   In which of the following will customers and suppliers necessarily note a difference?
      A.   a holding company
      B.   a subsidiary
      C.   absorption
      D.   maintaining two separate entities

D   20.   A subsidiary relies on the parent company for:
      A.   sales efforts
      B.   inventory
      C.   marketing research
      D.   financing

D   21.   The only common ground when _____ is ownership.
      A.   creating a holding company
      B.   creating subsidiaries
      C.   absorbing ventures
      D.   maintaining separate ventures

C   22.   Another name for the holding company arrangement is:
      A.   association
      B.   conglomeration
      C.   consolidation
      D.   unification

A   23.   One example of a _____ factor affecting the assimilation of a new venture into an existing one is the continuation of the venture's name.
- A.   strategic
- B.   personnel
- C.   tax related
- D.   motivational

C   24.   Decisions of structure may be directly related to _____ because of the effect on the current and future profitability.
- A.   legal issues
- B.   taxes
- C.   costs
- D.   motivation

C   25.   One example of an indirect cost factor in regard to organizational structure is:
- A.   staffing
- B.   tax treatment
- C.   performance controls
- D.   relocation

D   26.   The _____ structure may best ease the transition to a larger organizational unit for top managers.
- A.   conglomerate
- B.   separate entity
- C.   subsidiary
- D.   holding company

B   27.   The acquiring firm's management must be concerned about motivation of acquired personnel and about:
- A.   the guidelines for promotion.
- B.   management control issues.
- C.   compensation of its own managers
- D.   resource allocation

True/False

T   28.   Some inefficiencies in business organizations are eventually traced to inappropriate structures.

F   29.   In an acquisition situation, the two companies usually have similar cultures and organization styles and therefore make a natural match.

T   30.   A board of directors is as important for small ventures as it is for larger corporations.

F   31.   It is important to plan the structure of a new venture well since it is the least malleable when it is new.

F   32.   The basic structure offers flexibility when the venture is small or faces an unstable environment.

F   33.   If a key person does not work out in a new venture, other parts of the firm can absorb the effects of the problem.

F   34.   Confusion about who is in control of certain decisions can be resolved if the entrepreneur simply delegates authority.

F   35.   The key to management-level growth is the passage of time and the increasing size of the venture.

F   36.   In a functionally structured organization, employees are urged to seek the entrepreneur's approval for decisions.

T   37.   The basic structure and the functional structure are the two structure types used by most ventures.

F   38.   The average entrepreneur spends 35% of the time in planning for the venture's growth while spending only 10% of the time arranging financial backing.

F   39.   Because of the autonomy inherent in the entrepreneurial lifestyle, only 33% of surveyed entrepreneurs reported working more than 50 hours per week.

T   40.   Growth ventures begin to suffer inefficiencies resulting from their basic structure when the owner/manager becomes unable to make timely decisions.

T   41.   Though delegation may improve operation efficiency, many entrepreneurs are hesitant to take advantage of the opportunity to do so.

F   42.   The only way to improve efficiency in an overburdened venture is to restructure.

T   43.   Some ventures can keep the basic structure indefinitely.

T   44.   When a new venture is launched, the family venture typically benefits from the institutional overlap.

F   45.   During the maturity stage, the firm's social dynamics are highly organic, with all employees reporting directly to the entrepreneur.

F   46.   As more and more family members become involved in the venture, the family norms and values are solidified.

T   47.   When absorbing a new venture into the structure of an existing venture, the name of the new venture could remain the same as it was.

F   48.   Informal advisory boards, because they are generally more actively involved with a venture than formal boards of directors, provide a greater threat to the entrepreneur's power.

F   49.   It is illegal/unethical for board members to refer customers to the new venture since they are strictly advisers to the entrepreneur.

Essay

1.   Compare and contrast the functional management structure and the divisional structure. When would each best be used?

2.   When the basic structure of a venture becomes overstressed, certain signals of inefficiency spring up. What are the four basic areas of concern, and give some examples of each. How can inefficiency in these areas eventually lead to the failure of the venture if left uncorrected?

3.   Why do you suppose entrepreneurs have difficulty delegating authority? Imagine you are an employee in someone else's entrepreneurial enterprise. How would you approach the owner/manager if you believed there were some tasks you could handle in order to ease the stress?

4.   The text states that "establishing rules, procedures, and relationships detracts from the key strength of entrepreneurial firms." What is the key strength? How do rules, etc. detract from that strength? How does the choice of a firm's structure interplay with an entrepreneur's strengths and weaknesses?

5.   How does an acquired venture's location play into the strategic outlook and structural makeup of the overall firm? Give examples.

6.   Discuss the motivational aspects of assimilation. How could a merger benefit the people in the "old" venture?

CHAPTER 13

<u>Multiple Choice</u>

B   1.   The growth period for a new venture typically lasts up to _____ years (according to John Ward).
    A.   three
    B.   five
    C.   seven
    D.   ten

A   2.   In the _____ phase, the entrepreneur must work to enable the venture to produce at maximum capacity.
    A.   growth
    B.   stability
    C.   maturity
    D.   rejuvenation

B   3.   In the _____ phase, the entrepreneur works to extend the sales momentum for as long as possible.
    A.   growth
    B.   stability
    C.   maturity
    D.   rejuvenation

C   4.   The rate of growth achieved simply by meeting the increasing demand for the product is called the:
     A.   constant rate of growth
     B.   law of supply and demand
     C.   natural rate of growth
     D.   increasing supply/demand ratio

D   5.   During the growth phase resources must be continually increased to allow the production and _____ of the product to meet its demand.
     A.   promotion
     B.   packaging
     C.   pricing
     D.   distribution

C   6.   Growth _____ actions are those that attempt to continue the growth rate past the typical peak.
     A.   enabling
     B.   maintaining
     C.   extending
     D.   rejuvenating

B   7.   _____ is the overall limiting factor in maintaining the growth rate of a venture.
     A.   Marketing
     B.   Financing
     C.   Distribution
     D.   Plant capacity

B   8.   _____ growth suggests that the venture should grow as fast as possible given the entrepreneur's guidelines or parameters.
     A.   Extending
     B.   Controlling
     C.   Enabling
     D.   Rejuvenating

D   9.   Back ordering may be a sign of a _____ problem.
     A.   order entry
     B.   pricing
     C.   promotional
     D.   distribution

A   10. Hiring additional staff members is often done in a/an _____ manner.
- A. step-wise or incremental
- B. smooth or continual
- C. premature
- D. equitable

B   11. Which of the following is NOT a suggested method of "hedging" the need for additional production facilities?
- A. Facility rental or leasing
- B. Restricting demand
- C. Subcontracting
- D. Additional shifts

A   12. Which of the following companies frequently uses product variations as the primary method of extending growth?
- A. MacMillan Publishing Co.
- B. Autotire Car Care
- C. McDonalds
- D. Wal-Mart

A   13. The acquisition of direct competitors not only eliminates adversaries but can also offer growth extension opportunities through adding additional:
- A. products or distribution channels
- B. suppliers
- C. personnel with skills we need
- D. financing opportunities

A   14. Which method of control best eliminates the need for the entrepreneur to decide on routine matters?
- A. Establishment of effective policies and procedures.
- B. Centralization of authority.
- C. Selective hiring processes.
- D. Consideration of strategic decisions.

C   15. The most important aspect of the control process may be:
- A. strict reporting requirements
- B. selective hiring
- C. the use of budgets
- D. personal visits

A   16.   Venture capital is basically needed to:
           A.   enable growth
           B.   create growth
           C.   limit growth
           D.   maintain growth

B   17.   Which method of control eases the administrative burden on the entrepreneurial team?
           A.   Establishment of effective policies and procedures.
           B.   Selective hiring process.
           C.   Centralization of authority.
           D.   Consideration of strategic decisions.

C   18.   Which method of control can serve to motivate employees?
           A.   Establishment of effective policies and procedures.
           B.   Selective hiring process.
           C.   Delegation of authority.
           D.   Effective use of budgets.

D   19.   Concentric expansion to an ever-expanding circle of regions has the advantage of:
           A.   reaching all populated areas
           B.   providing ease of marketability
           C.   natural progression
           D.   minimizing distance from headquarters

A   20.   _____ are/is a frequent source of growth financing.
           A.   Venture capital
           B.   Loans
           C.   Stock options
           D.   Bond issues

C   21.   Which of the following is NOT a result of stress?
           A.   Illness
           B.   Increased energy
           C.   Eased relations
           D.   Turnover

C   22.   The primary cause of lower stress levels in entrepreneurs versus other
            managers/workers is the:
            A.   greater financial rewards received.
            B.   nature of the managerial team.
            C.   autonomy of the job.
            D.   entrepreneur's organizational skills.

D   23.   Which method of control helps stabilize the venture's direction?
            A.   Establishment of effective policies and procedures.
            B.   Selective hiring process.
            C.   Delegation of authority.
            D.   Consideration of strategic decisions.

B   24.   Which of the following strategies is probably easiest to control?
            A.   High growth, single product
            B.   Slow growth, single product
            C.   High growth, multiple products
            D.   Slow growth, multiple products

A   25.   Recent studies show that self-employed individuals who put in longer hours
            per week experience _____ when compared with corporate
            managers:
            A.   less psychosomatic symptoms.
            B.   more general life dissatisfaction.
            C.   less job satisfaction.
            D.   reduced productivity.

C   26.   College expenses, marriage, and moving are examples of:
            A.   venture-caused stress
            B.   venture-related stress
            C.   unrelated stress
            D.   lifestyle stress

B   27.   _____ results from differing priorities.
            A.   Venture-caused stress
            B.   Venture-related stress
            C.   unrelated stress
            D.   lifestyle stress

True/False

F   28.   Maintaining a growth pattern is easier than the initial achievement of growth.

F   29.   The level of growth achieved by a venture is based solely on the growth of the primary target market.

T   30.   Too much growth can cause a venture to fail.

F   31.   The goal of any growth-oriented firm should be to maximize growth in a given time period.

F   32.   Rapid growth maximizes sales revenues and produces the greatest net profits.

T   33.   Solutions to distribution problems are based primarily on the type of product sold, rather than on the geographical reach of the venture.

T   34.   In order to secure supplier production capabilities, the venture may pursue vertical integration.

F   35.   Human resources must be increased at a rate just above the rate of product sales growth.

T   36.   Rapid growth ventures often face a tapering off of sales growth not because of declining demand, but because of their inability to grow.

F   37.   Second stage financing efforts generally do not pose a threat to the entrepreneur, while third stage financing opportunities carry the risk of "dethronement." (e.g. Steve Jobs)

T   38.   Rejuvenation can sometimes be achieved simply through repackaging.

F   39.   Geographic expansion to contiguous regions enables a firm to capture the largest possible markets for the product.

F   40.   The introduction of ancillary products can help extend growth indefinitely.

T   41.   Acquisition is the most common method of expansion among service ventures.

F   42.   Controlled growth will usually be somewhat quicker than uncontrolled growth would be.

F   43.   If there is little hope of rejuvenating a venture's product, production should normally stop as soon as possible so all efforts can go to more profitable product offerings.

F   44.   Entrepreneurs in high growth ventures ignore minor budget variances at their peril.

T   45.   When hiring additional staff, the entrepreneur should seek balance in team skills and weaknesses.

F   46.   A new venture should quickly follow a product introduction with a full line of complementary products in order to meet any possible consumer needs.

F   47.   Venture-related stress is more likely to be felt in high growth ventures than in low growth enterprises.

Essay

1.   Discuss some stress management techniques. Since studies have shown that entrepreneurs experience lower stress levels, why is it important for an entrepreneur to be wary of stress?

2.   How can controlling mechanisms aid growth? How can control hinder growth? How can an entrepreneur recognize when the amount of control has "crossed the line?"

3.   What are the means of implementing control in entrepreneurial ventures? Give specific examples showing how these measures can help foster controlled growth.

4.   You own a _____ enterprise. What are some methods of extending your venture's growth beyond the normal growth cycle? What are the limitations you may face?

5.   What are the requirements for growth? How can an entrepreneur circumvent some of these needs?

CHAPTER 14

Multiple Choice

C   1.   Intrapreneurship differs from individual entrepreneurship in that it is:
     A.   developmental
     B.   stagnating
     C.   restorative
     D.   structured

B   2.   One similarity between intrapreneurship and individual entrepreneurship is:
     A.   availability of capital
     B.   focus on new products or services
     C.   focus on employee satisfaction
     D.   focus on corporate culture obstacles

D   3.   Individual entrepreneurship focuses on:
     A.   overcoming corporate culture obstacles
     B.   growth restoration
     C.   employee satisfaction
     D.   new product development

B   4.   The focus of intrapreneurship is on:
     A.   overcoming corporate culture obstacles
     B.   growth restoration
     C.   employee satisfaction
     D.   new product development

D   5.   Size is a factor in the ability to foster intrapreneurship for all the following reasons EXCEPT:
- A.   the need for control
- B.   layered hierarchy
- C.   additional worker contacts
- D.   physical distance

B   6.   Which of the following is true regarding the need for control in a growing business?
- A.   Planning takes priority over paperwork.
- B.   Performance reports are sometimes more important than performance results.
- C.   Entrepreneurial behavior overshadows rules and policies.
- D.   More flexible standards help foster the growth

D   7.   The corporate culture of a traditional company has a climate and reward system that favors _____ in decision-making.
- A.   Adaptability
- B.   Rigidity/inflexibility
- C.   Liberalism
- D.   Conservatism

A   8.   The key to the survival of new entrepreneurial ventures is:
- A.   Cash flow
- B.   Short term profit
- C.   High stock prices
- D.   Cost reduction measures

C   9.   Which of the following is a reason why organizations discourage true entrepreneurs?
- A.   The entrepreneur's resistance to change
- B.   The entrepreneur's focus on corporate goals
- C.   The entrepreneur's dislike for authority
- D.   The entrepreneur's poor attendance record

A   10.   One problem with rewarding intrapreneuship in an organization is the:
- A.   definition of productivity.
- B.   unwillingness to pay high salaries.
- C.   unavailability of managerial positions.
- D.   ambiguity of goals.

D   11.   Only the _____ can commit the organization to corporate entrepreneurship.
    A.   frontline workers
    B.   line managers
    C.   board of directors
    D.   chief executive officer

B   12.   Intrapreneurship thrives when both the encouragement and _____ are given to all levels of the organization.
    A.   structure
    B.   authority
    C.   control
    D.   discipline

D   13.   The _____ of a corporation dictates that changes in strategy/culture must come from top management.
    A.   organizational charter
    B.   managerial policy directives
    C.   code of ethics
    D.   hierarchial structure

C   14.   Another reason for top management direction is that corporate entrepreneurship will necessitate changes in the _____.
    A.   hierarchial structure
    B.   line of succession
    C.   reward system
    D.   code of ethics

C   15.   The intrapreneurial structure which requires direction at the vice-presidential level is the _____ structure.
    A.   subsidiary
    B.   organic
    C.   divisional
    D.   venture capital

A   16.   The corporate structure which merits an autonomous unit is the _____ structure.
    A.   subsidiary
    B.   organic
    C.   divisional
    D.   hierarchial

B   17.   The intrapreneurial structure which requires the highest level of
            management involvement is the _____ structure.
            A.   subsidiary
            B.   organic
            C.   divisional
            D.   venture capital

D   18.   A section within the _____ department assists in training for intrapreneurial
            activity.
            A.   management
            B.   corporate entrepreneurship
            C.   venture capital
            D.   human resources

C   19.   The model of intrapreneurial structure selected is a function of the size and
            age of the firm, and of:
            A.   its manufacturing technology
            B.   its hierarchial structure
            C.   its industry
            D.   its training needs

B   20.   _____ refers to the fact that intrapreneurs appoint themselves rather than
            being chosen by the organization.
            A.   "Doer decides"
            B.   Self selection
            C.   Corporate slack
            D.   Multiple options

C   21.   "Ownership" serves as a real motivator to a project originator. This is the
            logic behind _____.
            A.   "doer decides"
            B.   self selection
            C.   "no handoffs"
            D.   freedom from turfiness

D   22.   In order for _____ to exist, there must be separate corporate funds that are
            not budgeted and are available.
            A.   tolerance of risk
            B.   multiple options
            C.   patient money
            D.   corporate slack

A 23. Suggestions for achieving an intrapreneurial company include restructuring and:
  A. changing compensation methods
  B. increasing the number of layers of management
  C. purchasing supplies
  D. eliminating several layers of middle management

C 24. Corporate entrepreneurs must have the ability to do all the following EXCEPT:
  A. market the project idea
  B. work with others
  C. acquire resources
  D. finish a project

D 25. The _____ aspect of a reward system may be the most important from the viewpoint of the intrapreneur.
  A. salary
  B. unstructured
  C. risk-based
  D. recognition

B 26. _____ is the freedom to use increasing amounts of corporate resources to fund additional product development.
  A. Discretionary spending
  B. Intracapital
  C. Corporate slack
  D. Non-budgeting

A 27. One problem with evaluating internally developed proposals is:
  A. subjectivity
  B. objectivity
  C. creativity
  D. politics

C 28. Assignments of new projects are based on all of the following except:
  A. fit with strategy
  B. overall intrapreneurial structure
  C. departmental location of the innovator
  D. value of development inputs

True/False

F	29.	Corporate entrepreneurship requires business units independent of the parent company.
T	30.	Entrepreneurship is difficult to achieve in not-for-profit organizations.
F	31.	The enemy for both the individual entrepreneur and the corporate intrapreneur is the parent company.
T	32.	One central irony of entrepreneurship is that the very goal to succeed and grow can destroy the innovative spark that powered growth.
F	33.	Traditional corporations often waive short term performance standards and/or reports in order to promote the benefits of entrepreneurial activities.
T	34.	Innovation in organizations is a bottom-up process.
T	35.	It is unlikely that the chief executive officer in most organizations is a believer in the benefits of corporate entrepreneurship.
F	36.	Some departments in an organization will not be affected by the move toward a corporate entrepreneurial attitude.
F	37.	The formal structure of corporate entrepreneurship is not as important as the advantageous placement of innovative projects.
F	38.	An entrepreneurial culture is one in which entrepreneurship is allowed to flourish in designated areas of the organization.
F	39.	In an intrapreneurial environment, the inventor or initiator always retains developmental responsibility throughout the project life.
F	40.	Corporate slack refers to the willingness to invest funds in intrapreneurial projects without an expected immediate return.
F	41.	The "home run philosophy" ensures the development of the most prosperous ideas by encouraging as many people as possible to engage in intrapreneurial activity.
T	42.	"Turfiness" is a win/lose situation when trying to foster corporate entrepreneurship.

F 43. Intrapreneurship efforts are only considered successful when the end-product is sold on the open market.

F 44. Creative individuals make good intrapreneurs.

F 45. All aspiring entrepreneurs would make good venture owners.

T 46. Creative corporate workers may not seek to develop their ideas because they may lack vision.

F 47. Through bonus payments, the intrapreneur indirectly reaps the benefits of innovation as the project provides additional profit to the corporation.

T 48. A venture champion may be someone besides the project innovator.

T 49. Entrepreneurship does not flourish in not-for-profit organizations because managers tend to be program-oriented.

Essay

1. As head of an organization, how would you instill entrepreneurial attitudes into the corporate culture? What values, methods, policies would you encourage? Give an example of when this might NOT work.

2. In contrast to your answer to the above question, how would you put into practice your faith in the entrepreneurial spirit if you were a department manager? What would you do if the overall corporate culture did not support this attitude?

3. How would you handle failure in an innovative attempt?

4. Why must the commitment to corporate entrepreneurship come from the top?

5. What are some of the indicators of an intrapreneurial culture?

6. As the Vice-President in charge of developing an entrepreneurial culture in your organization, you are charged with identifying those employees who possess entrepreneurial instincts. What characteristics would you seek? How would you go about discovering these?

7.   Discuss the dual promotion system (as exemplified by the 3M Corporation). How does this system help foster entrepreneurial activity? Do you foresee any problems with using this type of system?

8.   What are the criteria for intrapreneurial proposals? How can corporate politics influence proposal acceptance or rejection?

9.   In the Post-It Note story in the appendix to Chapter 14, how much of the credit should be given to Art Fry's creative ability and how much should be given to 3M's intrapreneurial culture?

CHAPTER 15

<u>Multiple Choice</u>

B   1.   Lenders will often utilize a/an _____ method of valuing a venture.
     A.   market based
     B.   asset based
     C.   capacity utilization
     D.   net present value

D   2.   Why should the venture be valued before an initial public offering?
     A.   To satisfy legal requirements
     B.   To project future sales
     C.   To offer a fair market price
     D.   To maximize returns

C   3.   Any individual who makes an effort to value the venture is referred to as a/an:
     A.   financier
     B.   actuary
     C.   value analyst
     D.   capital analyst

D   4.   Which of the following is NOT assessed by the seller in the valuation of a venture?
     A.   Assets
     B.   Return on investment
     C.   Product market
     D.   Needed additions

C 5. The buyer will likely give a/an _____ value to the firm.
   A. optimistic
   B. highly accurate
   C. conservative
   D. subjective rather than objective

D 6. Which of the following is NOT considered by the financier when valuing a venture?
   A. Projected cash flow
   B. Projected profit
   C. Assets
   D. Human resources

D 7. One problem in valuing inventory is the difference between the actual and desired:
   A. retail price
   B. wholesale price
   C. product lines
   D. quantity/quality

B 8. Merchandise that an owner buys but is unable to sell is referred to as:
   A. depreciated inventory
   B. dead inventory
   C. salable merchandise
   D. undervalued inventory

B 9. If an entrepreneur has planned to sell a venture for some time, the _____ may be artificially low.
   A. asking price
   B. inventory
   C. stock price
   D. morale

C 10. Purchased inventory may present a problem because it:
   A. is old
   B. adds to the cost of the venture
   C. takes up shelf space
   D. comes prepackaged

A   11.   Historical analysis of a venture's revenue stream may indicate a value higher than appropriate if:
A.   the market is becoming saturated
B.   the market has room for growth
C.   costs are decreasing
D.   prices are deflated

C   12.   No other issue in valuation involves as much subjectivity as _____.
A.   market trends
B.   market size
C.   goodwill
D.   industry growth

C   13.   Which of the following is NOT an example of an intangible asset that is often included in the valuation process?
A.   Lease terms
B.   Purchase contracts
C.   Computer hardware
D.   Copyrights

B   14.   The approaches used to value a firm should reflect _____ for similar firms.
A.   contract prices
B.   open market prices
C.   public offerings
D.   lending terms

A   15.   The _____ approach to valuation offers the advantage of giving a true value to a firm.
A.   net present value
B.   market comparables
C.   replacement value
D.   comparable firms

A   16.   Which of the following is a variation of the asset based valuation approach?
A.   Adjusted book value
B.   Comparable firm's value
C.   Present value
D.   Price/earnings value

A   17.   The balance sheet value of the assets less depreciation is called the:
           A.   book value
           B.   market value
           C.   present value
           D.   liquidation value

B.   18.   Which of the following methods is most useful in determining the amount a purchaser would pay for the assets at the present time?
           A.   Book value
           B.   Market value
           C.   Replacement value
           D.   Liquidated value

B   19.   The _____ is preferred in that each individual asset is valued at the rate it could be sold to another similar business.
           A.   book value
           B.   market value
           C.   replacement value
           D.   present value

C   20.   _____ gives the value of the assets if they were to be purchased new.
           A.   Book value
           B.   Market value
           C.   Replacement value
           D.   Present value

D   21.   _____ can give an artificially high value for the venture.
           A.   Book value
           B.   Market value
           C.   Present value
           D.   Replacement value

B   22.   _____ typically gives the lowest value of all the asset-based valuation methods.
           A.   Book value
           B.   Liquidated value
           C.   Replacement value
           D.   Present value

A   23.   _____ ratios of similar firms can be used to estimate the worth of the firm being valued.
- A. Price to earnings
- B. Profitability
- C. Debt to equity
- D. Rate of return

C   24.   The _____ approach includes the discounted cash flow method of valuation.
- A. book value
- B. market value
- C. present value
- D. liquidation value

C   25.   The _____ approach develops the value of the firm based upon market risk assessment.
- A. book value
- B. market value
- C. present value
- D. comparable firms

True/False

F   26.   The correct price is the correct value.

F   27.   There is only one true value of a firm.

T   28.   In an agreement for purchase of a firm, there is a correct price.

T   29.   The buyer is often unknowledgeable about the value of the venture he wishes to purchase.

F   30.   It is pointless for an entrepreneur to value a venture before going to a lending agency; these agencies will do this themselves.

F   31.   The value determined by the seller will likely be higher than the initial asking price.

T   32.   Assets will often be appraised based on salvage value by lending financiers.

F   33.   Debt providers will tend to value the venture using a cash flow basis.

F   34.   An easy way to determine the value of inventory is to designate a certain percent of the wholesale price.

T   35.   Market related factors do not directly appear in valuation formulas.

F   36.   Market related factors may be used to quantitatively adjust the "final" calculated value of the venture.

T   37.   No other issue in valuation involves as much subjectivity as goodwill.

F   38.   The comparable firms valuation method is the single best indicator of a firm's value.

F   39.   The balance sheet value of the assets less depreciation is called the book value.

T   40.   Asset-based valuation methods typically do not include the earnings potential of the assets.

F   41.   The present value method assumes that a dollar earned tomorrow is worth more than a dollar earned today.

T   42.   The present value approach is a long run approach to valuation.

F   43.   The historical relationships reflected in the five year average approach adequately reflect the investor's current expectations about the future of the firms in the industry.

F   44.   The average price to market value of equity ratio measures the market value of the assets of the firms in the industry less outstanding obligations against those firms.

T   45.   Many entrepreneurs use ten years when calculating cash flow because the uncertainty in a longer time period is too high for an accurate valuation.

Essay

1.   What is goodwill? How could two parties manipulate this aspect of a firm to defend their individual valuations?

2.   Discuss the difference between price and value. Is one more important than the other?

3.   Name some venture-specific factors that may enter the valuation process.

4.   Discuss the differences between asset-based valuation methods and present value. Is either method of valuation more preferable than the other? Why or why not?

5.   What valuation method would be best suited for a service venture? For a small corner grocery? For a high-growth computer store? Support your answers.

6.   What are some other factors that may affect the negotiations for the sale price?

CHAPTER 16

Multiple Choice

C   1.   The method of changing ownership which causes the business to cease to exist is:
A.   direct sale
B.   merger
C.   liquidation
D.   leveraged buyout

B   2.   If the venture owner does not have time to develop a pre-harvest strategy, then the business must be valued based on:
A.   the past performance
B.   the present condition
C.   the future outlook
D.   portfolio analysis

A   3.   _____ is the most common method of harvesting.
A.   Direct sale
B.   Merger
C.   Liquidation
D.   going public

C   4.   Which of the following is required in the direct sale of a venture?
A.   Name transfer
B.   Non-complete agreement
C.   Asset transfer
D.   Consulting/employment contract

D   5.   The simplest way to harvest a venture is a:
           A.   public offering
           B.   leveraged buyout
           C.   bankruptcy proceeding
           D.   direct sale

D   6.   The method of harvesting which has a ready market for the venture is:
           A.   going public
           B.   liquidation
           C.   merger
           D.   ESOP

B   7.   The harvest strategy which may offer the best alternative for an
           entrepreneur who still has psychological ties to the venture is the:
           A.   direct sale
           B.   management buyout
           C.   leveraged buyout
           D.   merger

B   8.   The harvest strategy which yields the least amount of outward changes to
           the venture is the:
           A.   direct sale
           B.   management buyout
           C.   Chapter 7 bankruptcy proceeding
           D.   merger

D   9.   The strategy that is usually undertaken to avoid a hostile takeover of a
           publicly held firm is:
           A.   a direct sale to friendly buyers
           B.   liquidation
           C.   a transfer to another family member
           D.   a leveraged buyout

C   10.   A _____ strategy entails the acquisition of debt in the name of the venture.
           A.   direct sale
           B.   bankruptcy
           C.   leveraged buyout
           D.   merger

D   11.   An entrepreneur may feel the most rewarded when pursuing a/an:
         A.   direct sale to friendly buyers
         B.   leveraged buyout
         C.   ESOP
         D.   public offering

B   12.   The harvest strategy which necessitates the shut-down of a firm is:
         A.   bankruptcy
         B.   liquidation
         C.   leveraged buyout
         D.   management buyout

D   13.   The harvest strategy which usually arises as an opportunity rather than as a planned event is:
         A.   liquidation
         B.   a public offering
         C.   a leveraged buyout
         D.   a merger

A   14.   The entrepreneur will most likely stay active in a:
         A.   merger
         B.   leveraged buyout
         C.   management buyout
         D.   direct sale

B   15.   The harvest strategy which is done to gain protection from creditors is:
         A.   a merger
         B.   bankruptcy
         C.   a leveraged buyout
         D.   liquidation

C   16.   The harvest strategy which can serve as a motivation to many of the firm's employees is:
         A.   a merger
         B.   a management buyout
         C.   an ESOP
         D.   a public offering

D   17.   The first step in developing a harvest plan is to:
         A.   determine the target date for the harvest
         B.   value the company
         C.   acquire the necessary expertise
         D.   determine the type of harvest desired

B   18.   It is important to establish a _____ in order to plan the necessary actions to develop the harvest strategy.
            A.   value for the firm
            B.   harvest window
            C.   priority list
            D.   rapport with key outsiders

B   19.   In general, one of the last steps which should be taken before harvesting the venture is:
            A.   converting operational strategies
            B.   communicating to employees
            C.   determining the players involved
            D.   establishing rapport with key outside players

C   20.   The harvest strategy which offers the best opportunity for growth (from a financial standpoint) is the:
            A.   merger
            B.   direct sale
            C.   public offering
            D.   leveraged buyout

B   21.   Which of the following methods of harvesting a business is commonly used when an entrepreneur's expectations have not been met?
            A.   ESOP
            B.   liquidation
            C.   merger
            D.   leveraged buyout

D   22.   An entrepreneur will pass ownership of the venture to another family member for which of the following reasons?
            A.   Unmet expectations
            B.   Personal wealth
            C.   Facilitate growth
            D.   Change in personal situation

C   23.   When planning his/her estate, an entrepreneur will usually choose to harvest the venture through a/an:
            A.   merger
            B.   public offering
            C.   direct sale
            D.   ESOP

C 24. A merger will be undertaken when an entrepreneur decides to:
    A. gain personal wealth
    B. plan his/her estate
    C. facilitate growth
    D. pursue other interests

A 25. A direct sale will be pursued for which of the following reasons?
    A. Change in personal situation
    B. unmet expectations
    C. pass on to heirs
    D. facilitate growth

True/False

F 26. Only healthy businesses may be harvested.

F 27. Harvesting refers only to the termination of a business venture.

T 28. Ventures should be run as if they were to be harvested soon.

F 29. The intrapreneurial venture does not need a harvest strategy because it is an internal effort.

T 30. Only a small percentage of businesses are taken public.

T 31. More low-growth businesses are sold because of changes in personal situations than for any other reason.

F 32. Bankruptcy is a synonym for business failure.

F 33. Entrepreneurs generally do not buy and sell ventures; they would prefer to refine the mission of the current operation.

F 34. Low-growth entrepreneurs seldom invest in new venture opportunities.

F 35. Harvesting refers to a short term period of activity.

F 36. In a family business, the actual date of legal transfer of the venture is more critical than when operational control is changed.

F   37.   The change in life cycle stage usually has a significant lead time for preparation.

F   38.   An entrepreneur's standards dictate that a marginally profitable venture should be harvested.

T   39.   It is common for growth oriented ventures to grow through acquisitions.

F   40.   When passing on the family venture, the owner and the successor avoid the conflicts that might arise in other forms of harvesting.

T   41.   An entrepreneur may harvest a venture in order to facilitate its growth.

F   42.   A leveraged buyout offers unlimited liability to the purchasers of the venture.

F   43.   The management buyout offers an alternative to pension plans.

F   44.   The venture owner may retain ownership in a management buyout.

F   45.   The key to a liquidation harvest is that a buyer purchase the physical assets as operating assets.

Essay

1.   What are the recent phenomena in the business environment which have made retirement seem attractive to entrepreneurs?

2.   What are some personal reasons an entrepreneur might adopt a harvest strategy? For the reasons you have named, what are the best avenues of harvesting?

3.   What are the ten steps to a harvest plan?

4.   Assume you are an entrepreneur who has decided that a change in your personal situation requires you to pursue a harvest strategy. What method of harvesting might you choose? What steps would you take to ensure a successful harvest?

4.   What are the two types of bankruptcy? How can they play a significant part in the harvest of a venture?

5. Do all businesses need to plan for a harvest? Why or why not? What are the repercussions (good or bad) if a harvest plan is not developed?

6. Assume you are the owner of a venture which you have tentatively decided to harvest through a public offering in the next five years. How and when would you inform your employees of the upcoming change in the organization? Would it differ if your intended strategy was a management buyout? Why or why not?

7. Discuss the pros and cons of communicating intentions to sell the venture. What are the primary disadvantages of communicating intentions too early?

8. Develop a strategy for passing on your business to the next generation when three of your children have been active in the venture for a number of years.

CONTENTS

391

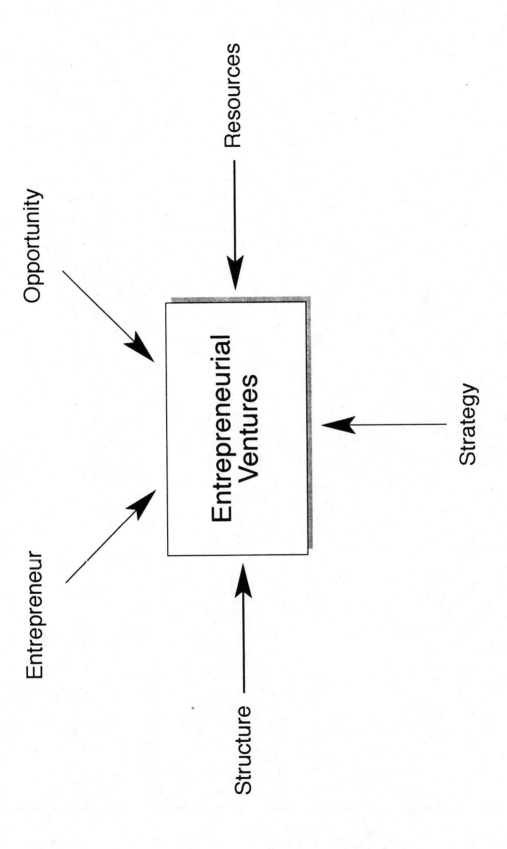

Transparency 1 (Figure 2-1)
The Five Components of Entrepreneurial Ventures
© 1993 West Publishing Company

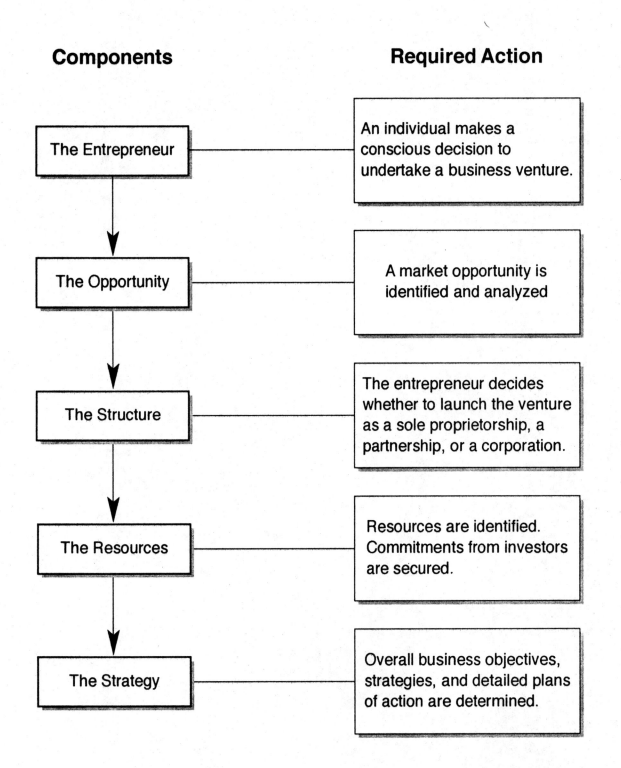

Components   **Required Action**

The Entrepreneur ————— An individual makes a conscious decision to undertake a business venture.

The Opportunity ————— A market opportunity is identified and analyzed

The Structure ————— The entrepreneur decides whether to launch the venture as a sole proprietorship, a partnership, or a corporation.

The Resources ————— Resources are identified. Commitments from investors are secured.

The Strategy ————— Overall business objectives, strategies, and detailed plans of action are determined.

Transparency 2 (Figure 2-2)
The Entrepreneurial Process
© 1993 West Publishing Company

The entrepreneurial motivation, $M = \Sigma A_i \times \Sigma T_j$, where

A_i = antecedent variables, and

T_j = triggering variables.

Antecedent Factor	$\times$	Triggering Factor	$=$	Motivation to Start a Venture
Creativity		Loss of job		
Background		Invention or idea		
Personality		Offer from partner		
Past experience				
Education				

Transparency 3 (Table 2-2)
Entrepreneurial Motivation Equation

Venture Launch Likelihood, $L = \Sigma A_i \times \Sigma T_j \times \Sigma E_k$, where

A_i = antecedent variables,

T_j = triggering variables, and

E_k = enabling variables.

Antecedent Factor	× Triggering Factor	× Enabling Factor	= Likelihood of Venture Launch
Creativity	Loss of job	Opportunity	
Background	Invention or idea	Resources	
Personality	Offer from partner		
Personal experience			
Education			

Expanded Entrepreneurial Equation

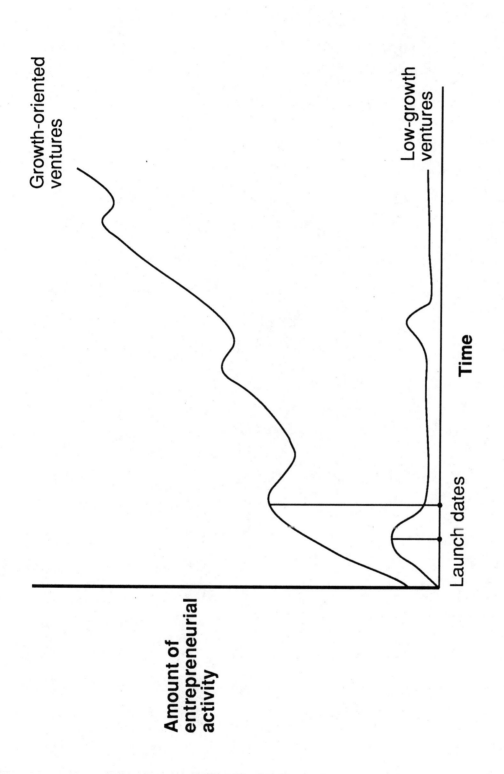

Transparency 5 (Figure 2-5)

Entrepreneurial Activity in Low-Growth and Growth-Oriented Ventures

© 1993 West Publishing Company

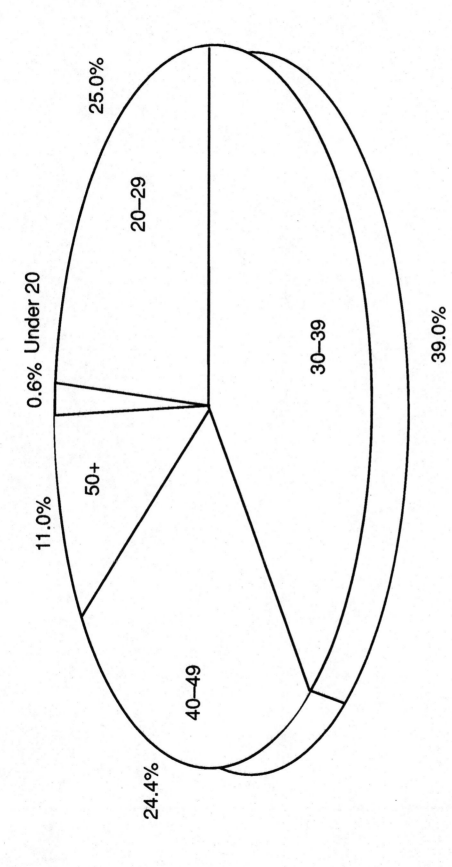

25.0%

20-29

0.6% Under 20

11.0%

50+

24.4%

40-49

30-39

39.0%

Transparency 6 (Figure 3-1)
Age of Entrepreneuer at Time of Launch
© 1993 West Publishing Company

Source: Arnold C. Cooper et al., New Business in America: The Firms and Their Owners (Washington D.C.: The NFIB Foundation, 1990), 19.

Characteristic	Small Business	Growth
Family background	Blue collar	White collar
Education	Technical	Broad
View of risk	Risk-avoider	Moderate or calculated risk-taker
View of planning	Does little long-range planning	Plans for the future
View of growth	Not desired	Moderate to rapid growth desired
View of harvest	None until near retirement	May or may not have harvesting as a goal
View of delegation	Does not delegate well	Delegates operational control but monitors closely until the firm is larger
View of funding	Distrusts outside sources but may use bank financing	Uses multiple sources depending on rate of growth desired
View of success	Comfortable living	Profitable, competitive force or profitable harvest

Transparency 7 (Table 3-1)

Difference Among Entrepreneurial Types

© 1993 West Publishing Company

Strategic Plans

Prepared by top management and key operating managers

Read by management and key employees

Focus on strategy and operations

Require information about the economy, industry, and competitors

Revised at least annually

Document length is as needed to discuss strategy

Financial Plans

Prepared by top management with help from CPA firms and/or the firm's financial staff

Read by investors outside the firm

Focus on sources and uses of funds

Require projections of sales, expenses, profits, and losses

Revised whenever additional funding is needed

Document length is 20–40 pages and no more than 50

Transparency 8 (Table 4-1)

Differences Between Strategic Plans and Financial Plans

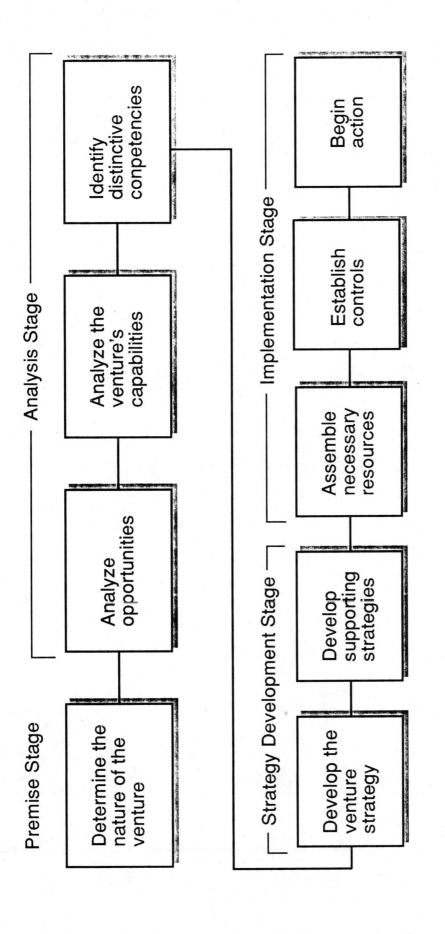

Transparency 9 (Figure 4-1)

The Strategic Planning Process for Entrepreneurial Ventures

I. Mission
   A. Nature of the venture and its products or services
   B. Venture philosophy

II. Analysis of the venture's external environment
   A. Analysis of the economy, social trends, and government regulation
   B. Analysis of competitors, customers, key suppliers, and other factors directly affecting the venture

III. Analysis of venture strengths and weaknesses
   A. Marketing
   B. Personnel
   C. The product or service
   D. Production processes
   E. Financial condition
      1. Cash flow
      2. Income and expenses
      3. Borrowing capability
      4. Need for equity capital

IV. Venture strategy
   A. Overall strategy
   B. Marketing strategy
   C. Production strategy
   D. Financing strategy
   E. Human resource strategy
   F. Community involvement strategy

V. Specific goals and objectives
   A. Goals for the next year
   B. Goals for five years from now

VI. Financial projections
   A. Cash flow projections
   B. Pro forma income statements
   C. Projected balance sheet

Transparency 10 (Table 4-5)
Suggested Format for a Strategic Plan
© 1993 West Publishing Company

I. Executive summary

II. Nature of the venture
   A. Background
   B. The product/service
   C. Location of venture

III. Description of the market
   A. Market trends
   B. Demographic trends
   C. Current competitors
   D. Comparison of proposed venture to competitors

IV. Description of the product/service
   A. Uniqueness of product/service
   B. Advantage over competing products
   C. Alternative uses of product/service

V. The management team
   A. Description of role each team member will play
   B. Resumes of each team member

VI. Objectives and goals
   A. Long-term objectives
   B. Short-term goals

VII. Venture strategies
   A. Marketing strategy
   B. Product strategy
   C. Human resource strategy
   D. Financial strategy
   E. Overall strategy for growth

VIII. Financial data
   A. Historical data (if any)
      1. Balance sheet
      2. Income statement
      3. Cash flow statement
   B. Financial projection
      1. One year by month
      2. Five years by quarter
   C. Break-even analyses

Transparency 11 (Table 4-6)
Financial Plan Outline
© 1993 West Publishing Company

Entrepreneur's Perspective

	Favorable	Unfavorable
Favorable	Launch venture	Reformulate management team
Unfavorable	Downscale or locate other types of investors	Look for other opportunities

Investor's Perspective

Transparency 12 (Figure 5-2)
Venture Evaluation from Entrepreneur's and Investor's Perspective
© 1993 West Publishing Company

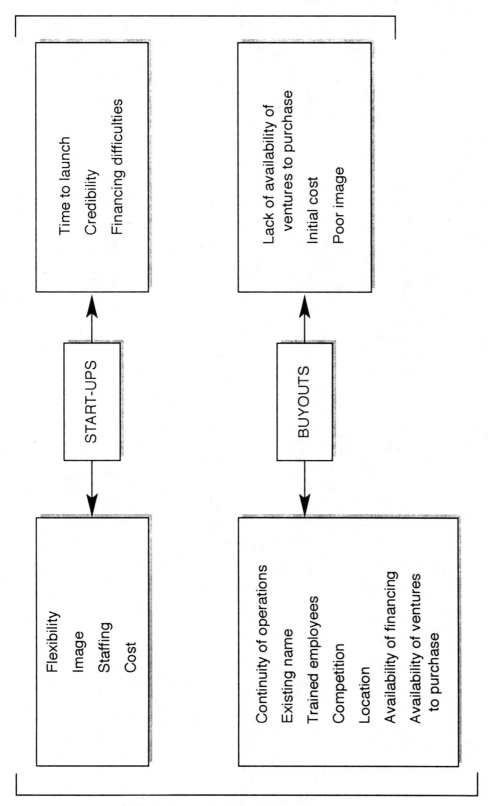

Transparency 13 (Figure 6-1)
© 1993 West Publishing Company

Advantages and Disadvantages of Startups and Buyouts

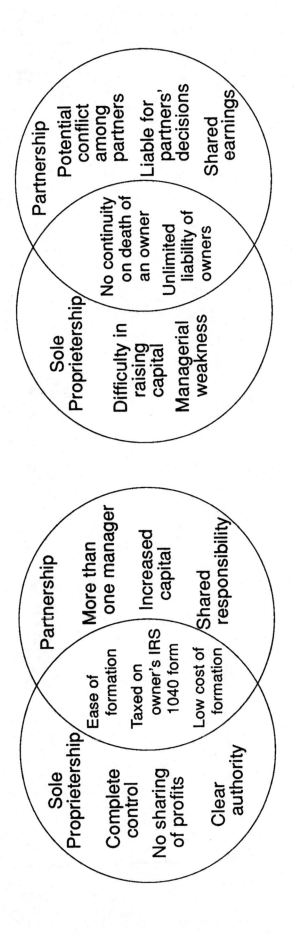

ADVANTAGES

Partnership
- More than one manager
- Increased capital
- Shared responsibility

Sole Proprietorship
- Complete control
- No sharing of profits
- Clear authority

- Ease of formation
- Taxed on owner's IRS 1040 form
- Low cost of formation

DISADVANTAGES

Partnership
- Potential conflict among partners
- Liable for partners' decisions
- Shared earnings

Sole Proprietorship
- Difficulty in raising capital
- Managerial weakness

- No continuity on death of an owner
- Unlimited liability of owners

Transparency 14 (Figure 6-2)
Advantages and Disadvantages of Sole Proprietorships and Partnerships
© 1993 West Publishing Company

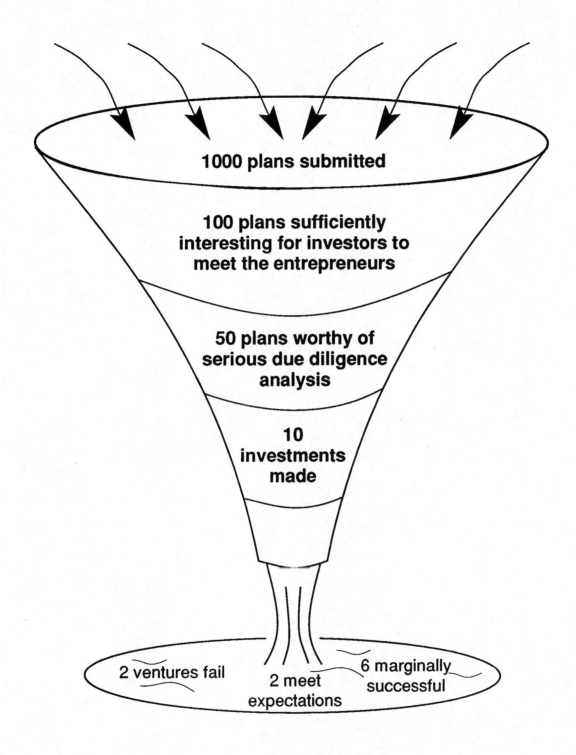

1000 plans submitted

100 plans sufficiently interesting for investors to meet the entrepreneurs

50 plans worthy of serious due diligence analysis

10 investments made

2 ventures fail

2 meet expectations

6 marginally successful

Transparency 15 (Figure 7-1)
Disposition of Business Plans Submitted to Venture Capitalists
© 1993 West Publishing Company

Source: Adapted from A. David Silver, Venture Capital: The Complete Guide for Investors (New York: John Wiley & Sons, 1985), 51.

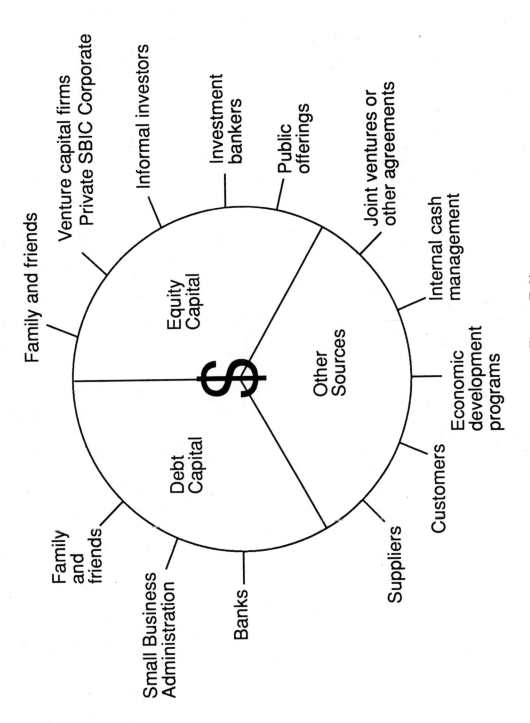

Equity Capital
- Family and friends
- Venture capital firms Private SBIC Corporate
- Informal investors
- Investment bankers
- Public offerings
- Joint ventures or other agreements

Other Sources
- Internal cash management
- Economic development programs
- Customers
- Suppliers

Debt Capital
- Family and friends
- Small Business Administration
- Banks

Transparency 16 (Figure 7-2)
Types of Financing for New and Growing Ventures
© 1993 West Publishing Company

Stage of Development	Low Growth	Moderate Growth	High Growth
Pre-start-up	Personal funds,* friends+	Personal funds, friends, banks	Personal funds, informal investors, existing ventures
Start-up	Same as above, plus banks	Same as above, plus informal investors	Same as above, plus venture capital
Post-Start-up	Same as above	Same as above, plus IPOs	Same as above, plus IPOs, additional stock offerings

*Personal funding refers to equity dollars from sole owner or partners regardless of whether the venture is a sole proprietorship, partnership, or corporation.
+Friends refers to contributions from families and friends, regardless of whether it is debt or equity.

___

Transparency 17 (Table 7-4)

Most Common Sources of Financing for Venture Stages and Growth Rates

© 1993 West Publishing Company

1. New product or service

2. Parallel competition

3. Franchise

4. Geographical transfer

5. Supply shortage

6. Tapping unused resources

7. Customer contract

8. Becoming an additional supplier

9. Joint ventures

10. Licensing

11. Market relinquishment

12. Selloff of a division

13. Favored purchasing

14. Rule changes

Transparency 18 (Table 8-1)
New Venture Entry Wedges
© 1993 West Publishing Company

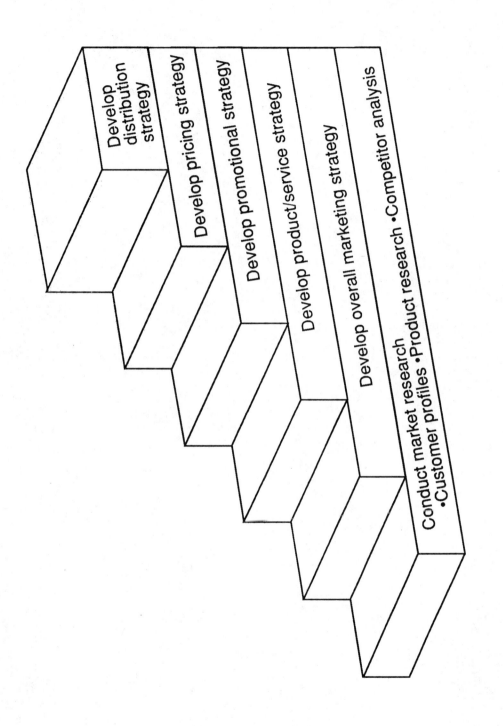

Transparency 19 (Figure 9-1)
Steps in Developing a Marketing Strategy
© 1993 West Publishing Company

The figure shows stacked blocks labeled:
- Develop distribution strategy
- Develop pricing strategy
- Develop promotional strategy
- Develop product/service strategy
- Develop overall marketing strategy
- Conduct market research •Product research •Competitor analysis •Customer profiles

Strategy

Strategy	Significance
Cost based	Takes cost of product into account, but may not consider competition.
Demand based	Assumes downward sloping demand curve. Not specific without experimentation.
Competitor based	Takes competition into account. Encourages discounting, which may result in losses.
Skimming	Charges highest possible prices when product is first introduced. Helps recover development cost if there is little competition.
Prestige pricing	High prices imply high quality. May attract upscale customers if product differentiation is possible.
Penetration pricing	Low prices designed to capture market share. Can be effective, but costly.

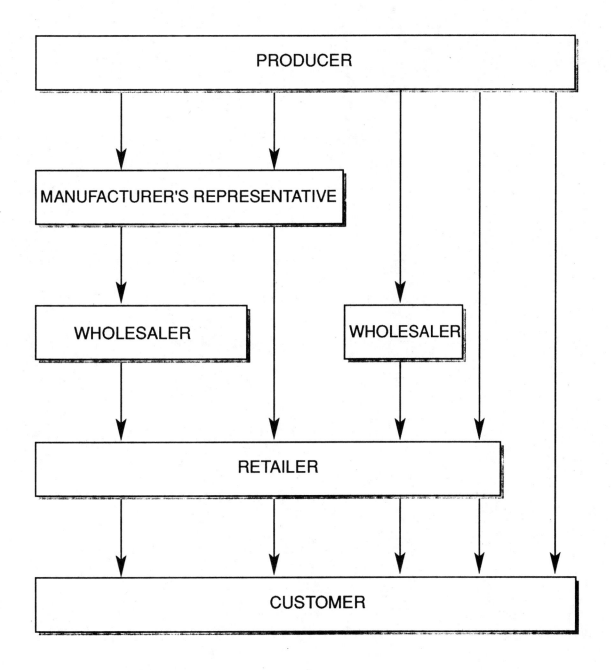

Transparency 21 (Figure 9-2)
Distribution Systems
© 1993 West Publishing Company

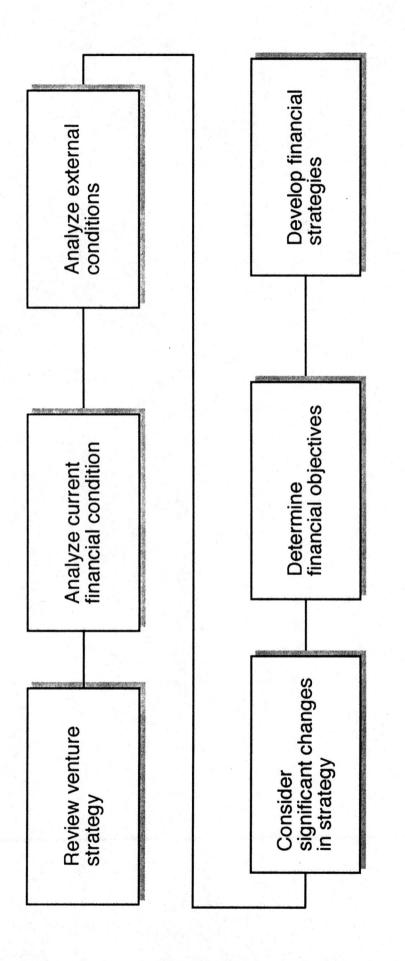

Transparency 22 (Figure 9-4)
The Financial Planning Process
© 1993 West Publishing Company

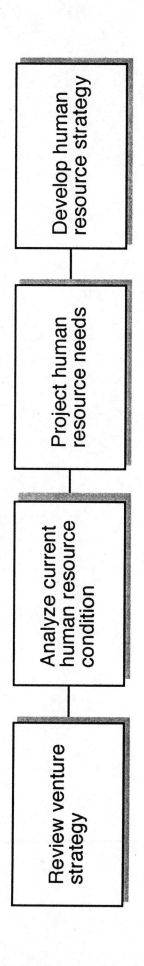

Review venture strategy

Analyze current human resource condition

Project human resource needs

Develop human resource strategy

Transparency 23 (Figure 9-5)
Human Resource Strategy Process
© 1993 West Publishing Company

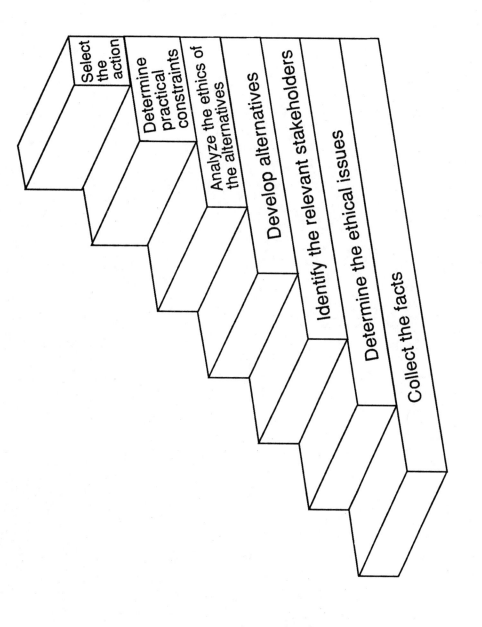

Transparency 24 (Figure 9-7)

Steps In An Ethical Decision-Making Process

© 1993 West Publishing Company

The steps shown in the figure, from bottom to top, are:

- Collect the facts
- Determine the ethical issues
- Identify the relevant stakeholders
- Develop alternatives
- Analyze the ethics of the alternatives
- Determine practical constraints
- Select the action

Source: Manuel Velasquez and Norman Bowie, lecture materials for Arthur Andersen seminars on teaching business ethics, Chicago, Arthur Andersen Corporation. Used with permission.

Automotive Products & Services	38,561
Auto/Truck/Trailer Rental	10,613
Business Aids & Services	42,734
Convenience Stores	17,467
Construction/Home Improvement	28,270
Educational Products/Services	13,265
Employment Services	7,552
Hotels/Motels/Campgrounds	11,103
Laundry/Drycleaning	2,629
Miscellaneous	8,402
Real Estate	16,995
Recreation/Entertainment/Travel	10,344
Rental Services	3,358
Restaurants	102,135
Retailing—Food	25,374
Total	392,854

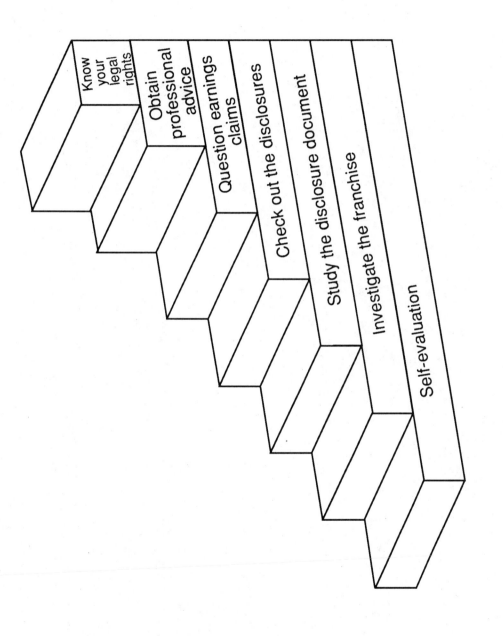

Transparency 26 (Figure 10-1)

Seven Steps for Protection before Franchise Investment

© 1993 West Publishing Company

Source: *Franchise Opportunities Handbook*, U.S. Department of Commerce, (Washington, DC: U.S. Government Printing Office, 1984), xxx–xxxii.

Franchising fee

Quality control

Advertising

Products and/or services available

Royalties

Equipment

Location requirements

Facilities

Maintenance

Signs

Business hours

Decor

Reporting

Bookkeeping

Supplies

Personnel (appearance and training)

Franchisor-franchisee relationships

Transparency 27 (Table 10-4)

Typical Elements Covered in a Franchising Agreement

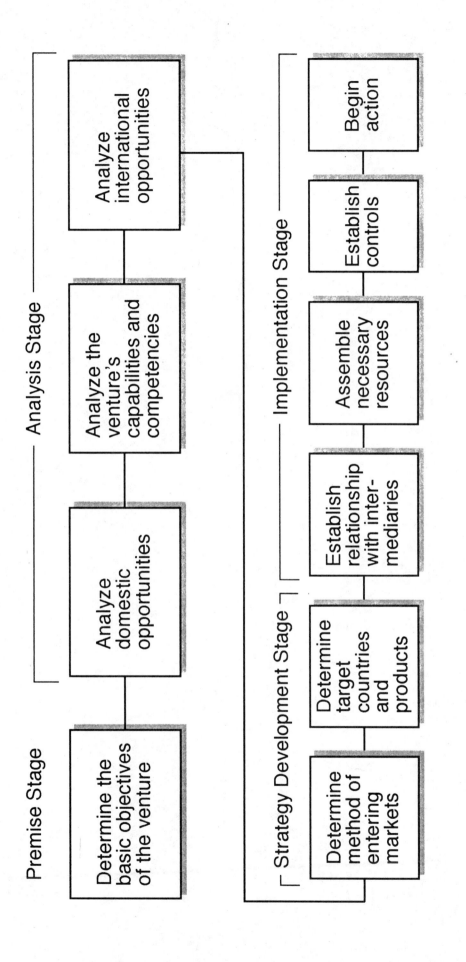

Transparency 28 (Figure 11-1)
The International Strategic Planning Process
© 1993 West Publishing Company

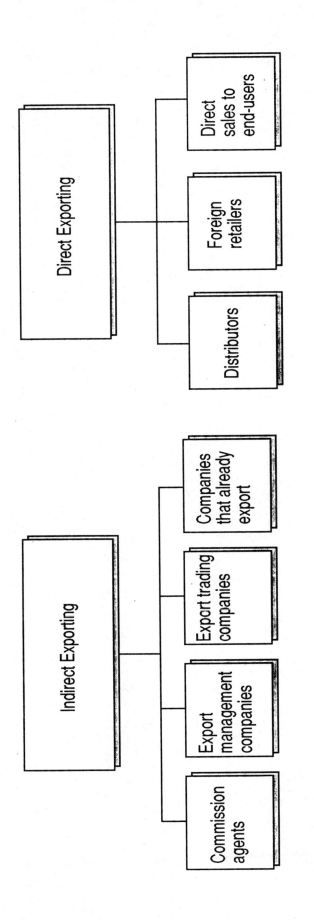

Transparency 29 (Figure 11-2)

Methods of Entering International Markets

© 1993 West Publishing Company

Source: *A Basic Guide to Exporting* (1992), 4-1 to 4-4.

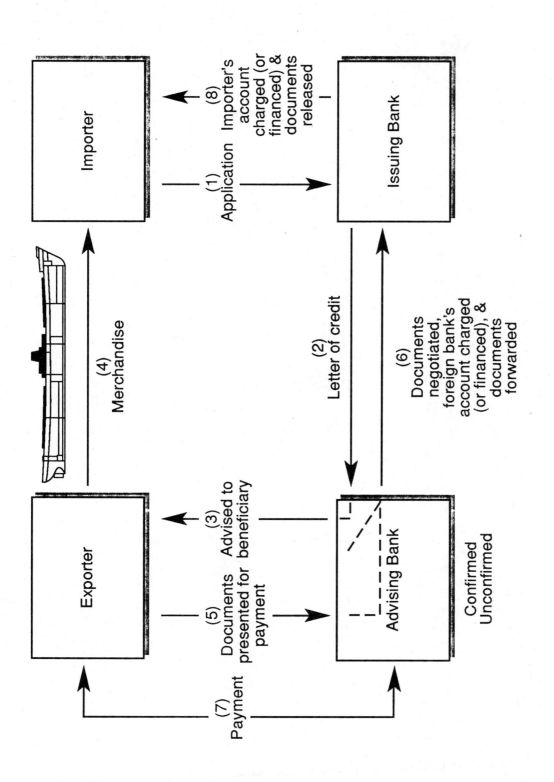

Transparency 30 (Figure 11-3)
Letter of Credit Transaction Process

© 1993 West Publishing Company

Source: *Letters of Credit*, Hongkong Bank.

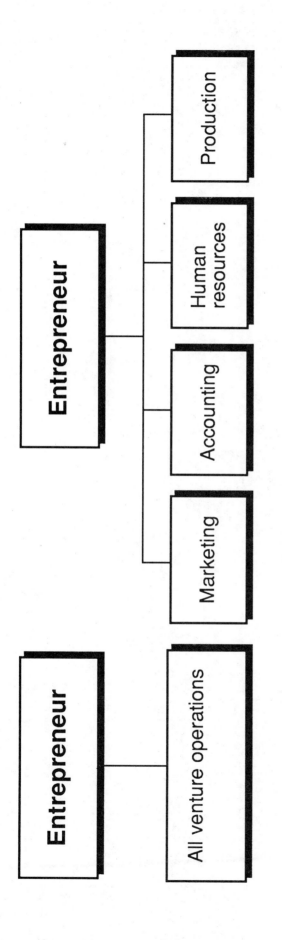

Transparency 31 (Figure 12-1)

Differences between Basic Structure and Functional Management Structure

© 1993 West Publishing Company

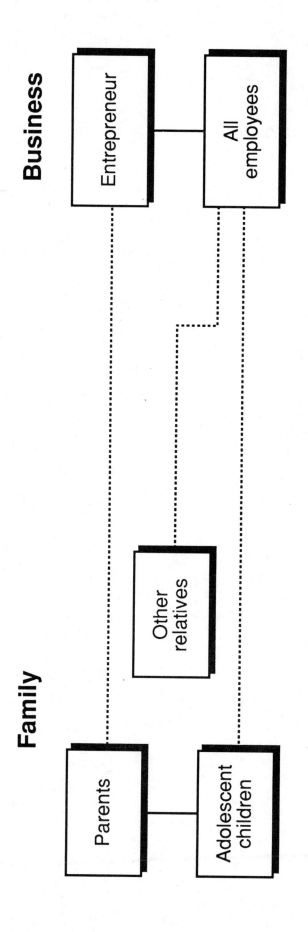

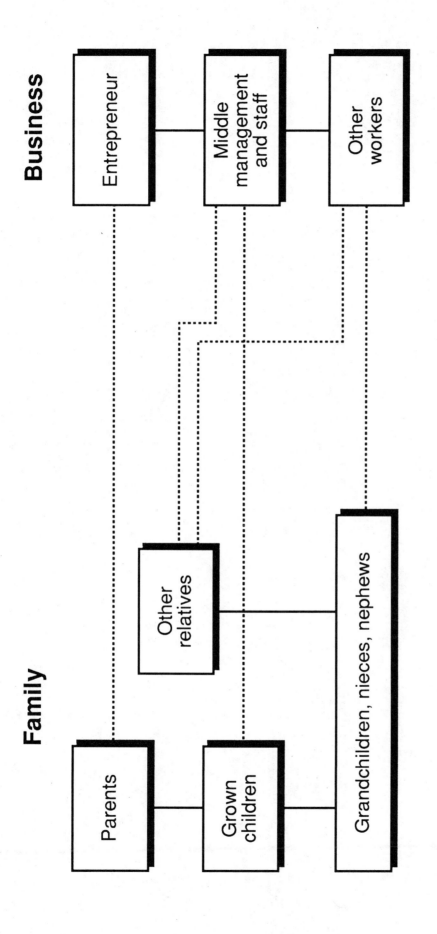

Business

Entrepreneur

Middle management and staff

Other workers

Family

Parents

Grown children

Other relatives

Grandchildren, nieces, nephews

Transparency 33 (Figure 12-3)
Family/Venture Relationships in a Mature Business
© 1993 West Publishing Company

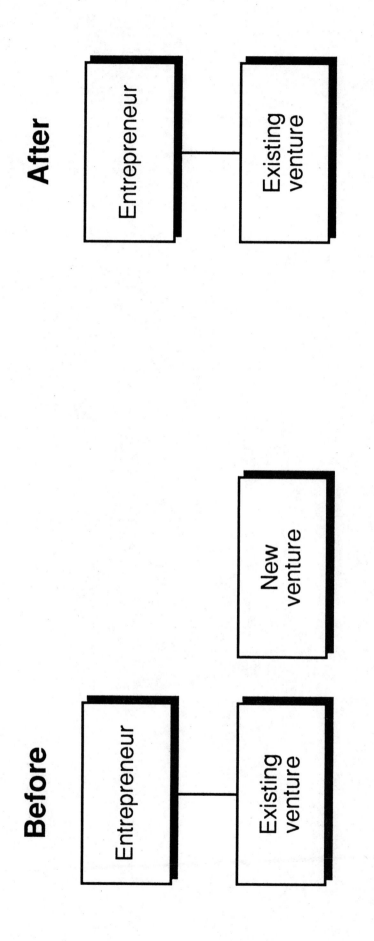

Transparency 34 (Figure 12-4)
Absorbing the New Venture into an Existing Venture
© 1993 West Publishing Company

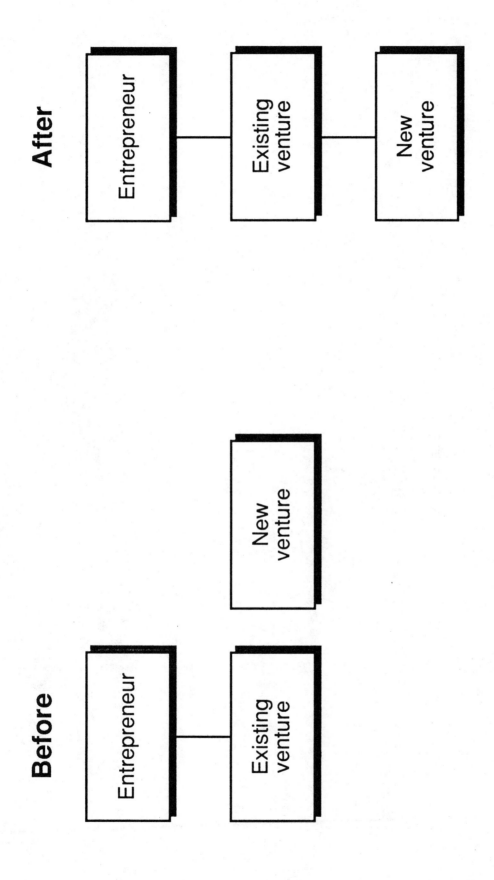

After

Entrepreneur

Existing venture

New venture

Before

Entrepreneur

Existing venture

New venture

Transparency 35 (Figure 12-5)
Creating a Wholly Owned Subsidiary
© 1993 West Publishing Company

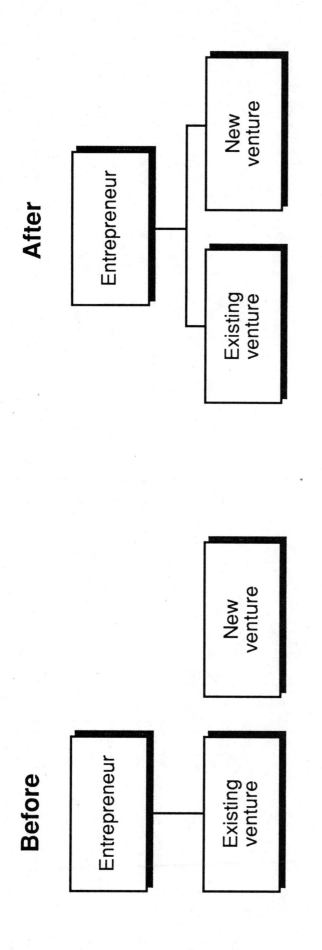

Before

After

Transparency 36 (Figure 12-6)
Maintaining Separate Ventures
© 1993 West Publishing Company

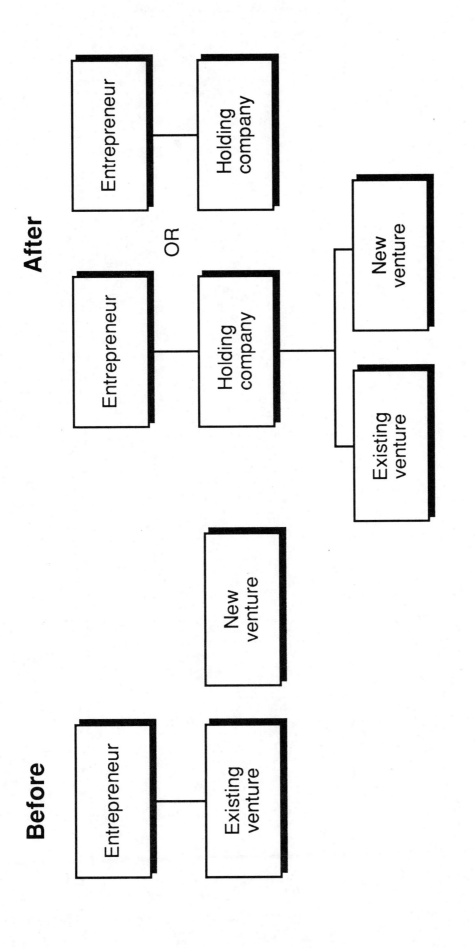

Transparency 37 (Figure 12-7)
Creating the Holding Company

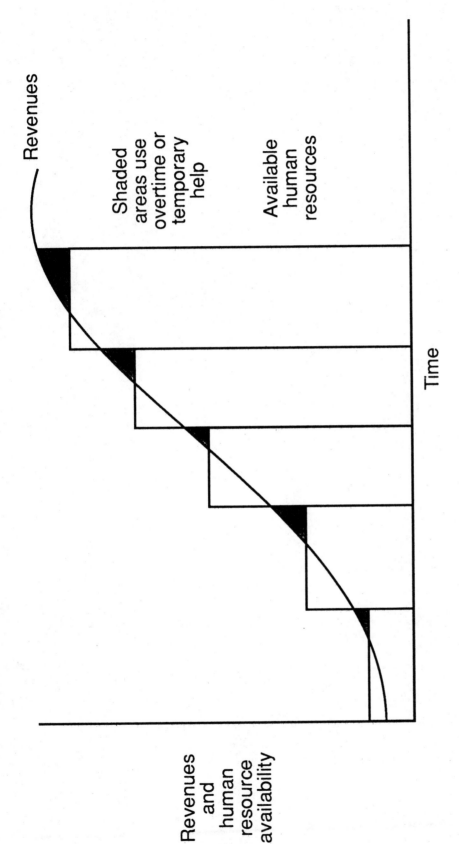

Transparency 38 (Figure 13-2)

Human Resource Availability Compared with Increasing Revenues

© 1993 West Publishing Company

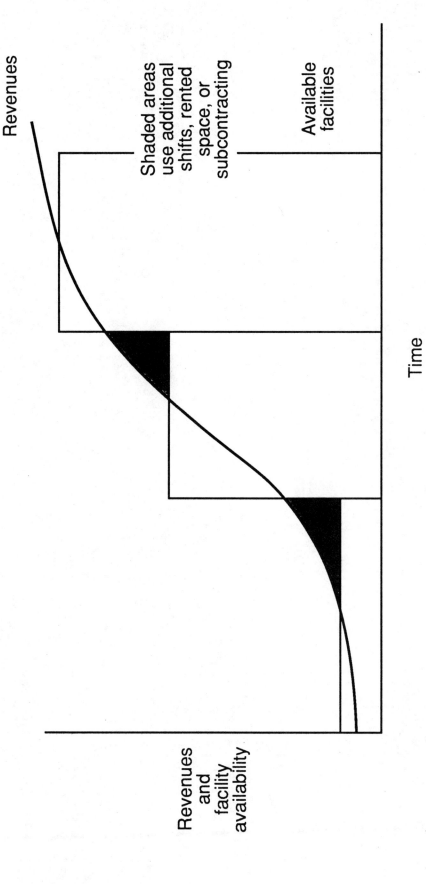

Transparency 39 (Figure 13-3)
Facility Availability Compared with Increasing Revenues
© 1993 West Publishing Company

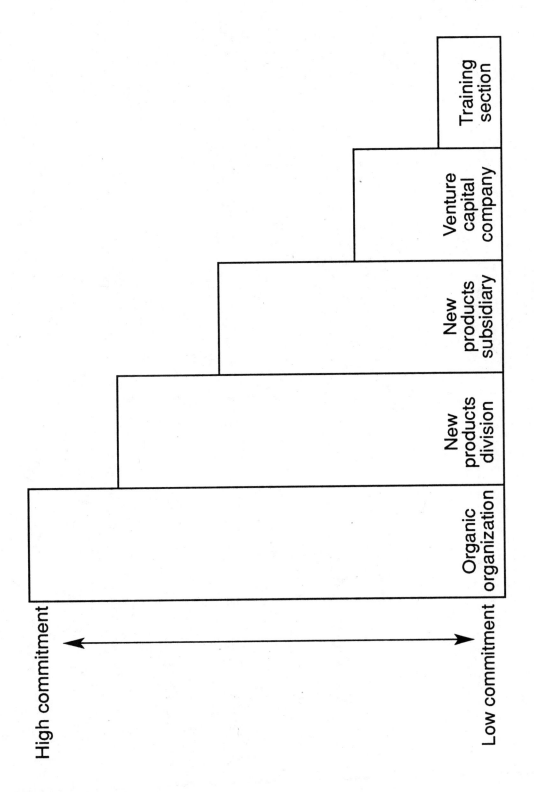

Transparency 40 (Figure 14-1)

Intrapreneurial Structure Compared with Commitment

© 1993 West Publishing Company

1. Analyst's perspective
   - Seller's perspective
   - Buyer's perspective
   - Financier's perspective
2. Nature of assets
3. Value of inventory
4. Nature of the market
5. Goodwill
6. Other intangible assets
7. Venture-specific factors

Transparency 41 (Table 15-1)
Factors Affecting Value
© 1993 West Publishing Company

Changes in personal situation

- Retirement
- Relocation
- Life cycle changes
- Stress

Unmet expectations

Pursuit of other opportunities

Personal wealth

Passing on the family venture

Estate planning

Facilitate growth

Transparency 42 (Table 16-1)
Reasons to Harvest a Venture

Direct sale

Employee stock option plan

Management buyout

Leveraged buyout

Merger

Going public

Liquidation

Bankruptcy

Passing venture to family members

Transparency 43 (Table 16-2)
Methods of Harvesting a Venture
© 1993 West Publishing Company

Methods

Reasons

Methods	Change in personal situation	Unmet expectations	Pursue other interests	Personal wealth	Pass on to heirs	Estate planning	Facilitate growth
Direct sale	X	X	X	X		X	
Employee stock option plan	X			X			
Management buyout	X		X	X	X	X	
Leveraged buyout	X		X	X		X	
Merger							X
Public offering				X			X
Liquidation	X	X	X			X	
Bankruptcy		X					
Pass to family	X		X		X	X	

Transparency 44 (Figure 16-1)
Methods and Reasons for Harvesting